the

BEAST

that walks like

MAN

the

BEAST

that walks like

MAN

The Story of the Grizzly Bear

HAROLD MCCRACKEN

ROBERTS RINEHART

Published by Roberts Rinehart Publishers
An imprint of The Rowman & Littlefield Publishing Group, Inc.
4501 Forbes Boulevard, Suite 200
Lanham, MD 20706

Distributed by NATIONAL BOOK NETWORK

The Hanover House edition was previously catalogued by the Library of
Congress as follows:

McCracken, Harold, 1894–1983.
The beast that walks like me : the story of the grizzly bear / Harold
McCracken.
p.   cm.
Includes bibliographical references.
1. Bears.   2. Bears—Legends and stories.   I. Title.
QL737 .C2 M2
599.74446

ISBN 1-57098-394-1

♾ ™ The paper used in this publication meets the minimum requirements
of American National Standard for Information Sciences—Permanence of
Paper for Printed Library Materials, ANSI/NISO Z39.48-1992.

Manufactured in the United States of America.

Contents

Foreword

THE STORY of the American grizzly bear is an
extraordinary heritage of legendary lore and historic melo-
drama, that goes back to the time when the saber-tooth tiger
and the mastodon roamed where our farms and cities thrive
today. That was a long, long time before the first primitive
Indian ever set foot in the New World. "Old Ephraim" has
come down to us through a million years or more, give or
take a few hundred thousand, the most powerful and pugnacious of all the present-day carnivorous creatures on earth.
No other animal has been more respected and feared through
all the generations of red men and white men who have known
him; and none has been subjected to such an intensive attrition
of extermination.

It is the purpose of this book to present a chronology of
the best of all information relating to the grizzly bears, from
the earliest times. Here will be found some of the rich ideolo-
gies and ceremonial practices of the primitive American Indians, who believed that this beast that walks like man was
their paternal ancestor. There are the accounts of the first
white men of record to meet Old Ephraim, and the exciting
experiences of buckskin-clad pioneers who tackled these dangerous beasts with single-shot, muzzle-loading, flintlock pea-

rifles—and fought them to a finish with only a knife. Here are the sanguine bear-and-bull fights, which were the feature attraction of religious festivals around the missions when California was a Spanish colony, and the stories of the most notable explorers and hunters, from Jedediah Smith and Kit Carson to fabulous "Grizzly" Adams and Teddy Roosevelt. Here also are the obituaries of the last of Old Ephraim's tribe, as the species passed into history in areas where they once roamed abundant and supreme.

This writer has undertaken to tell the whole story of the grizzly bear—the romantic, the melodramatic, and the serious. An attempt has also been made, by relating certain instances and facts, which may in a small way permit the reader to see behind the hairy visages of these silent and sagacious creatures. There is also appended a check list of all the eighty-six varieties of grizzly and big brown bears in North America which have been described in scientific nomenclature.

What is set down here is the result of an intensive interest that goes back through more than fifty years, personal experiences with well over three hundred grizzlies in their own wild native haunts, and supplemented by extensive research into many phases of the subject.

Credit is duly acknowledged to the many sources and persons which have contributed to the preparation of this book. The footnotes, which are to be found in the Appendix, give their own recognition and may lead the reader to go deeper into some of the aspects which are presented but briefly. Special acknowledgment and appreciation is made to the many rustic naturalists—guides, trappers, and hunters, both white and Indian—who have imparted their observations, which have given me a better undertanding of grizzlies: Captain Charlie Madsen, Andy Simons, "Bear River Charlie," and others in Alaska; Joe Saul, the Cree Indian, who gave me the first lessons in bear hunting, when I was a lad of eighteen in British Columbia; and many more of their kind. Also those who have so graciously aided in the widespread research into the records of the past: Virginia Walton, Historical Society of Montana; John Willard, of Helena, Montana; the Fish and Game departments and the local offices of the Fish and Wildlife Service in the various western states; Venia T. Phillips, the Academy of Natural Sciences of Philadelphia; Donald D. McLean, California Department of Fish and Game; Dr. Alfred M. Bailey, Denver Museum of Natural History; George Mushbach; H. Conrad McCracken; Dr. James L. Clark, The American Museum of Natural History; Ivor Avellino, American History Department, New York Public Library; E. Marie Becker and S. L. Vigilante, Library of the New York Historical Society; Edward Eberstadt & Sons; and, last but not least among many more, my father James Owen McCracken, newspaperman and rancher of the early days of the West, whose stories about grizzly bears so deeply impressed me in early childhood that it set my ambition to become a professional grizzly-bear hunter.

It is hoped that the following chapters will provide a better understanding of the character and history of Old Ephraim and his tribe, and that it may excite a sympathetic interest which will lead to the preservation of the species in some regions of the United States, where these creatures are today so close to extinction.

HAROLD MCCRACKEN

Douglaston, L.I.

Harold McCracken in Alaska, ca. 1916. Courtesy Marjorie Goppert

A Bear of a Man: Dr. Harold McCracken

H AROLD McCRACKEN was an independent spirit with an adventurous thirst for knowledge. A strong sense of the romantic and the spectacular led him early in life to hunt Alaskan big game for use as museum specimens and to learn aerial photography in the early days of open cockpits and silk-winged biplanes. In midlife, he made adventure, travel, and sports films and worked to educate himself to become a recognized scholar and author. Late in life, he assumed the mantle of museum director and worked to build the finest collection of Old West art ever assembled. So successful was his unorthodox life that his prolific writings and scholarly achievements were rewarded by five honorary doctorates.

Born in Colorado Springs in 1894 to James Owen McCracken, a newspaperman, and Laura Crapsey McCracken, a trained artist, Harold grew up with his family on a small, remote ranch near Payette, Idaho, along the Snake River. There in his early childhood he often roamed sagebrush flats with his faithful dog Shep, experiencing the freedoms of the natural world and adventures that included his first chance encounter with a wild black bear. Living far from formal schools, he was educated at home by his mother in the arts of civilization and learned to love learning for its own sake at a young age. Moving with his family to Des Moines, Iowa, he attended his first public school classroom at age nine, but this proved so traumatic that it spawned a rebellious distaste for regular educational routines that stayed with him for the rest of his life. He learned best from his own studies at home, in libraries and museums, and from other persons whom he respected.

Museums in particular had a pronounced effect on Harold Mc-Cracken's life. As a young teenager he spent considerable time studying exhibits and interacting with museum personnel. While his family was, for a short time, living in Philadelphia, he often visited the museums of the University of Pennsylvania. When the family again returned to Des Moines, he introduced himself as a high school student to the staff of the Iowa State Historical Society museum. There he volunteered and learned to properly collect and prepare ornithological specimens. In his junior year of high school, he wrote to several prominent men as part of an English class assignment, asking their opinion of what it took to succeed in the world and the relevance of a college education. Author Jack London wrote back to him with the advice, "No extraordinary man who has a call can do anything other than answer that call." McCracken did not graduate from high school, but he did discover and begin his studies of the research bulletins of the Smithsonian Institution and the U.S. Biological Survey, being far more motivated by his own educational goals than by those of the public school system.

In 1913, at age eighteen, McCracken found himself having to choose between beginning seminary classes at Drake University, as his parents advised, and his own desire to become a professional bear hunter. With his small savings and the blessing of his parents, he purchased a one-way train ticket to British Columbia to live for a year and a half with his aunt and uncle. So began an adventure that set a pattern for the rest of his life. The North Thompson Valley where he stayed had not yet been reached by railway and was still very much a part of the old frontier. One of his first friends there was Joe Saul, a Cree elder who shared a lifetime of hunting and wilderness living expertise with him and helped him with the local Chinook Jargon. In the fall of 1913, McCracken realized his desire to go bear hunting, but his greenhorn experience of actually shooting a bear on his own proved that he still had a lot to learn about bears and hunting. That winter McCracken was hired to run a trading post on the Clearwater River that had mostly Cree trappers and their families as customers, an experience that gave him valuable skills in dealing with native peoples. He wrote his first short story in a company ledger book and began seriously entertaining the idea of becoming a professional writer.

In 1914 McCracken traveled to Columbus, Ohio, where his parents had relocated. Here he met Dr. William C. Mills of the Ohio State Archaeological Museum and found part-time employment that allowed him to work in the museum. That fall, he entered Ohio State University as a student and found additional work at the OSU Geology Museum, where he cleaned and preserved the bones of a mastodon skeleton. For the next year he took only classes that interested him, including paleontology and journalism, but was disappointed when he was unceremoniously kicked out of the school of journalism and told by the dean that he didn't have what it takes to be a writer. At that time, he resolved to find a way to go to Alaska and hunt grizzly bear, and the means by which he did so were characteristic of his innate gall and sheer brass. Deciding that Ohio State University needed a museum of natural history, for which he would collect the first specimens of Alaskan grizzly bears, he began a personal campaign to convince the OSU administration of this glaring need and even induced an Ohio senator to introduce a bill in the Ohio legislature to do so. Although the measure did not pass, McCracken did succeed in finding modest funding for his Alaskan collecting expedition from his own dentist and the publisher of *Hunter-Trader-Trapper* magazine. Dr. Mills at the Ohio State Archaeological Museum had no funding to give but instead gave his blessing to the expedition, which permitted McCracken to use the name of the university, thus providing credibility for the adventure in local newspapers.

Preparing for his specimen collecting, McCracken visited the American Museum of Natural History in New York to learn from naturalist Carl Akeley just exactly what one does in order to properly preserve a large animal for a museum once it has been shot. In May 1916, his dream became reality as he traveled to McCarthy, in the St. Elias Alps of Alaska. Low on cash but finding a guide recommended to him by the Alaskan governor, McCracken accepted an offer to provide cover for a secretive copper-prospecting survey under the guise of his scientific expedition. This allowed McCracken to ride up into the remote Chitina Valley as part of a well-equipped camp. There he spotted, stalked, and shot the first grizzly bear that he found, and so successfully collected the first museum specimen of his expedition.

3

Within a few weeks after returning from the Chitina Valley, however, McCracken found his very modest funds nearly expended and had to choose between traveling back to OSU with one bear and continuing his grand expedition without further funding. By signing on as a "galley slave" on a small tramp freighter, he found a way to earn his passage out to the Alaskan peninsula for the winter of 1916–1917, where he determined to continue his quest regardless of his bank account. That winter he shot several more of the brown bears, one of which proved to be the largest on record for several decades thereafter. In the spring, he sent stories of his Alaskan adventures to *Hunter-Trader-Trapper* magazine, which became his first published articles.

The advent of the United States' involvement in World War I led to McCracken volunteering to become a combat pilot. Turned down because of his eyesight, he instead joined the Signal Corps Aviation Section to learn aerial photography. Assigned to a newly formed officers' training school at Columbia University, he learned about photography but was unexpectedly recruited to help develop a secret thermal radiation detection device capable of long-distance identification of heat sources. It was hoped that the device would be useful in locating enemy planes during bad weather, but army tests made during the war without the benefit of the original researchers did not prove its ultimate usefulness.

After the war, McCracken made return trips to Alaska in 1919 and 1921. During the latter trip, which lasted several years, he began taking motion picture footage of his journeys, with emphasis on traditional Aleut life and grizzly bear behavior. During these years, his attitude toward the bears evolved as he grew to know their habits in general and many of the bears as individuals during one summer-long filming expedition. This extended field experience proved valuable to him when he researched bear populations in the lower forty-eight states.

A new phase of McCracken's life began in 1923 when he moved to New York City and created a movie from his raw film footage about his Alaskan adventures. This was enough of a success that he gained employment as a motion picture photographer, specializing in dangerous aerial footage and sporting events. This was supplemented with income from serving as an associate editor for *Field and Stream* magazine. McCracken soon married his student sweetheart from Ohio State University, and they began the responsibilities of a family life together. Friendships with staff of the American Museum of Natural History continued, and he became a member of the renowned Explorer's Club. The resources of the New York Public Library proved useful for continuing his own self-directed education.

Yet Alaska still beckoned, and 1928 saw him leading the Stoll-McCracken Siberian-Arctic Expedition to collect archaeological and natural history specimens for the American Museum of Natural History. This time he had a truly official, well-funded expedition with a full crew, taking twenty persons with him. Following stories he had heard years before, he tracked down the location of ancient burial sites in the Aleutian Islands and found well-preserved mummies in a log sarcophagus. During this trip, he also shot his thirteenth and last brown bear before returning to his family in New York with the validation of having successfully led a major museum-funded exploring expedition to the Arctic.

Upon McCracken's return to New York, he accepted an offer to work as an editor for G. P. Putnam and Sons for a line of adventure books. When the stock market crash of 1929 critically weakened the company, he began writing books of his own, starting with fiction for young adults based on his Alaskan adventures. His first book was *Iglaome: The Lone Hunter*, published in 1930. At this time, he also began research on the artist Frederic Remington, a line of study that would eventually change his life. But his early years as a writer were difficult, as he discovered that the royalties from his books were far lower than he had hoped.

During the 1930s, McCracken published four more books and made many motion pictures. A few of the movies were produced under his own imprint, but most were with larger companies such as RKO. One, a documentary about the 1755 expulsion of Acadians from Nova Scotia entitled *The Land of Evangeline*, won a Grant Shorts award in 1939. His writings met with commercial success in 1942 as he created a series of books for juveniles about Alaskan wildlife. During World War II, he also made motion pictures for the U.S. military to help with soldiers' morale. While filming for the U.S. Navy, he briefly found himself on a ship hunting for German submarines.

After the war, McCracken found time to finish and have published *Frederic Remington: Artist of the Old West* in 1947. This was the first comprehensive attempt to provide a scholarly account of Remington. The book was well received, making McCracken a recognized authority on western American art. That same year he again published in the area of natural history with *Trapping: The Craft and Science of Catching Fur-Bearing Animals*, with Harry Van Cleve as coauthor. McCracken also started researching and writing more history books that appeared in the 1950s, including *The Charles M. Russell Book: The Life and Work of the Cowboy Artist* and a history of the sea otter fur trade in Alaska, *Hunters of the Stormy Sea*. However, the book that established him as an authority among natural history writers was *The Beast That Walks Like Man: The Story of the Grizzly Bear*. His sustained writing efforts received recognition in 1957 when Hope College of Holland, Michigan, awarded him an honorary Doctor of Literature degree. At age sixty-three, the thought of a retirement supported by his now adequate book royalties and devoted to further research and writing must have been on his mind.

The summer of 1958 found McCracken living in a small log cabin on the Valley Ranch, deep in the Rocky Mountains upriver from Cody, Wyoming, and working on a new book about western artist and writer George Catlin. Irving H. "Larry" Larom, the owner of the ranch and a friend of McCracken's, was also a trustee of the Buffalo Bill Memorial Association, which had just erected a new museum building, the Whitney Gallery of Western Art. When leaving Cody to fly back to New York, McCracken was met at the airport by several board of trustee members, and to his surprise he was offered the position of director of the new art museum and of the Buffalo Bill Historical Center (BBHC) as a whole. He accepted the offer, welcoming the opportunity to move back to the Rocky Mountain West of his youth while challenged to start a new career as a museum director.

Beginning his new position in Cody in January 1959, he found a bare gallery and was charged with developing an exhibit to open that spring that would put the new museum on the map. Fortunately, several important art collections were expected to arrive, including the recently purchased Frederic Remington Studio Collection, a donated collection of Charles M. Russell paintings, and additional Russell paintings on special loan. There being no other acquisition funds, McCracken used his personal influence as a western art expert to borrow the remainder needed to fill the gallery. An entire semi-truck trailer from New York City arrived in time for the official opening of April 25, 1959. Over 3,000 visitors attended from all parts of the country at a time when the population of Cody still numbered fewer than 5,000. The Whitney Gallery of Western Art gained considerable momentum from the successful opening, attracting national attention and support. It also helped to define and elevate the place of western art around the world.

Harold McCracken had found his place in the West, and his museum directorship became an important part of his personal and professional identity. Under his guidance, the BBHC continued the tradition of William F. "Buffalo Bill" Cody by presenting authentic western history, and the Whitney Gallery became known for documentary art of the Old West. McCracken continued his art history studies in addition to regionally collecting prehistoric specimens for the BBHC from Wyoming archaeological sites. These were active years of growth for the BBHC, and Harold McCracken was a strong player with the board of trustees in developing the vision of the historical center. In 1974 McCracken turned eighty years old, but retirement that year still proved difficult for him. Given his devotion to the BBHC, an exhibition was held to recognize his many contributions, "The Art of Frederic Remington: An Exhibition Honoring Harold McCracken at the Whitney Gallery of Western Art." Furthermore, in 1980 the BBHC officially dedicated the Harold McCracken Research Library to perpetuate his memory. This was fitting and appropriate, as libraries and museums had been the primary means by which he had educated himself throughout his life.

Harold McCracken passed away in Cody in 1983. He has been remembered for his contributions by the University of Alaska, which awarded him a Doctorate of Literature in 1966 and established an annual Harold McCracken Literature Award for students. Other universities that have similarly acknowledged him include Colorado State University, Doctor of Humane Letters in 1972; University of Wyoming, Doctor of Laws in 1974; and St. Lawrence University, Doctor of Human Letters in 1980.

Nathan E. Bender, Housel Curator
McCracken Research Library
March 2003

REFERENCES

Bartlett, Richard A. *From Cody to the World: The First Seventy-five Years of the Buffalo Bill Memorial Association.* Cody, Wyo.: Buffalo Bill Historical Center, 1992.

Goppert, Deborah. "Dr. Harold McCracken Director Emeritus Buffalo Bill Historical Center." *The Cody Enterprise* (June 12, 1974): 2–8.

Hedgpeth, Don. *The Art of Frederic Remington: An Exhibition Honoring Harold McCracken at the Whitney Gallery of Western Art.* Exhibition catalog. Cody, Wyo.: Buffalo Bill Memorial Association, 1974.

"In Memory: Dr. Harold McCracken 1894–1983." In *Annual Report.* Cody, Wyo.: Buffalo Bill Historical Center, 1983.

McCracken, Harold. *Roughnecks and Gentlemen.* Garden City, N.Y.: Doubleday and Co., Inc., 1968. This is McCracken's autobiography.

———. Letter to Mrs. Henry H. R. Coe, October 13, 1982. Harold McCracken Vertical File, McCracken Research Library, Buffalo Bill Historical Center, Cody, Wyoming.

Mead, Jean. "Harold McCracken." In *Wyoming in Profile,* 21–27. Boulder, Colo.: Pruett Publishing Co., 1982.

The Grizzly Today

I<small>N HIS</small> biographical essay, Nathan Bender reveals why Harold McCracken was so well qualified to write this book and make it the most authoritative work on the grizzly bear at the time that it was published. Chronicler of the American West and the Far North, student of the native people of the New World, art historian, and well-traveled sportsman and wilderness adventurer, McCracken combined all the traits necessary to produce precisely the book suited to the tastes and needs of his time. Even today, it remains one of the most readable accounts of the discovery, wonder, demise, and ultimate worth of the grizzly bear. But it was, and is, more than that. It is a measure of its times and the times to come. *The Beast That Walks Like Man* was published at a pivotal moment in the history of its subject. In several ways, the North American grizzly bear was about to see the trends of its career redirected. In fact, the next half century—from 1955 until today—has seen a remarkable change in grizzly–human relations in North America.

THE NEW IDEA OF THE GRIZZLY BEAR

First, there is a far different mood about the conservation of grizzly bears than there was in McCracken's time. Though he expressed boundless admiration for the bear and at least some hope that it would survive, *The Beast That Walks Like Man* had the mood of a eulogy, even an obituary, for a species that was on the ropes. The glory days of the grizzly bear, and of the people for whom the bear played some important role in their lives, were regarded as the past. The remaining pockets of grizzly bear presence in the lower forty-eight states were small, perilously uncertain in their status, and presumed to be shrinking. Chapter 26, "Last of Old Ephraim's Tribe," is a roll call, state by state, of extinction events and gloomy forecasts for the remaining animals.

A revealing example of how this steady loss of bears occurred and can still occur is provided in McCracken's comments on his "own native state of Colorado" (pages 264–265). The idea that the grizzly bear hardly seemed to be holding on in Colorado in 1955, which was expressed by various state officials and McCracken himself, has been replaced by a forlorn hope. There are people who believe that grizzly bears are still there, but many more do not. And once a bear population reaches that stage where its only possible survivors are "stealth bears" that exist almost entirely in a few human imaginations, it is usually too late to do whatever is politically and biologically necessary to turn the decline around and restore a reasonably secure population.

His account of the status of the remaining grizzly bears in Yellowstone National Park is especially revealing, not the least because these were the bears closest to McCracken's base in Cody, Wyoming. In his discussion of these bears (pages 262–263), he was torn between trusting the official statements from National Park Service staff that the bears were still hanging on and believing the ever-present and far more seductive local antifederal folklore that the government had secretly killed them off already. (This rumor had been locally popular for at least half a century when McCracken published his book and continues to thrive today; it has always been fiercely independent of how many bears were being seen at the time.)

I single out the Yellowstone region here not because it was Mc-Cracken's home base or because it is mine, but because the grizzly bears of Yellowstone must serve, at least symbolically, as the representatives of the species who played the greatest role in the reversal of the bear's course toward extinction and, quite literally, in the redefinition of the animal as an idea in American society.

It was in Yellowstone, four years after *The Beast That Walks Like Man* was published, that a team of researchers led by twin brothers

John Craighead and Frank Craighead, Jr., launched the first long-term ecological study of the grizzly bear anywhere. In ten years, they not only clarified many of the long-standing mysteries about the biology and behavior of the grizzly bear but also led the way to creating a whole new image of the animal.

As the story stood when McCracken published his book, the bear had accumulated a substantial romantic aura about it, but for practical purposes, especially in grizzly country, it was still widely viewed much as it had been a century earlier—as a dangerous competitor to humans at worst and as an infernal nuisance at best. For all too many westerners, the grizzly bear symbolized the evils of a wilderness land that needed taming. This certainly was the case on the lands near Yellowstone when I first came to work in the park about thirty years ago.

But American society has at times a surprising intellectual agility. We really can change our collective mind. In an extraordinarily short period of time, thanks to the work of the Craigheads and a growing number of other grizzly bear students (their numbers are now legion), and thanks to the many people who followed the fate and doings of this fascinating animal, the grizzly bear was transformed from the demon of the howling wilderness into just the opposite. It became the symbol of good wilderness—of a beautiful, natural wildness that must be saved not merely for its own sake but also because it has so much to offer the human imagination and spirit. The bear was poised on the brink of that change when McCracken's book had come out earlier, though as with most other observers of his time it must have seemed to McCracken that the only brink the bear faced was that of extinction. Perhaps his book was one of those immeasurable social forces that tipped the scales just the little bit that it took to turn things around. I like to think so.

CONSERVING THE NEW GRIZZLY BEAR

I do not mean to suggest that the bear's troubles were over. The Craigheads' study eventually resulted in a still-smoldering controversy, starting in the late 1960s, over the best way to conserve the grizzly bears of Yellowstone and, by logical extension, the other remaining bear populations. No doubt this and subsequent bear-management controversies (every grizzly bear population has and seems to require its own bitter public and political battle) strengthened the bear's new public image as a wilderness poster child, but they likewise entrenched the animal ever more deeply in the western mind as yet another kind of nuisance. The grizzly bear has become symbolic of interference by "outsiders" in what had for a long time been mostly a local, western concern—the management of the federal lands upon which the bear depended for survival. Local resistance to the reestablishment of a grizzly bear population in the Bitterroot Mountains along the Montana–Idaho border has been little short of ferocious and, so far, successful in preventing the addition of a key bear population in the northern Rockies.

We may have stopped taking big chunks of land away from the bear, but we continue to whittle at the edges of the remaining viable habitats, and we are willfully reluctant to give back any land they've lost. The grizzly bear population of the lower forty-eight states is almost certainly not lower than McCracken's 1955 estimate of 850–875 animals (page 265), but nobody is claiming that it is much higher than that, either. For the genetic well-being of the bears, for the ecological diversity and health of the western wildernesses, and most of all for the spiritual and aesthetic needs of the American people, that is nowhere near enough grizzly bears.

The change in public mood about grizzly bear conservation has been complex and difficult to sort out. Perhaps it is only because so many of those people most hostile to grizzly bear conservation in the West have passed away, or maybe it's because public education continues to improve or because bear managers have gotten better at their jobs. For whatever reason or combination of reasons, there is now far more sympathy for the needs of the grizzly bear on the part of people actually living in grizzly bear country. Grizzly bear conservation is no longer driven primarily by people living far from actual grizzly bears.

With this change and with our fast-improving understanding of the needs of the grizzly bear, there continues to be hope for the remaining populations: the bears of the Greater Yellowstone Ecosystem in Wyoming, Montana, and Idaho; the Northern Continental Divide Ecosystem of Glacier National Park and wilderness lands to its south in northern Montana; the Cabinet–Yaak area along the northern Montana–Idaho border; the Selkirk Mountains along the northern Idaho–Washington border; and the North Cascades National Park area in northern Washington. Some of these populations are quite small, and I tell you that the welfare and stability of none of them dare be taken for granted.

Thus, it remains uncertain if even the grizzly bear's increasingly powerful symbolism and mighty congregation of admirers provide the wherewithal necessary to protect it over the next century in a region that is still resource-gobbling and growth-crazy. Among the good things that can be said about the longtime human inhabitants of grizzly country whom McCracken neighbored with is that there weren't so many of them that their very numbers threatened the bear. The same cannot be said of all the hordes of new immigrants now moving to the West for precisely the kind of "amenities"—read "open, sparsely populated country"—that the bear also requires.

Scientific Definitions

It would take far more space than a short essay provides to introduce all of the important and exciting revisions that have occurred in our understanding of the grizzly bear since McCracken's book appeared, and no such revision is necessary here. You aren't reading this book for the latest scientific facts anyway. *The Beast That Walks Like Man* is not offered as some kind of definitive word (such a thing may never exist); it is offered as a compelling personal statement of the worth of a singular species and as a broad and eloquent historical description of the animal's place in human culture.

Still, it is worth alerting new readers to a point or two. Most of all, you should know that the formal delineation of the grizzly bear species has been completely revamped since McCracken's time. He responsibly and dutifully appended Clinton Hart Merriam's 1918 classification of dozens of North American grizzly bear species (see pages 291–304). But it is refreshing that McCracken did point out that Merriam realized that some would view his long list as "preposterous" and that he quoted Merriam's somewhat self-serving comment that "it is not the business of the naturalist to either create or suppress species, but to endeavor to ascertain how many Nature has established." A half century of additional consideration, aided by everything from field observation to incredibly well-resolved DNA technologies, has done away with all of Merriam's fanciful definitions of separate grizzly bear species. Even in Merriam's time, someone needed to say to him that it is also the business of the naturalist to make sense. His list never did (it was, amazingly and absurdly, possible for him to define siblings in a single litter as members of different species), and it is now happily gone. Only in the case of the huge brown bears of Kodiak Island is there yet a serious question about the possibility of more than one species of brown bear in North America. North American brown and grizzly bears have a lot of superficial variety, especially in local variations, in appearance and physiological traits and behavior. But it now looks like there is just one clearly distinguishable species, and not all that genetically diverse a species (far less diverse than the American black bear, for example) at that.

BEAR HEROES

As I write this, it's early spring in Yellowstone. Well, some days it's early spring, and other days, like during last week's blizzard, it's still winter. Whatever we may call it, the bears know what time it is. We are getting our first reports of big male grizzly bears emerging from their dens (thus settling, by the way, the question McCracken ruminates over on pages 222–223 about which bears emerge first; it's the big males, almost without exception). As with each year in the past century or so, when they leave their dens and wander down the slopes and beyond the park boundaries, they will find a few more humans than they did the year before—a few more second homesites along or right in the middle of their old paths, a few more miles of roads out on the edges of the Yellowstone Ecosystem. Maybe this will be the year that they'll finally find such increased concentrations of humans enough of a bother that they will abandon some spot permanently or only return to its edge every year or two, just to reassure themselves that they no longer have any business there. That's how the losses happen. The same pattern of incremental loss is occurring through most of the remaining actively occupied grizzly bear habitat in the lower forty-eight states, as well as all too much of it in the Canadian Rockies.

Here in Yellowstone, as elsewhere in Montana to the north, there are also more promising developments. Since 1995, there's been a new and enormously interesting scent on those first breezes that the bears inhale when they emerge. They once again, for the first time in several decades, share their domain with a sizeable population of wolves, who not only make life more exciting in general but also unwillingly provide the bears with a lot of free meat when bears take a fresh kill away from a wolf pack or scavenge an older kill. Life continues to change for the grizzly bears, and, as with the changes in human attitudes about them, the changes are often good.

The bears themselves have changed little. They are enormously adaptable, but when it comes to accommodating huge numbers of people in their country, they pretty quickly run up against changes they just can't make. The changes are up to us. And we have been making them. I have lately been pointing out to audiences I encounter that not only has our idea of the bear changed, but our idea of the human in the bear's world has also changed. Two hundred years ago, to be a "bear hero" was almost entirely a measure of your ability to kill bears. One hundred years ago, individuals like Theodore Roosevelt, William Wright, and several other sportsmen–naturalists displayed a new kind of heroism. They not only hunted bears, but they also studied them and fought for their conservation. Today, the bear hero is rarely a hunter; the prototype for the modern form was provided by the Craighead brothers—they were still hardy wilderness adventurers, but they "hunted" the bear to study it, to admire it, and to conserve it for the future. That's a remarkable makeover in one animal's relationship with humans in only two centuries.

The hunter–conservationist has not faded from our society, but the brand of heroism practiced by sportsmen from Roosevelt's time to McCracken's time and beyond has largely been lost on the general public. We are still redefining the bear hero as a human type, and with so few bears around it's getting harder and harder to reconcile any kind of killing, even the most enlightened forms of sport, with our idea of the grizzly bear as a rare treasure. Many of us hope for a day when grizzly bears will again be common enough to accommodate hunters as well as other bear enthusiasts. It will be interesting to see how we resolve this particular complication of the bear–human relationship in the future.

In the meantime, we are hard-pressed to find individuals who bring more of the necessary qualities for bear conservationists—who will serve us as better exemplars of the kinds of friends the bear will need—than Harold McCracken. We are all products of our times, and no doubt future bear protectors will need and embrace new ideas and new sensibilities that have eluded us so far, just as we have abandoned some of the things that McCracken knew to be true. But it's a sure thing that it will be in an all-encompassing breadth of awareness—everything from the bear as art, as brother, as icon, and as quarry to the bear as scientific marvel and barometer of wilderness health—that we will best serve the species in the future. Harold McCracken proved that.

Paul Schullery
National Park Service
Yellowstone, 2003

REFERENCES

Craighead, John J., Jay S. Sumner, and John A. Mitchell. *The Grizzly Bears of Yellowstone*. Washington, D.C.: Island Press, 1995.

Paetkau, D., L. P. Waits, P. L. Clarkson, L. Craighead, E. Vyse, R. Ward, and C. Strobek. "Variation in Genetic Diversity across the Range of North American Brown Bears." *Conservation Biology* 12, no. 2 (April 1998): 418–29.

Russell, Andy. *Grizzly Country*. New York: Alfred Knopf, 1967.

Schullery, Paul. *The Bear Hunter's Century*. New York: Dodd, Mead & Company, 1988.

———. *Lewis and Clark among the Grizzlies*. Guilford, Conn.: Globe Pequot Press, 2002.

Servheen, Christopher. "The Status and Conservation of the Bears of the World." *Eighth International Conference on Bear Research and Management Monograph Series* 2 (1990).

Chapter I

THE BEAST THAT WALKS LIKE MAN

Stories about grizzly bears were a rich part of the lore and legend of the Old West which fired the imagination of my youth—just as they have for many other youngsters born with a natural interest in the out-of-doors and the excitement of adventure. I have never lost that deep fascination which Old Ephraim inspires; and in the matter of personal experiences with these marvelous creatures, out in their natural haunts, I have been considerably more fortunate than most men.

Raised through boyhood on a little ranch in Idaho, my father had previously been a newspaperman in various sections of the West, and his specialty had been interviewing notorious characters of the old days and writing feature stories about them. He had also picked up a lot of stories about grizzly bears. These were mostly about somebody getting badly torn to pieces, or about giant cattle-killing bears that were too smart for the best hunters to shoot or catch in traps. In the evenings, when Dad's work in the fields and with the stock was done, and the coyotes were howling in the darkness around the unpainted little ranch house, he would relate these stories to me, and often my dreams were filled with the excitement of myself playing a part in those fabulous adventures. My actual encounters with real live bears began when I was eight years old. During the more than half a century which has passed since that first impressive boyhood adventure, fate has been very generous to me in opportunities to become intimately acquainted with grizzlies. By the time I was twenty-two I had killed six grizzlies, one of which was among the largest on record.

On one trip I went into the big-bear country on the Bering Sea side of the Alaska Peninsula by dog team in the middle of February (1922) and lived right out among those largest of all the grizzlies from the time the first of them came out of their hibernation dens until the snows of another winter came. With one companion I lived very much as the bears did, sleeping in the middle of the days and prowling around the salmon streams from afternoon to morning. According to a carefully kept diary, and trying not to count the same bear twice, I observed 197 different Alaska brown bears—188 of them within a period of forty days; 28 in a single day; and on one remarkable occasion I watched 12 big fellows all in sight at the same time and all catching salmon in a short stretch of the same stream. Some of the bears were seen on so many different occasions they were given appropriate nicknames—such as "Nick Carter," "Grandpa," "The Three Musketeers," "Grouchy," "The Murphy Family," "The O'Flaherty Family," and the like. This was undoubtedly one of the rarest privileges ever enjoyed by any serious observer of grizzly bears going about their natural and unmolested personal and family pursuits of daily life.

At first I had an intense desire to kill grizzlies and took great pride in doing so. The fact that most of them were shot as natural-history specimens for museums was principally because that was the most practical means by which it was possible for me to realize such experiences. For a number of years I made my living at that sort of thing. But it was not very long before I lost my desire to kill and changed my gun for a camera—finding a much more satisfying interest in these marvelous beasts of the frontier.

The first wild bear I ever met out on its own haunts was only a little black bear. He was going along quite peaceably, minding his own business, a mile or so from our ranch on the Idaho side of the Snake River, a short distance south of where the Payette flows into it. As quickly as I could get my long slender legs to working properly I lit out in a frantic race for home, and it is doubtful if I have since covered the same distance on foot in a shorter period of time. Nor did I stop when I reached the house. My mother had to follow me clear to the attic to find out what had scared me so badly. Later Dad came in from trying to shoot the bear and consoled me by saying: "Why, son, that wasn't anything to get so frightened about. A little black bear wouldn't hurt you. But if that had been a *grizzly* . . ." From then on, when I wandered around the ranch and out into the sagebrush, I often made believe that my shepherd dog was a giant grizzly bear—and very secretly decided to become a professional grizzly hunter.

It was not until I was eighteen that I shot my first bear. My folks had always taken for granted that I should become a minister of the gospel. But after a rather bad attempt to become a theological student at Drake University in Des Moines, Iowa, I left home and went to live with a relative in the Canadian Rockies of British Columbia. My cousin was married to a grand old character who had spent many years as a trapper and fur trader around the headwaters of the North Thompson River and Mount Robson country and had settled down up there on a little mountain ranch.

From time to time my father got family letters from his cousin, which told about the wild and beautiful mountain country in which they lived. I wrote to her. "Are there any bears up there? Any grizzly bears?" The reply that came back knocked the wobbly props out from under any inclinations I had for classrooms or becoming a minister. "Yes, there are lots of bears around the ranch. All kinds of them . . . black, brown, and grizzlies." That settled it. I quit school. I worked in the basement of a Des Moines department store selling boys' pants until I got the price of a one-way ticket to Kamloops, the nearest point on a railroad. The ranch was about a hundred miles up the North Thompson River from there. With a shoe box filled with sandwiches and boiled eggs, and five five-dollar bills sewed up in the collar of my black sateen shirt, I left home and started out seriously to become a bear hunter—grizzly bears in particular. I took along the choicest of the natural-history books I had collected; and I had a commission to collect birds for the museum of the Iowa State Historical Society—which gave my leaving the only dignity it possessed.

I reached the ranch in early April 1913. That was the year they started building the Canadian National Railway along the North Thompson for the transcontinental route. The ranch wasn't very much of a layout; just a big sprawling log cabin, nestled in a picturesque amphitheater of the mountains. But it was made to order for me. Archie McCorvie was a rugged old Scotch-Highlander, and he was very sympathetic to a young fellow who was much more interested in following game trails than in studying to be a minister. The first thing he did was to give me his .30–.30 rifle and put me in the charge of a Cree Indian, one of the best hunters on the river, with instructions to take me into the mountains "Indian style" and teach me the principles of his craft—which proved to be the most valuable outdoor training of my life.

There were grizzlies around all right, although the first bear I shot was a big brown bear. I was alone at the time, and what happened was of such an undignified character that I didn't even tell about it. I had gone out at daybreak and taken a stand near a well-used trail that went down into a dense swampy area where the bears retired to spend the day. All of a sudden this big brown fellow walked out in plain sight. I couldn't have missed him. But at the shot he reared up, making such a wild fuss and noise that I fled like a scared rabbit. Some subconscious impulse just took control of my legs, and they carried me away through the brush. When I stopped from sheer fatigue, I was afraid to go back. It was more than a week afterward that a combination of guilt and curiosity took me once again to the same spot. The dead bear was found, a short distance from where it had been shot; but it was a good many years before I told anyone about that undignified experience.

I did not get my first grizzly until the spring of 1916, although I shot five more of them in the fall of that same year. After about fourteen months in British Columbia I had returned home and entered Ohio State University, to study to become a naturalist or archaeologist. I was enrolled as a special student. But I stayed only long enough to promote my first expedition, which was an ambitious two-year project in Alaska and the Yukon to collect big-game specimens which were to have begun a natural-history museum at the university. Principal on the agenda were the grizzlies and giant Alaska brown bears. The fact that I was only twenty-one and had never even seen a wild grizzly was no deterrent at this stage.

The spring of 1916 found me with a string of pack horses leaving the little Alaskan town of McCarthy, near the Kennicott Copper Mines at the end of the Copper River and Northwestern Railroad, headed for the interior margin of the great Malaspina Glacier, to hunt mountain grizzlies and the rare blue glacier bears. During the summer I planned an attempt to be the first person to climb Mount Logan, second highest peak in North America.

The meeting with my first grizzly came very quickly. It was the climax of a thousand dreams and ten years of hoping. I was alone on this memorable occasion, as I had been when I met my first wild bear and had shot my first brown one. It was the beginning of what has led me through the years to the compiling of this book.

We had been traveling three days; swam our horses across the Nazina River and crossed a couple of smaller ones; climbed over one divide and had spent the previous night in another high mountain pass. Getting an early start, we expected to make our first camp in the upper valley of the big Chitina valley, up which we would travel to the Malaspina. It was still early when we came out, quite suddenly, on the west side of the pass. Across the broad valley rose one of the most magnificent arrays of snow-capped, cathedral-like mountain peaks to be found anywhere on this continent—the beautiful St. Elias Alps. There was the stimulating feeling that came from a realization that only a few white men had ever been in this whole country before, and there were many valleys where no white man had ever set a foot.

As we began the long descent into the valley, several large bands of white mountain sheep (*ovis dalli*) were grazing peacefully on grassy ranges along the side of the mountain, on both sides of the pass. We stopped the horses to put our binoculars on these beautiful creatures. Almost immediately I decided to go after them and let the rest go on. I could save the skin and it would be mighty good to have fresh meat. We decided to establish camp on the flat valley floor beside a wooded stream that ran out to the river, which made it easy for me to rejoin the party; and, taking my rifle, I started out.

This was high above timber line. The large grassy ranges were broken by deep rocky canyons and backed by towering peaks. It was my first chance at hunting in Alaska, and I could not have had a more beautiful place. The brisk freshness of the clear spring morning added an extra touch to my enthusiasm. I went to the south, because the wind was from that direction. It would also put me closer to the camping place. There was a band of about twenty wild sheep feeding up close to the high cliffs a half mile or so away, which became my objective.

I had just crossed a deep canyon and began to climb higher up when I saw my first grizzly. He had walked out of a shallow ravine onto a ridge a short distance beyond the sheep—which were immediately forgotten. My first impulse was to hurry back and overtake the pack train for assistance. But it was already down out of sight in the timber, and after some debating I decided to tackle the bear alone.

There was another large ridge between us; and, moving a little higher up, I was able to get down into the ravine without being seen. Hurrying as fast as I could, I finally crept up to get another view. Lying stretched out beside an outcropping of rock, I put my binoculars on the grizzly. My hands trembled a little as I focused the glasses. He looked terribly large, sitting there very placidly on the crest of the grassy ridge, gazing with apparent thoughtfulness out across the valley. Still too far away to risk a shot, I just watched him.

Since that day when I had met my first bear near the Snake River in Idaho, I had heard a lot about grizzly bears and I had read a great deal about them. I had learned from the science books that they are the largest, most powerful, and most formidable of all the carnivorous animals on earth today. But I had remembered most vividly the impressions of the tough pioneer hunters of the Old West who had been chewed and torn into a bloody mess by these pugnacious beasts. There was no doubt in my mind about the danger of firing a rifle slug into a grizzly; and the fact that I was alone was no particular aid to my courage. Nor had any of my previous experiences proven that I was anything of an intrepid bear hunter. But I had waited too long for this moment and I somehow found the courage to go through with it.

"*Close-um, tillicum. . . .*" ("Get close, my friend.") The words of my Cree Indian tutor kept ringing in my ears. I knew the logic of this advice. It is not original with the Crees. There is an old viking adage of wisdom for young warriors: "If you go in close enough, your sword will be long enough." I thought of this too. "Yes," I encouraged myself, "I'll get close enough to be sure and hit him just where I want to. . . ." Again the advice of my Cree tutor came back. "Heart shot sometimes no good, when shoot big bear . . . Side head good . . . but sometime no hit side head. *Break-um down best.*

Shoot-um shoulder . . . plenty big mark . . . easy hit-um there."

He sat longer than I had expected, and there was no alternative but to wait and watch. It was impossible to get closer without being seen. If he moved in my direction, I could just lie there until he got close enough. If he went the other way, I could hurry across the wide ravine as soon as he was out of sight. In the meantime I had plenty of opportunity to study him and to do a lot of thinking. With my powerful binoculars it seemed that I could almost reach out and run my fingers through his coarse grizzled hair. He had been out of hibernation long enough to regain a good share of his robust figure. He gave the appearance of being completely given over to that pleasant self-satisfaction which comes after a hearty meal. Sitting in the slouched-over position so typical of lazy bears and men, with hind feet stuck out in front, arms dangling, and stomach bulging, he gazed out across the valley. I wondered what he had eaten during the night. There were a good many hoary marmots and ground squirrels around, but digging out a full meal of these seemed like such a futile way for even an energetic grizzly to get his groceries. Certainly he had not raided the band of sheep which had been grazing so peacefully such a short distance away. Probably he had filled that big stomach of his with fresh green grass and maybe some palatable roots or tubers which grew up here, that I didn't know about.

A couple of times he got up and moved his position, as if to find a more comfortable place to sit. Once he spent quite a little time alternately scratching his stomach and running his long brown claws idly through the grass in front of where he sat.

There had been a good many previous occasions when I had wondered what mental functions were going on within the hairy heads of other animals; although never before had I been afforded such an opportunity as this, to watch and speculate about such a marvelous wild creature. He appeared so amiable and good-natured—not at all what I had expected of a grizzly. I had spent ten years of wishful planning, and actually traveled more than five thousand miles, with the serious intent of killing this bear. Just how far would the very same motive have caused this animal to travel—or would his disposition have inspired such a motive? If he had become aware of our camp down on the floor of the valley, would he have left this high, peaceful range and made that short trip down there for the express purpose of tearing one of us to pieces; or would he move farther away and mind his own business? Just who was the greater savage? Had any grizzly ever traveled that far for the express purpose of killing a man? Yet I had known a good many men who had traveled several thousand miles just to kill a grizzly.

At last the bear started wandering up the ridge, in a lackadaisical sort of way which indicated he had not entirely made up his mind as to where he would go for a midday sleep. I noticed the flat-footed manner in which he laid down his big moccasin-like feet, heel first, just like a man, and an Indian in particular. It reminded me why the early pioneers in our West had nicknamed the grizzly "Old Ephraim" and "Moccasin Joe," from this manner in which he walked and the tracks that were made by his feet. Watching him intently through the binoculars, I marveled at the smooth flow of massive muscles underneath the heavily coated hide; the easy grace with which his big body moved along; and the primitive dignity of his whole bearing.

Instead of coming in my direction, as I had hoped, he wandered over the ridge and disappeared. As soon as I felt reasonably sure he was not coming in sight again, I began hurrying in a wide swing higher up. I was confident he was going to find some shady place to lie down, and I was anxious to keep him below me, in case of a fight.

Reaching the crest of the ridge almost up where the rocky cliffs began, I moved cautiously on to where it was possible to get a good view down the ravine. There was a low gravel bank running part way down the near side, and I soon saw the bear moving along leisurely close to the base of this. Freezing motionless, my eyes were kept fastened upon him, as I very slowly moved my rifle into a better position. He was about seventy-five yards away, and if he walked out a little farther I would shoot. Instead, however, he stopped; and, after using his claws to level off a place, he lay down.

Picking a well-defined spot at the top of the bank directly above the bear, I slipped back to make a closer approach.

Within a few minutes I was walking very cautiously out to look down upon him, gun ready for instant action. The first glimpse of his shaggy brown hair, not more than twenty-five feet directly below me, sent a sudden chill through my whole body. The great moment had come. Believing he was stretched out on his stomach, I moved up my gun as I took another step . . . and then another. I would put a bullet through the top of his head. Suddenly, however, I realized that the grizzly was lying flat on his back, and his little piglike eyes stared straight up at me. At almost the same instant he made a lurch to get onto his feet, as I pulled up my rifle and fired. He must have jumped six feet, landing on all fours, and I was conscious that the hair was up on his back. Whether he made any sound or not, I don't remember. In more a state of panic than methodical procedure I fired again. Close as he was, I believe I missed him completely the second shot. At this he wheeled and went racing away down the grassy ravine. I fired again and again, realizing at each shot they were not doing any damage. Then, quickly getting control of myself, I waited long enough to really put the sights on him, and when the gun blasted the bear came to an abrupt stop. He had already traveled well over a hundred yards; but, hit squarely in the backside, his hind quarters were paralyzed. He now set up a terrible noise and began ripping and tearing up the low juniper bushes and the ground with claws and teeth.

Trembling so violently that I could hardly hold a cartridge in my fingers, I reloaded the gun. It was now pretty certain that the bear would not get away, but I sat down and, steadying elbows on knees for a careful aim, another shot was put into his neck. Then I started hurrying close enough to finish him off, if still another shot was necessary. My legs were so wobbly and weak, however, that I could hardly walk. But I was so jubilant that I wanted to shout an old-fashioned Indian war-whoop that would echo to the white mountain tops. I had gotten my first grizzly—and done it all alone.

Skinning out that bear was the most satisfying experience I had ever enjoyed. It was not a large grizzly, even for the Alaskan mountain variety. I made sketches in my notebook and took all sorts of measurements, even opened the paunch to find it crammed with grass, roots, and a trace of ground squirrels. But the thing that impressed me the deepest was how much the skinned body resembled that of a human being. It reminded me of the old-time Indian legends, which proclaim the grizzly bear as the ancestor of their race. "Him arms and him legs, jus' like Indians. . . ." my Cree tutor had tried to explain to me. "Him stomach . . . him heart . . . him everything all-same. Him walk like Indian too." Surely, I thought to myself, there is something here that goes deeper than mere physical coincidence.

Relating the accounts of my personal conquests in killing grizzly bears is one of the least important parts and purposes of this book. Looking back through the years, I have become less and less proud that I killed so many. Others have killed many more; and, while I have by no means become an anti-hunter, I have come to realize how vastly more there is to be learned about these marvelous creatures than merely the most destructive spot to hit them with the slug from a high-powered rifle. We know so very little about any of the animals around us—practically nothing of their language or any of their psychological functions—although man has lived in such close association with them for a million years or more.

Observing and studying grizzly bears, unmolested in their own native haunts, has proved to be far more gratifying than all the hunting I have done. Also, through the years I have tried to learn everything I could from the writings and experiences of others. It is my purpose, therefore, to set down in this book as complete a story as possible about the grizzly bears of North America, from the very earliest times of which there is any available information; their legendary association with the Indians, before the days of the white man; the most important and most exciting phases of our pioneer explorers and bear hunters; the grizzlies' futile struggle for survival throughout the United States; and, probably more important, the most comprehensive explanation that I can give of their lives, personality, and temperament, drawn from my own experiences and the observations of other naturalists.

Chapter II

BIRTH OF A NOBLE LEGEND

W<small>HEN</small> the last grizzly bear has been dead a thousand years or more, perhaps the stories that will survive about these mighty animals will put him in the category of an incarnate demigod of the past. There is a great deal that recommends the grizzly to the fabric of a lasting legend, and the symptoms of such an investiture are already evident. By thousands of campfires and other places where outdoorsmen get together, since the first of our frontier adventurers encountered these pugnacious creatures on the plains and in the mountains of the Far West, men have told glowing stories about the grizzly—stories that have all the raw glamour of their subject and so easily rise to the height of an epic. The bravest, toughest, and most distinguished of these men have spoken with the greatest of pride about their conquests of the grizzly—Lewis and Clark, Zebulon Pike, Kit Carson, Stonewall Jackson, General Custer, Theodore Roosevelt, and many more. Not one has held him lightly; and most have honestly respected him in their hearts—just as the old-time Indian considered it an accomplishment of greater bravery and distinction to have killed a grizzly than to have taken the scalp of any human enemy. One can cast aside all the yarns of the neophytes and the fabrications of imaginative journalists who never really knew the grizzly; and one can fully discount all the honest doubts and theories; and still Old Ephraim stands realistically in all the impressive admiration which might be expected of the largest and most powerful of all carnivorous creatures on the earth today.

There is much about the grizzly and his characteristics which highly recommends him to our historic lore. He is American to the backbone and as noble, roughhewn, and fearsome as the emblematic lion of England, the winged bull of Assyria, dragon of China, sphinx of Egypt, or any of the other fabulous animalistic demigods of history. He is far more symbolic of the characteristics of our frontier forefathers and the men who have given our nation the respect which we enjoy in the world today than the eagle which has become our heraldic emblem—a fit companion, in the proud parade of our historic lore, along with all the colorful characters in homespun and buckskin, with Kentucky rifles, fur-ladened pack horses, and covered wagons on one-way journeys westward across a trackless wilderness. Like the Indian, however, the grizzly has been maligned and persecuted; and, like the vast herds of buffalo, he has been virtually exterminated throughout most of the wide range where he once roamed supreme. But as sure as the hills will be emptied of all their gold, the guided waters will make gardens of the deserts, and new conditions of life will come to pass, time and again, over all the lands from Manhattan to Hollywood, still the stories of the grizzlies, as part of the old frontier, will be listened to with an ever increasing attention by America's grown men and growing boys.

The grizzly bear, it should be remembered, was an old resident of America when Europeans discovered the New World. He had been here, even along the eastern seaboard, for many thousands of years before the first Indian set foot on any part of this continent. It is a well-established fact that he roamed over wide areas of North America as long ago as the Pleistocene period, which goes back about 1,250,000 years. He was a coinhabitant of our fair land along with the mastodon and the saber-tooth tiger; and he was here when the Great Ice Age brought musk ox down onto our now-fertile midwestern plains. Archaeologists have diligently searched this continent for evidences of primitive man, and they are now pretty well agreed that the first humans came to America more recently than the last glacial period at the *end* of the Pleistocene, or *only* about 10,000 to 15,000 years ago—which gives the grizzly a rather amazing seniority.

The evidences of Pleistocene bears on this continent are based upon skeletal remains found over such widely separated locations as California, Oklahoma, Iowa, Mississippi, Maryland, Florida, and Wyoming. Some of these and the associated manifestations of their antiquity have been critically studied over a period of almost half a century by highly accredited paleontologists, and several scholarly papers have been published regarding them.

During the excavations carried out in 1906 by the University of California in the famous *Rancho La Brea* asphalt pits, now within the metropolitan area of the city of Los Angeles, there were found the remains of a grizzly bear of extraordinarily large size.[1] The scientists who have studied these remains have named this beast *Arctotherium californicum* (Meriam); and they state that it was "one of the largest and most powerful known carnivorous animals of Pleistocene time"—exceeding in size the saber-tooth tiger, the *Rancho La Brea* lion, or even the great cave bear (*Arctotherium simum*) of northern California. Both of these prehistoric grizzlies were considerably larger than the Alaska brown bears of today.

Another of these grizzlies that roamed North America untold centuries before any human foot had left its track upon our continent is represented by two fossil specimens found in the vicinities of Lawton and Cheyenne, Oklahoma. They are scientifically described as *Ursus horribilis oklahomaensis*, in a paper published by the University of Oklahoma in 1935.[2] Other prehistoric grizzlies have been described from fossil remains found in Iowa,[3] Maryland,[4] Mississippi, Florida, and elsewhere.

It is quite evident from the considerable number of fossil remains which have been examined by highly competent scientists that there were wide variations in size among the ancient grizzly bears of North America—even to a greater degree than in recent times—although the general characteristics of these animals have changed very little through the many thousands of years. It is reasonable to believe, from the carefully reconstructed evidence, that some of the Pleistocene bears were of tremendous size. The *Rancho La Brea* grizzly, for example, considerably exceeded a full ton in weight and stood more than twelve feet in height when he rose up to stand on his hind feet. There must have been many others of like proportions, probably even larger ones, that roamed through the mountains and over the plains of the West.

The grizzly bear is certainly the most pugnacious and extraordinary survivor of that prehistoric era. Just why and how the mastodons and the saber-tooth tigers, and all those other mighty creatures of the bygone past, became doomed to complete extinction by nature's inexorable laws of survival is still one of the many unsolved mysteries which man would like to understand. It is not that the grizzly was smarter or that he clawed the others into the dust. Such things have repeatedly happened through the eons of time; and there is no evident rhyme, reason, or plan in the pattern by which species have been wiped from the face of the earth.

While the grizzly proper is restricted to North America, with only the counterpart of the Alaska brown bear now found in Kamchatka, eastern Siberia, other varieties of bears are indigenous to most parts of the earth. It seems more than probable that Old Ephraim originally migrated from Asia, when there was an extensive land bridge which geologists claim once existed where Bering Sea now lies. Other of our native animals, along with the humans, no doubt came to this continent the same way. Just when these various migrations took place we are not certain and probably never will know.

It should be pointed out that some of the animals and birds

which are today common around our homes, farms, and wooded hinterlands may have come to North America even before the grizzly arrived. Such creatures as moose, mice, robins, buffalo, wren, and cottontail rabbits didn't just spring into being like the fictional "Topsy." They may have been as they are today when the culture of our ancestors was but little higher than that of the other animals. This is mentioned merely to emphasize that while the grizzly is a very old resident of North America, and lived as a neighbor to the mastodons and other fabulous and extinct beasts of the prehistoric past, he is by no means the only one of our wild creatures who deserves such a distinction—although he still remains the mightiest of all the flesh-eating animals on this or any other continent.

These brief and very cursory facts are given merely as something of the background of this marvelous creature.

Now he too faces the unfortunate and quite inevitable fate of joining the disappearing species. But his extermination is not through any of the unexplained laws of nature. Like the vast herds of buffalo that once roamed our Western Plains, the grizzly has become a victim of the white man's devastation and of the natural progress of our type of civilization. And, now that Old Ephraim begins to take his place in our frontier lore and legend, the interest which he has created and the glamorous saga which his rugged and ruthless character has made for himself take on new and more historic importance. Aside from all this, his struggle for survival is one of the most exciting chapters in the story of the Old West.

Chapter III

"THE GRIZZLY WAS OUR ANCESTOR"

LONG before the first European came to this continent the North American Indians had their own theories regarding the origin of the human race. Most of the tribes held to a belief that they had sprung from one or another of the animals or birds of the primeval wilderness, by some more or less divine creation; and the grizzly was a widespread and favorite traditional ancestor among the red men.

There was much to recommend the mighty bear as a progenitor. He was the embodiment of all the virile virtues which primitive man aspired to—strength, courage, and cold belligerence. "The chief thing is to be brave," was the Indian's dogma of human ethics. "To be brave is what makes a man. . . . Do not fear anything. To be killed in battle is no disgrace. When you fight, try to kill. Go up close to your enemy. As you charge, you must be saying to yourself all the time, 'I will be brave; I will fear nothing.' "[5] The grizzly bear was the personification of all this, and he was more.

The best of the Indian braves were never a favorable match for the grizzly, even when several of the tribesmen attacked together, using the best of their weapons of warfare—and warfare was the most distinguished profession of the Indians. The grizzly had developed a haughty disdain for their arrows, spears, and stone axes, which were so effective against their human

34

enemies. They did occasionally kill the mighty bear, but this was far more dangerous, and far more honorable, than the taking of any tribal scalp.

Even the acquisition of the horse, from the early Spanish conquistadors in the middle of the sixteenth century, did not put the Indian on an equal with the grizzly. The horse advanced the red man's culture fully as abruptly and dramatically as the auto or the airplane has improved our own modern means of transportation; and yet the grizzly remained the arrogant and supreme brutal master of the Indian's world. To be sure, tradition was born when the red man's history was much too young to be remembered, and that was a long time before the coming of the horse; but this undiminished superiority of the mighty bear gave new dimensions to his place in the romantic fabric of the Indians' flowering culture.

There were other and equally realistic reasons for this ancestral association. The Indian was a keen observer of nature. He recognized the traits and peculiarities of all the creatures of the wilderness around him, as well as the many differences in species among the mammals and birds—far more clearly than the average white man of today who has not had zoological training. He recognized the close physical affinity between the animals and his own race. He realized the fundamental similarity between the long claws of the bear, and other wild creatures, and his own fingernails; that they had fingers and toes and ribs and a backbone, just as the Indian had. He knew they had a brain, heart and blood system, stomach and genital organs, and all the rest—of the same constitution and physical function as his own and his wife's. In conception and birth, throughout the sustaining of life, and the passing into the limbo of death, there was very little difference between them. When the bear stood erect, he walked like a man. But the grizzly was always the mightier of the two. And the bear was smart. "A bear is wiser than a man," an old Abnaki Indian sage once philosophized, "because a man does not know how to live all winter without eating anything."[6]

The red man considered all living creatures as "other people," rather than the "dumb animals" by which we moderns degrade them. Many of the tribes believed that the animals had tribes, just as the Indians had, with head chiefs and councils, and that some of them were supernaturally endowed with powers by which they could help human individuals in their daily pursuits, problems, and physical ailments. The Indian had a healthy religious belief in a Great Power. "He is in the birds and wild animals, lakes and streams, prairies and mountains. He brings the leaves in the spring. He makes the grass and the berries grow; and upon them the birds and the animals depend for life . . . The Thunder is a great bird. It flies with the clouds and brings the rain. From its eyes the lightnings flash. And the Blizzard is a person, who runs before the storm and shoots his arrows."[7] This is taken from the Blackfoot philosophy of "the power of the sun," although it represents the general belief of the Great Plains tribes.

Few of the earth's races have been so rich in lore and legend as the North American Indians. They were brilliantly colorful and dramatically spectacular. And, while much has been written about them, their story has unfortunately been presented preponderantly from the white man's viewpoint—a viewpoint that has not been particularly sympathetic or understanding to the red man's ideals. There is much that the white man never learned, and much in error has come down to us regarding the whole ethos of their lives.

This book is primarily concerned with the Indian's traditional attitudes, beliefs, and religious ceremonies directly associated with the grizzly bear. Some of these may seem a bit fantastic and difficult for us to accept as more than interesting fabrications of primitive man. It is only natural to draw disrespectful conclusions to human manifestations which are radically different from those inherited as our own. Just as the ancient Hellenic philosophers proclaimed that "the world is divided into two classes—*Greeks and barbarians*," so has practically every other race held high its own national ego. But, before we make ourselves the pedantic judges of those beliefs which the Indian held sacred, we might first consider a few of our errors which have already become an undisputed part of the record.

Everyone knows that the Indian was so named because he was thought to be a native of India, which the early Spanish explorers believed they had reached by sailing westward from Europe.[8] There are other similar examples of the errors which have persisted in spite of correction. We misnamed the American buffalo, which scientifically is not a buffalo at all but a bison, related to the European variety. The true buffalo is a short-haired creature without a prominent hump on his shoulders, such as the African buffalo and similar varieties found in southern Asia. But the vast herds of wild bovine in our West were named buffalo by the early plainsmen, buffalo they lived and died, and buffalo they will always continue to be known. The animal they named a moose is really an elk; our elk is not an elk at all; our mountain goat is not a goat; our wild sheep is not strictly a sheep; and even our antelope, sad to say, is likewise not a member of the antelope family. The explanations are too involved to go into here, and the layman is supposed to take the scientists' word for it.

This does not mean that all we know about the Indian is contrary to the true facts, nor that we are not entitled to our own opinions regarding anything in the red man's repertoire. We should, however, accord their devout beliefs the tolerant courtesy to which every race is justly entitled.

The red man devoutly believed in his animal ancestry. Most of the tribes, clans, families, and individuals held some close affinity of one kind or another with some particular mammal or bird, and it is a common occurrence to find the bear referred to with a connotation of human relationship among the primitive peoples throughout this continent as well as in other parts of the earth. This is ably set forth in detail by A. Irving Hollowell in his scholarly thesis *Bear Ceremonialism*.[9]

Both the grizzly and black bear were given ancestral relationship among the American Indians, although the wide differences between these two animals were fully recognized and the grizzly occupied the pre-eminent position. Among the Abnaki, who inhabited the present state of Maine when the English and French first visited that region, it was common practice, when signs of the black bear were seen in the woods, for the hunters to say, "These are our cousins' tracks."[10] The Têtes de Boule, a tribe of wandering hunters who roamed over an extensive region on the upper branches of the Ottawa, Gatineau, and St. Maurice rivers of Quebec when visited by the Jesuits in 1671, referred to the bear as "grandfather." This same term, with such close variations as "grandmother" and "great-grandfather," is found all the way across the continent, from the Ojibways to the Luiseños of Southern California and the Tsimshians and Tahltans of the northwest coast regions, as well as among the tribes of eastern Siberia. Among the Plains Crees the grizzly was referred to as "four-legged human" and sometimes as the "chief's son"; the Sauks called him "old man"; the Menomini term meant "elder brother"; while the Blackfoot name translates into "that big hairy one"; and to other tribesmen the grizzly was "the old man in a furred cloak."

It has already been indicated that the grizzly was at one time a resident of the United States from coast to coast, and there is some evidence that this animal inhabited our eastern coastal regions at a period which was not too distant, historically, before the coming of Europeans to the vicinity of Manhattan. "The grizzly bear formerly resided in this state [New York], according to the traditions of the Delaware and Mohican indians, who say that the last was seen on the east side of Hudson's river; and they to this day terrify their children with it." This statement was made by the distinguished scholar, statesman, and naturalist, the Hon. DeWitt Clinton, in an address before the Literary and Philosophical Society, in New York City, on May 4, 1814.[11] He was president of the society at the time; and the text, which was published the following year, includes interesting addenda, among which is

"Note 14," here quoted: "The reverend John Heckwelder states, that the Mohican indians had a tradition of an animal they called the big naked bear. They say that the last was seen on the east side of Hudson's river, where the indians killed him after great difficulty; that it was remarkably long bodied, and larger than the common bear; and all over naked, except for a spot of hair on its back, of a white color; that it was very destructive to their nation, killing and devouring them. And such was the terror it inspired, that they often say to their children, when crying, 'Hush, the naked bear will hear you, be upon you, and devour you.' "[12] The use of the word "naked" in this instance may be a case of faulty translation of the original Indian word or phrase, or it may be a glamorization or exaggeration used by the primitives to give more dramatic emphasis upon their obstreperous youngsters—even as we do in similar instances today.

DeWitt Clinton refers to this as a grizzly bear, and it is clearly demonstrated that he was thoroughly familiar with what a grizzly was, although his statements were made a year before that animal received its accredited scientific classification by George Ord.[13] Some zoologists have felt that DeWitt Clinton should have enjoyed the distinction of having his description accepted in scientific nomenclature instead of that of Ord, who added his name to the Latin designation—*Ursus horribilis* Ord.

DeWitt Clinton expressed the belief that the grizzly "has retreated from the eastern parts of the continent, and occupies that wide and expansive range of country upon all the waters which form the sources of the Missouri; where he exists the terror of the savages, the tyrant of all the other animals; devouring alike man and beast, and defying the attacks of whole tribes of indians."[14]

There is little else to substantiate the Delaware and Mohican story of their great "naked bear" as being an incarnate grizzly, who made his natural habitat "on the east side of Hudson's river" in times so recent that the local Indians would tell stories about the animal, although his existence in that region at a much more distant time seems beyond doubt. It is also possible, of course, that a far-wandering grizzly or family of these animals might in those early days have strayed that far east, or the bedtime bogeyman story of the naked bear might easily have been brought, in one way or another, by Indian travelers from farther west. There is also the possibility that the Hudson River red men may have brought this story with them when they first migrated eastward across the continent.

The gossamer threads of primitive history such as this cannot be passed over lightly, however, any more than they can be taken at face value without discount or serious researching. Here is just another example of our lack of knowledge and understanding of the North American Indians and of the vast void which casts a deep black shadow over their pre-Columbian past. Even if one makes no serious attempt to pick these stories to pieces and get to their basic realities, one should keep in mind as clear a picture as possible of the background in which they were created and have survived; and, when they concern the grizzly bear, one should not forget the particular position which this fearsome creature had always occupied in the lives of those particular people. Before the European explorers of the sixteenth and seventeenth centuries came to break down the Stone Age curtain that imprisoned the Indians in their dark ages of complete primitiveness, their whole culture was all that Stone Age implies.

The mighty grizzly being what he was through so many centuries of the Indians' experience, it is only natural that he should occupy an extremely important and glamorous position in their memorabilia of the past. Little wonder is it that so many of them should choose him as a legendary ancestor; and whether or not we agree with the Indians' ideas, in part or in whole, the lore and legend with which he has surrounded the grizzly has had a strong influence upon our present-day opinions and the place which we have accorded this animal among the permanent legends of the future.

Chapter IV

SAGAS OF LONG AGO

THE Great Spirit made Mount Shasta first of all.[15] That was thousands of summers ago, when there was no life of any kind upon the earth. There were no animals, for there was nothing for them to eat; and no birds, for there were no trees or flowers in which they might build their nests; and no fish, for the streams and rivers had not yet been made. But one day, as the Great Spirit looked down from his home up among the stars, he decided to come down to have a closer look at the earth. So he pushed down snow and ice through a hole in the blue sky, until he had made a mountain so great that it was easy to step down upon it from a big white cloud.

As he stood on top of the great mountain and looked around, the Great Spirit saw that the earth was entirely barren and lifeless. He decided to make the earth beautiful and create living things to enjoy it. Walking down out of the snow, he put his fingers onto the bare ground, and green trees, grass, and flowers instantly sprang up and began spreading into forests that quickly covered the valleys and low hills. Then he told the sun to shine a little more brightly, to melt some of the snow on the great mountains, just enough so that the water would run down to nurture the forests and the flowers. With the end of his walking stick he marked out a place for the streams and rivers, which began carrying water out to fill the sea. Then he broke off the small end of his walking stick, which he crushed into small bits in his hand, and, casting these into the streams, they became fish which swam away to spawn. Picking some leaves from the trees, he held them in the palm of his hand and, blowing them into the air, they became birds of many kinds which flew away singing, to build their nests. After this, very pleased with what he had done, the Great Spirit broke off some more of his walking stick and, casting larger bits of it about, they became animals of many kinds. He made them of many sizes, some weak and some swift of foot, and each one a little stronger or a little swifter than others, so they would each have a good chance of survival. And when he came to the large end of his walking stick, the heavy part that he always held in his right hand, he held it thoughtfully for some time, deciding just what sort of creature he should make out of this last sturdy piece; and then he made an animal that was to be mightier than any of the others and was to rule over all the rest. This was the grizzly bear. But, when this animal took form and life, it was so strong and aggressive that the Great Spirit had to climb hurriedly back to the mountain-top, to find a safe place to rest after performing all his labors of creating life upon the earth.

Thus begins the story of creation as related by the Shasta and Modoc Indians, who lived in the region which is today northern California and southern Oregon. These people had been old residents there for hundreds and hundreds of years before Sir Francis Drake's crew of the *Golden Hind*, on June 17, 1579, "landed in what is now Marin County, California . . . just north of the Golden Gate and lying between San Francisco Bay and the broad Pacific,"[16] and they claimed the territory for Queen Elizabeth of England. The Spanish came later, built their missions, and took possession; and then they lost California to the aggressive frontier determination of the United States. But the Shastas and Modocs knew little or nothing about what was going on beyond the shadow of towering Mount Shasta and the limited horizon of the wooded mountain ridges around them. They had their first contact with the white men in the early part of the nineteenth century, when an occasional trapper came into their territory;[17] but the development of gold mining in the 1850s and '60s, and the shortly following conquest of the upper Sacramento Valley by white settlers in a greedy scramble for new farm lands, overran the ancestral domain of these red men and brought about the hasty processes of their extinction as a race. The grizzly bears in that district have also become a memory of the past. But the great Mount Shasta still rises in all its magnitude and beauty, and the primeval story which it inspired so many centuries before the coming of the destructive white man still survives as one of the classics of Indian legendry.

The Great Spirit, when he first came down from the sky, made the earth such a beautiful place that he decided to stay for a while. So he converted Mount Shasta into a great tepee, built a fire inside to make it a pleasant place to live, and brought down his family from up among the stars. The fire glowed upward out of the tepee top against the dark sky at night, and by day the smoke rose lazily to drift with the clouds. The Indians knew this was so, because their ancestors had seen it when the fire and the smoke were there many hundreds of summers ago.

It was not very long after the Great Spirit brought his family down to live in Mount Shasta that one day his youngest and fairest daughter wandered down into the woodlands that spread far out around the base of the mountain. It was in the springtime, when all the flowers were in blossom; the birds were all singing and building their nests; the salmon were coming up the streams from the sea to spawn, and animals were with their newborn young.

The beautiful little girl wandered farther and farther, with the spring breezes blowing through her long red hair and putting an extra bit of color into the soft skin of her cheeks. She had been so fascinated by the fragrance of the flowers and the forest, and the songs of the birds, that when the end of the day approached she could not remember the way back to her home. But she was not afraid, and finally, becoming very tired, she crawled under the spreading branches of a big tree and lay down to rest.

Not far from where the fairest child of the Great Spirit lay down a family of grizzly bears had their home. The mother bear had lately brought forth, and the father was out procuring food for the newly born. It should be remembered that in this time of so long ago the grizzly bears were somewhat different than we know them today. They were covered with the same heavy coat of hair, had their long sharp claws, and lived in caves; but they walked erect on two feet, talked among themselves in a language of their own, just as humans do today, and they used heavy clubs for weapons instead of their claws and teeth. Beasts that they were, and arrogant rulers of all the animal world, they had quite a pleasant family life.

As the father grizzly returned home, with his club on his shoulder and a young elk carried under his left arm, he saw the beautiful little girl lying under the tree, with her long red hair partly covering her bare shoulders. Not knowing what to make of this soft, gentle creature, he took her home to his wife, who was very wise in all such matters. The old grizzly mother was not only wise and kind, but she ran their household pretty much as she chose to. "We will keep this strange child," she said in a very determined voice. "I will share my breast with her and we will bring her up with the other children, and maybe some good will come of it. But we must never mention anything about it to anyone else."

And so it was. The little daughter of the Great Spirit was raised in this family of grizzly bears. The mother bear cared for her, just as she did for her own children; and the father went out through the forest with his club on his shoulder, to provide food for all of them.

Then came the time when all the young were grown up and must start families of their own. "Our son must have a wife," the old mother grizzly said one evening as they were all gathered together. "It should be our adopted daughter, the fair one with the pink skin and the long red hair, whom your father found under the tree." This met with the approval of everyone. "You are a very wise wife," said the father bear. "You are a very kind mother," said the girl. So the father went out with his club over his shoulder to get some special meat for the marriage feast.

All the other grizzlies were now told about it, and they came from many miles around to make the happy event a most memorable one. They celebrated as one family, for they were all very pleased, and together they built a great tepee for the pretty red princess and her grizzly bear husband. They built it close to that of her father's, and it can still be seen and is now called Little Mount Shasta.

The marriage was a happy one, and many children were born. The children, being partly the flesh and blood of the Great Spirit and partly that of the grizzly bear, were somewhat different from either of their parents. Their skin was reddish and bare, like that of their mother, and the hair of their heads was long but black, like that on the head of their father. They did not have long claws on the ends of their fingers, and in appearance they were more like their mother; but in many ways they partook of the nature of both parents. They were strong and brave, like their father, but they had the wisdom of their grandfather, the Great Spirit. Thus the red man was created, for these were the first Indians.

With the passing of years the time came when the old mother grizzly knew she was soon to die; and, realizing that she had done wrong in keeping the child of the Great Spirit and never letting him know what had happened, she worried about this until she decided to do something to correct the wrong and ask forgiveness before her days on earth were ended. So she called all the grizzlies together at the big tepee which had been built for the princess and her family and told them what she had decided to do; and as soon as she had said these things she sent her son, who had married the princess, to the summit of Mount Shasta to tell the Great Spirit where he could find his long-lost daughter.

The Great Spirit was so elated and so excited that he raced down the south side of the mountain, with such powerful strides that even to this day you can see the marks of his tracks. The grizzlies were all waiting for him. They stood in two great lines, with their clubs resting peacefully in their arms, and they made a lane through which the Great Spirit passed as in a tribal ceremony. He slowed his pace and walked with restrained emotion to where his daughter was waiting for him. But when he saw the children, and learned that the grizzlies had created a new race, he became very angry. It was only the Great Spirit's privilege to create new races of living things on the earth. His eyes flashed like the lightning as he stared at the old grizzly mother who had planned and been responsible for all this, and she immediately fell down and died on the spot. Seeing what the Great Spirit had done, all the other grizzlies became very incensed and, clutching their clubs in their right hands, they set up a loud howling of angry protest.

Becoming even more incensed at this, the Great Spirit took up his daughter and, holding her on his shoulder, his eyes flashed again. He ordered all the grizzlies to drop their clubs upon the ground, never again to use them; he forever silenced their voices, and he ordered them to get down on their hands and knees before him and so to remain until he released them from these orders. The grizzlies were unable to resist the will of the Great Spirit, and they all did as they were told.

Then he drove all of his daughter's children out into the world and bade them scatter in all the different directions, after which he tightly closed the door of the big tepee so they could not come back to live there. Then, carrying the fair one on his shoulder, he strode away, going back up the mountain. Never again did the Great Spirit return to the timber or release the bears from the orders which he had imposed upon them.

So it was that the Indians were created; and so it was that

the grizzlies lost their power of speech and the use of clubs as weapons, and forever since they have had to walk about on four feet instead of two. Like other beasts they have had to use their claws and teeth as weapons, and only when they are compelled to fight for the preservation of their own honor or their lives does the Great Spirit permit them to stand up and walk like men.

This is how the Indians came to be. We know it happened this way because the story has come down to us, from father to son and from uncle to nephew, since the very beginning. That the grizzly once stood erect and walked like a man, one has but to look at them. Their arms are a great deal shorter than their legs; they walk flat-footed, and the soles of their feet are like your own. They have no tails and in all respects are more like man than any other animal. All this is why the old-time Indians about Mount Shasta would never kill or interfere in any way with a grizzly; for, if it were not for these bears, there would be no Indians today.

There are many stories such as this, which are like windows into the Indian's philosophy of life and the interpretation of things around him. Call them legends or whatever you choose, but if stories like this had been accepted as the pattern for our popular conception of the red man, rather than his coldly realistic methods of warfare, we would be better qualified to understand these people.

The bear was not the only wild creature that figured in the Indians' hypothesis of animal personification and animal ancestry, for the red man's belief gave life and a soul like his own to most everything which he could identify with individuality. The bear occupied the most widespread and glamorous position, however, and to relate all the Indian legends, customs, and ceremonies relating only to these animals would fill a large volume. Making it even more difficult is the fact that the printed page is so inadequate a means of doing full justice to the red man's conception of these things, for his traditional lore was often invested in more of an opera than a mere expression in words. Song, dance, and pantomime were as important as the words, and the stage was as wide as the prairies and as high as the mountains, with all the props that an abundant nature could provide. Sometimes it took hours or days to express what the printed page might convey in a few minutes of reading time—but the printed page at its very best has never been a satisfactory medium of reproducing the drama of pantomime, the weirdly stimulating thump of primitive tom-toms and stamping feet, or the blending magic of moonlight with the story of a people whose philosophy we fail to understand.

The dance was far more than a dance to the Indians. Beyond the significance of its story and its deep religious implications it expressed the joys of biotic exultation, the exuberance of life and human emotions. It was rich in symbolism and mystic meaning, much of which was never revealed to the white man, and much of which was lost to even the red man in the long transition of time.

One of the most significant and dramatic ceremonies of the western Indians was the legendary Bear Dance of the Utes. These were a brave and warlike people who once occupied the central and western sections of present Colorado, spreading into eastern Utah and northern New Mexico. This dance was a very ancient one, among the oldest of all the Ute ceremonies, based on their traditional symbolism of animal worship and adoration of natural phenomena. It was generally an annual event, until around the end of the nineteenth century, although seldom witnessed by a white man, even after the tribe was incarcerated on a reservation. To the Utes, as to other tribes, nature was the omnipotent and all-providing mother, and their tribal beliefs were largely founded upon the evidences of nature as they saw them. They believed in the theory of ursine ancestry, and the Bear Dance was based on this concept.

Probably the first white man ever to witness the Bear Dance

of the Utes, and one of the few to be privileged to learn some of its tenets, was Verner Z. Reed. In March of 1893 he was permitted to attend the sacred ceremony held in the valley of the Rio de los Pinos, a beautiful little tributary of the great San Juan, in the southwest corner of Colorado. Incidentally, this is not far from one of the last rugged strongholds where both the grizzlies and the Utes are today struggling against complete extinction as species in that state.

"The Utes believe that their primal ancestors were bears [grizzlies]," reported Reed after learning what he was permitted to know about the significance of the ceremony and its traditional background. "After these [the bears] came a race of Indians, who, on dying, were changed back into bears, and as bears they roamed in the forests and mountains until they died, when they went to the Future Land and lived with the shades [spirits], preserving the forms of bears, but having human wisdom and participating in the pleasures of immortality. It is believed that this transmigration ceased a long time ago, but the bears of the present [1893] are believed to be descendants of the Ute bears of old, and are therefore related to the Indians. Bear worship, in one form or another, tinges many of their ceremonies."[18]

The Utes believed that the grizzlies possessed great magic powers and wisdom, which they were capable of transmitting over long distances, and they also believed that the bears were fully aware of the ancestral relationship between themselves and the Utes. The ceremony of the Bear Dance was therefore an aid to continuing and strengthening this friendship and also of charming the dancers as a means of protecting them from death by these mighty bears. There were also other motives involved in the affair. Important among these was the sending of messages to their dead relatives and friends who dwelt in the land of immortality; also to assist the bears to recover from winter hibernation, to find food, and to choose mates; and it was an occasion for springtime courting and lovemaking among the Indians themselves.

49

In the days before the Utes were herded together on a reservation, without regard to ancestral clans, each tribal division generally held its own Bear Dance, although they were carried out with the same ages-old formality and prescription. It was carefully supervised by a medicine man or chief, with the assistance of those whom he chose to appoint to the various required duties. Sometimes two or three months were devoted to the preparations. The time was always in the spring, usually during the month of March, when the bears were coming out of their winter dens in that particular area.

Most everything that was a part of these ceremonial fantasias of the Indians invariably had some deep motive or ritual meaning which was hidden to all but the orthodox practitioners of the faith. To the gentile outsider there was little beyond what met the eye. In spite of his unusual privilege to freely observe the Bear Dance of the Utes, and to talk to the participants about it, Verner Z. Reed makes it clear in his report that "all of the mysteries of the dance were not explained to me."[19]

As in most such primitive dance ceremonies, from arctic wastes to tropical jungles, the whole affair followed a prescribed program of formality. It required a formal request and appointment of the time to be held by the proper functionaries of the tribe. The following is given as the "almost verbatim" language of the southern Utes in requesting the chief to arrange for the dance which Reed witnessed in the Rio de los Pinos:

"Chief, it has been long since our people have all been in one place, and it would be good for us all to be together again. The times have been good with us; our children have been stricken with no disease; we have had no wars in which our men have been killed; we had much good fortune in our hunts; and we have plenty of food for a feast. The bears are our friends; the time has come for them to be awakened from the long sleep of winter. We have good friends above; it would be well to send messages to them to let them know that we on earth still love them and remember them . . . Let us, then, give a Bear Dance."[20]

When the arrangement was fully decided upon, the makers of songs and tellers of stories were officially called into session, and it was decided what histrionics should be included in the ceremony. These were mostly symphonies of animal worship and propritiatory supplications ages old and as wild and rugged as the rocky mountains around them and the grizzly bears to whom they were offered; but there were also somber incantations to the spirits of their own dead ones in the land beyond, with a mixture of interludes in a much lighter and highly romantic vein. Often sex played its own important part.

As soon as the program was fixed, the participants began practicing the songs and dances; and the squaws prepared "singing sticks" or *moraches*, made out of wood in the shape of an animal's jaw, with teethlike protuberances over which to grate hollow bones, or to be used on the drums, to add their primitive melody to this earthy extravaganza.

After due consideration the site for the dance was selected and men were appointed to get the stage properly set. They brought fresh timber and pine boughs from the forest and built an enclosure which was called the "cave of sticks" or *a-vik-wok-et*. It was generally 100 to 150 feet in diameter, depending upon the number of participants, circular in shape, and was meant to represent the den of a bear. Like a hibernation cave, it had one narrow entrance, opening to the south, facing the sun. The walls were made high enough so no one could look over the top; on one side of the bare ground interior the place for the musicians was marked by a cavernous hole carefully dug in the ground. This hole in the ground was very important. The opening was only a foot or so in diameter, and beyond it was hollowed out beneath the surface in a cavernous shape. This served as a sounding board for the special boxlike, bottomless drum that was to be placed directly over the opening, and the *moraches* properly grated over the drum would give forth like the throaty growl of a grizzly bear.

51

Day after day and week after week the musicians, singers, and storytellers devoted themselves to practicing their parts. It was believed that the immortal bears and the souls of departed Indians who dwelt together in the land beyond were fully aware of what was going on, that they would be preparing to hold a spirit Bear Dance of their own, and that the spirits would send messengers down to earth to whisper to the sleeping bears that they were soon to be awakened from the long winter sleep.

When the preparations were well under way, messengers were sent out to invite the tribal bands and families scattered throughout the territory, and at the appointed time they would come from far and near over the mesas and through the valleys, to set up their tepees in the panorama of the mountains and participate in the sacred ceremony. They would all be dressed in their finest regalia and everyone on their best behavior. The *a-vik-wok-et* was sacred ground during the days of the dance. No dogs or unbelievers were permitted to set a foot inside the enclosure. It was as sacred as a temple, and all who entered were required to participate as devotees of the faith.

The musicians and storytellers were always men and they always took the lead in starting the ceremonies, although it was the women who chose their own partners for the dances, and they had the privilege of choosing any male partner they desired, just as the female bears always do.

The grating of the *moraches* resounding in the cavelike cavern beneath the drum and the loud incantations of the singers and their stamping feet were believed to transport the message like thunder into the caves of the grizzlies in the mountains. But the bears do not awaken easily or quickly.

For the dances the women formed in one line and the men in another. As the music began the women chose their partners, without respect to family ties. At first the couples faced each other, merely stepping three steps forward and then three steps backward at the proper sounds of the music. The men made gesticulations with their arms, in imitation of motions being made by forepaws of the bears, urging the women to come close to them. Then, as they warmed to the spirit of the occasion, the couples held hands. As the days pass, however, the enthusiasm increases; the couples dance quite independently, until they embrace each other in the fashion of bears "hugging" in a tight embrace.

The first day the bears are merely awakened from their long sleep. On the second day they become more activated to the duties of life, leave the dens, and the females begin "dancing to trees"[21]—presumably a reference to amorous overtures on the part of the females. On the third day it was believed the bears had mated. Then they wander down into the forest to find food. On this day the Indians danced from early morning until sundown, with little cessation, and, after a short rest and supper, continued without interruption throughout the night and until noon of the following day. Fires were kept burning in the enclosure, and the music and dancing went on intensively until each individual was compelled by sheer exhaustion to stop and rest until able to continue. As each dancer dropped out their place was quickly taken by another, although some participants were able to continue throughout the whole eighteen hours. Then, at the end of the four-day ceremony, everyone relaxed and a great feast was held.

There were numerous sacred and earthy interludes in the ceremony of the Bear Dance of the Utes. It was also an appropriate time for making love, and when it was all over the feasting and merrymaking was often punctuated by younger couples being united in the simple marriage ceremony of the tribe. Within a day or so the bands began drifting away to their homes on the mesas and in the mountain valleys, carrying with them the pleasant memories of the music, the legendary cult of the distant past, and the earthy pleasantries of the present—one of the many interesting interpretations of the high place held by the grizzly bear in the ethos of the Indians.

Chapter V

LEGENDS MEAN MORE THAN STORIES

THE high place of respect and awe which was accorded the grizzly in the life of the Indians, particularly the western tribes, was a natural one, if for no other reason than the untold generations of realistic contests with crude stone-age weapons against superior claws and teeth. The philosophy of these highly imaginative people was strongly influenced by the harsh realities of nature, in which life has always been a constant struggle for survival and individuals seldom enjoy the privilege of a natural death. The Indian believed, and very devoutly, that the afterlife was a far more pleasant experience than the earthly interlude, and because of this they held life very lightly and held highly the circumstances of a dignified exit.

That the bear was accorded human relationship, and semi-divinity, with a spirit of a higher order than others, even above man in some instances, is borne out in the lore and legends of a great many primitive racial groups in North America and other continents as well.

The Bear Dance was practiced extensively throughout a large part of North America, and it took on various aspects among the widely separated tribes. The early Jesuit traveler and historian of New France, Pierre François Xavier de Charlevoix, in 1721 found it practiced among the nomads of the northeastern woodlands.[22] The dance which he described is interpreted to relate more closely to the hunting of these animals and a propitiation to the appeasement of their spirits. This is common to other early descriptions, from coast to coast, but these were little more than superficial observations of travelers who did not see behind the painted wooden masks of the dancing Indians.

Among the Blackfeet, who lived on the western prairies in the evening shadows of the Montana Rockies, they had a Grizzly Bear Dance which was closely associated with their sacred medicine pipe—because the magic powers of the pipe came from the grizzly bear.[23] This colorful nightlong ceremony included the singing of bear songs and imitating the sounds and actions of the grizzly bear. The participants, at one stage of the extravaganza, would march through the village carrying the sacred medicine pipe and other sacred medicine bundles, all dressed in their gay ceremonial paraphernalia of decorated buckskin, feathers, and ermine skins, and accompanied by the wild music of tribal drums. The spectators would loudly applaud when the prominent men performed their parts, singing and dancing and imitating the grizzly by holding their hands as the bear holds its paws, or moving backward and forward in short jumps, then pretending to dig into the ground or turn over stones in search of insects, then puffing and uttering wild sounds like the grizzly when it charges upon an enemy. In the big tepee when the important rituals were performed there was a more serious aspect; sweet pine was burned as incense, and the bear worship was carried out in religious sanctity.

Another side light on the bear relationship to the Indians, as interesting as it is important, is the Bear Mother story. This is in the nature of a mythological parable, which was expressed in several closely related themes and was widespread particularly among the tribes of the northern Rocky Mountains and North Pacific coast regions.[24] This theme variously relates how a young Indian woman married a grizzly bear and gave birth to twins of half-bear characteristics and thus created a new clan of Indians. Like many other symbolic stories of the red man, it was enacted with a great deal of frankness of realism and sex, in which the Indian had no more false pride than the animals of the wilderness which were his neighbors. The Bear Mother parable was often expounded by the storytellers at evening gatherings; clan chiefs orated it at the foot of totem poles when they were erected, often with a human slave dropped into the hole in the earth as a propitious sacrifice; and it was frequently accompanied by the ever-present ritual dance and singing of significant songs. Also, this was occasionally a subject of the totem poles themselves and other mediums of pictographic art practiced by the tribes of the Northwest coast regions. Here again there was far more than meets the ear or eye of the outside observer. Incidentally, some of the best known of the totem poles that illustrate this bit of Indian lore are still standing amid the remnants of once-proud villages of these people on the Skeena and Nass rivers in British Columbia; and there is one that was uprooted and transferred for the blind amusement of visitors to the Musée de l'Homme in Paris, France. There are also a number of black slate (argillite) Bear Mother effigy carvings by the Haidas of Queen Charlotte Islands gathering dust in several of our museums. These generally take some form of the half-bear offspring being suckled by their human mother.

The mythological twins of the Bear Mother had their reflection in the occurrence of normal twins that were born to tribal families. Among the Thompson Indians of British Columbia a woman who was about to be delivered of twins was supposedly made aware of the happy event by the repeated appearance of a grizzly bear in her dreams.[25] Maybe she was! When the twins arrived they were called "grizzly bear children" or "hairy feet," and they were regarded and treated quite differently from other children. The grizzly bear, it seems, was not looked upon as the actual father, although they were considered to be under his special protection and were endowed by him with the special attributes he possessed, such as great healing powers, control over good or bad weather, personal bravery, etc. At their birth the mother's earthly husband dressed himself in special ceremonial decorations and danced around outside the dwelling, singing the grizzly bear song. A young male "baby sitter" was also selected to attend the twins and sing loudly whenever they cried. He painted his whole face red and held fir branches in each hand. There were many prescribed details. If the twins were male and female, the young attendant must always carry a *male* fir branch in his right hand and a *female* branch in his left hand. The Indians designated between the sexes even in such things as flowers, plants, and the branches of trees.

After the birth of twins in the normal life of these people the parents must move with their grizzly bear children into a special lodge, some distance apart from the rest, and here the youngsters were raised under special care. They were not allowed to come in contact with other people, and when anyone passed near the place they always whistled so the grizzly-bear children could be kept out of sight.

There are also records of wild bear cubs being nourished on the milk from the breasts of Indian women, although just what connection this had with any ancient precept is not clear. Samuel Hearne, reporting on his journey from Hudson's Bay across northwestern America to the Arctic Ocean in the years 1769 to 1772, reported in a footnote of his book: "It is common for the Southern Indians to tame and domesticate the young [bear] cubs; and they are frequently taken so young that they cannot eat. On those occasions the Indians oblige their wives who have milk in their breasts to suckle them."[26] The Indian was far too realistic a hunter for food, particularly during the starvation months at the end of winter, to have kept any young game for mere amusement, and for any human female to suckle bear cubs was certainly a physical ordeal that only some important reason could dictate.

Among most if not all of the tribes the grizzly symbolized

mortal invulnerability and was believed to have great wisdom, spiritual powers, and healing abilities—all of which it was possible for him to bestow upon especially fortunate human individuals. There were also certain "medicine bears" which could not be wounded by any ordinary arrow (or bullet). The Pawnees, like many others, held to the belief that the grizzly knew how to cure himself of any physical injury that might be inflicted upon him. If only a little breath of life were left in his body, he knew the ways to overcome all the difficulties. He knew the secrets of medicinal herbs and how to keep the life blood, and the immortal spirits, from escaping from the mortal body. Nor was the Indian ever content with the prosaic or commonplace as a background for his ancestral beliefs. One of the touches of histrionics which he commonly added to this bit of legendary lore was that the grizzly "breathed out from his nostrils colored dusts—red, blue, and yellow—and spit out different colored earths, while performing his acts of healing."[27]

The healing powers of the bears were exemplified in a number of legendary forms. Each tribe generally had its own way of expressing its common beliefs, and in some tribes there was more than one legend, entirely different in concept but with the same basic precept. An example of this is "The Story of *Mikápi*" and "The Story of the Sacred Spear," both a part of the Blackfoot belief in the spiritual and healing powers of the grizzly bears. As was the case in most such Indian stories, they were built up to great length and invested with many details which to the outsider might seem quite irrelevant. In their original form, and at the hands of a particularly accomplished storyteller, they might take hours to relate; and, when the occasion demanded, they were accompanied by singing, dancing, and pantomime, in which the whole village would participate.

"The Story of *Mikápi*" (Red Old Man)[28] is that of a young warrior of the Piegan tribe of the Blackfoot confederacy who went alone into the country of their enemies, the Snake Indians. It was a mission of bravery and high honor, to avenge the death of his warrior friend, Fox-eye. It all happened, of course, in the long, long ago, in the days of the stone knife, many, many generations before the Indian knew there was such a thing as a horse to ride. The long preliminary to this narrative begins with the explanation that "Fox-eye had two widows; but their fathers and mothers and all their relatives were dead . . . and all of Fox-eye's own relatives had gone to the Sand Hills [that shadow land of spirits in the afterlife to which the souls of good Blackfoot people go] . . . So these poor widows had no one to go forth and avenge them." Aware of all this and the circumstances of his friend's death at the hands of the Snakes, *Mikápi* takes upon himself this affair of tribal honor. "So now, I say," he announces to the widows in knightly fashion, "I will take the sad load from your hearts. I will go to war and take many scalps; and when I return, they shall be yours. You shall paint your faces black, and we will all rejoice that Fox-eye has been avenged."

It would take many pages of the white man's talk to tell the whole story of *Mikápi* and his hardships in making the long and lonely journey to the land of the Snakes and of his phe-nomenal bravery in creeping right in among the many lodges of his enemies. "Slowly and silently he crawled through the grass and the darkness, closer and closer, until *Mikápi's* strong arm grasped an enemy tribesman around the neck and covered his mouth. A long jagged stone knife was thrust into his breast, again and again . . . and while the stars looked down and the evening fires burned in the lodges, *Mikápi* removed a scalp . . . and his heart was glad. Softly he sung to himself his favorite song of war. But he was not satisfied."

The village became alarmed and all the warriors raced out to find the bold intruder and exhaust all their vengeance upon him. But *Mikápi* was very brave and he did not run away. Nor did his enemies find him. Patiently he waited for the stars to come out again. Three scalps the young Blackfoot took and proudly tied to his belt in the silence of as many nights. But finally the desperate enemy warriors found him, and their arrows pierced his body in an exciting flight. Each time, however, he pulled out the sharp stone-pointed shafts, in a desperate struggle to escape, and finally he threw himself over a high rocky cliff, to find sanctuary in the darkness and the rushing turmoil of the river below.

All night he floated down the stream that tumbled between the rocks and the forest, and when morning came he dragged himself out on a sandy bit of the shore. Half-drowned and helpless, he lay in the morning sunshine. "Here I must stay and die, so far from my father's lodge," he said to himself. "The widows of Fox-eye will continue to mourn; and in their old age there will be no one to care for my father and mother." Then he made a prayer. "Oh pity me now, oh Sun! Help me, oh great Medicine Person! Look down upon your wounded and suffering child."

Even as he spoke the words there was a crashing in the brush near by and there stood before him a monster grizzly bear. "What does my brother here?" spoke the bear in a friendly voice. "Why does he pray to survive?"

After considerable conversation between the two, in which *Mikápi* expounded the virtues of his mission of pride and honor, the grizzly picked up the helpless warrior and carried him to a place where a magic mud was to be found, and, while singing a medicine song, the bear applied the muddy potion upon *Mikápi's* wounds. Then he carried the Indian back into the woods, where certain medicinal berries were gathered and given to the patient.

Mikápi became stronger, and when this came to pass the grizzly said: "Lie down, now, upon my back, and hold tight by my hair, and we will travel." And when *Mikápi* had got on and was ready the bear started off with long swinging strides. All through the night and through the days they traveled on without stopping, except when the grizzly administered to the Indian's needs. Finally *Mikápi* was delivered close to the lodge

of his own tribe, and the people saw them coming and wondered.

"Get off, now, my brother, get off," said the grizzly. "There
are your people." And as soon as *Mikápi* got down, without
another word, the big bear turned and went off up the mountain.

Mikápi's friends and relatives hurried out and carried him
into the lodge of his father. He untied the three scalps from
his belt and gave them to the widows of Fox-eye, saying: "You
are now revenged. I wipe away your tears." And everyone
rejoiced. All his female relations marched through the village,
shouting his name and singing his praise, and everyone prepared for the scalp dance. . . . "Long lived *Mikápi*. Of all
the great Blackfoot chiefs who have lived and died, he was
one of the greatest. He did many great and daring deeds; for
he was aided by a great and powerful spirit—the grizzly bear."

"The Story of the Sacred Spear"[29] was told by the same
Blackfoot storytellers as another vehicle for expressing their
tribal belief in the immortal powers of the grizzly bear. In this
instance there was a sacred talisman or "medicine bundle,"
known as the Bear Spear, in which these sacred powers had
been invested.

The story is built around an ancient character known as
Little Mink, the youngest son of a great chief of long ago,
when the Indian had only dogs to help them transport their
possessions from one camping place to another. While on a
journey one of the chief's favorite travois dogs was found to
be missing at the end of the day. Little Mink, very young but
brave and bold, insisted upon going back to find the dog. At
first the father refused, but at length consent was given.

The boy backtracked along the trail, until he came to a
camping ground at the edge of the Rocky Mountains, and
here he found the lost dog's tracks leading off into the mountains. On he went, until he came to the mouth of a big cave,
where he found the missing travois, but the dog was gone.

While Little Mink was wondering what to do next, there

was a mighty roar and a monster grizzly came rushing out of the cave. It clutched the lad in its arms and carried him into the darkness of the cave.

"My son, be not afraid," said the big grizzly. "I am the chief of all the bears, and my power is very great. Remain here with me while the snows are deep . . . and I will bestow my power upon you."

The story goes into considerable detail, and Little Mink remained with the big grizzly throughout the winter, doing just as the bear did. At last, with the coming of spring, it was time for the lad to return to his own people; and, true to his promise, the grizzly bestowed upon Little Mink his supernatural powers. He explained how to make the sacred Bear Spear, in which these powers would be invested—with sharp stone point; with the teeth and nose of a bear properly attached; decorated with red paint, and grizzly claws fastened to the wooden handle, to rattle and sound like the grizzly when he runs. "Whenever you go to war," the bear told him, "carry this Bear Spear. . . . Make a noise like a grizzly bear when you charge into battle. Thus my power will go with you; and your enemies will run away, because everything that lives fears the power of the grizzly bear." He also taught Little Mink how to heal the sick and how the Bear Spear was to be used in these ceremonies. Then he sent the lad back to his father's camp, and when they heard all the wonderful things that had happened a great feast was held in Little Mink's honor. He became a great chief—and this is how the Blackfoot got their Sacred Spear.

The Pawnees, who called themselves the *Chahiksichshiks* or "men of men" and who lived in the great valley of the Platte River, had a legend very similar but much more elaborate than the one previously cited. It was "The Story of *Ku ruks la war' uks ti*" ("Medicine Bear").[30] The hero of this interesting saga of Indian Americana was a certain poor boy of the Pawnee tribe. He was so poor that he is not even given a name at the beginning of the long story, and it is related that his whole family was so destitute that everyone looked down upon them. However, the lad decided to find honor or death; and he went to a fabled place among the hills, where there were many cedar trees and there were many skeletons of his people who had been killed in a mysterious manner. In the center of this strange graveyard he found the cave of a family of grizzlies. The father was not at home, but the friendly old she-bear said: "I am sorry that you have come here. My husband is the one who kills persons and brings them here for the children and me to eat. You had better go back to your people quickly, or he will eat you up. . . . He is one of those bad bears—a grizzly—medicine!" The poor boy, however, insisted on waiting to face this terrible man-eating bear.

When the monster returned and saw the bold young intruder, he pounded the earth with his great paws, snorted like thunder, and blew red dust from his nostrils. He shouted that he was chief of all the grizzlies and head of all the animal lodges, and there was no living creature on earth as strong or who had as much supernatural power. The poor boy was very frightened, but he bravely faced the demon, defying all his wrath and power. Greatly admiring this unusual courage, the grizzly finally promised to adopt the boy as his own and bestow all his powers upon him.

In this imaginative story there is a mingling of primitive drama, poetic justice, and mystic animal worship. To tell it briefly is only to spoil it; and even in all its translated detail it unquestionably loses a vast amount of its original conception, as it once was related in all its orthodox sincerity of complete belief by the tribal patriarchs of the proud Pawnees.

The grizzly invested the poor boy with invulnerability to being injured in any way by the weapons of his enemies, and he taught him the magic of literally wiping away the wounds inflicted upon others and of restoring life to those who had been killed.

When the lad finally returned to the lodge of his own father, the people quickly learned about what had happened. He had such great supernatural powers that he was able to go right into the midst of enemy warriors, without any fear of personal injury, and slay the tribal enemies with reckless abandon. And so it came to pass that "old men were calling his name, young women were singing his praise, and old women came to dance before him. People no longer made fun of his father or mother. Now they looked upon him as a great and powerful person." He was given the distinguished name of *Ku ruks la war' uks ti* or Medicine Bear, and sometimes they called him *Ku ruks ti carish*, which means Angry Bear. He brought great honor to his tribe, finally married the chief's beautiful daughter, and became a great chief in his own right—all because of the grizzly bear.

These are but a few of the Indians' legends in which the grizzly was accorded a worshipful distinction and homage and which show the influence of these animals upon the red man's culture.

Chapter VI

FIRST TO MEET THE GRIZZLY

JUST who was the first European to actually
meet the grizzly bear face to face may never be known. To
determine this fact is almost the same as establishing who was
the first white man to visit our western plains and mountains.
For these big and boldly unevasive animals were so plentiful
when the white man lifted the curtain of exploration on the
West that it would be next to impossible for anyone to pass
even hurriedly through the country without becoming well
aware of their presence and having some contact with them.

So far as the present boundaries of the United States are
concerned, it is evident that the first Europeans to meet the
grizzly were Cabeza de Vaca and his three companions,
Castillo Maldonado, Andreas Dorantes, and the latter's Moor-
ish Negro slave, Estevan. They were undoubtedly the first to
visit grizzly country in our present Southwest. Their remarkable experience between November 1527 and July 1536, including the long overland journey which took them slowly
in a wide swing through the interior of present Texas and
northern Mexico, could hardly avoid some contact with these
animals, although there is nothing in the Cabeza de Vaca journal to enlighten us on the subject. The same applies to the
expedition of Francesco Vasquez de Coronado, across the territory of New Mexico and as far into the interior as Colorado,

Kansas, and Nebraska, in the years 1540–1542. Here again there is practically nothing for the record beyond the mere mention of bears. What a rich privilege it would be to include in this book the whole story of that first Spanish conquistador who, in the true spirit of a Nimrod, took the first grizzly as a trophy. Maybe he was dressed in shining metal armor and used a crossbow as a weapon. Maybe his weapon was a long shiny spear that had seen service against the Crusaders in the Holy Land. But that story, like many others of even greater historical importance, must remain among the lost bits of unwritten records of our Old West.

In the American Northwest it was evidently a Frenchman who first met the grizzly bear. It may have been the early Jesuit missionary Claude Jean Allouez. If he did not actually come in contact with these animals, he does make what is probably the earliest references to them. In his *Mission to the Kilistinouc* in 1666, north of the present Assiniboine River, his journal tells of "another nation [of Indians] adjoining the Assinipoulac, who eat human beings, and live on raw fish; but these people, in turn, are eaten by bears of frightful size, all red, and with prodigiously long claws."[31] In a footnote by the editor, Dr. Louise Phelps Kellog, the following statement is made: "The Assiniboin are a Siouan tribe, offshoot of the Yankton family of the Sioux [Dakota]. Their habitat was on Lake Winnipeg and the river of their name. The animals here described are grizzly bears." In the writings of several of the very early French historians there are indications, if not substantial proofs, that the Jesuits traveled among the Sioux, and in grizzly country, even before the Allouez record of 1666.

Louis Joliet and Jacques Marquette are known to have explored the upper Mississippi River in the spring of 1673 and went down past the mouth of the Missouri (Pekitanoui) River; and René Robert Cavelier de La Salle was well down the Ohio, if not on the Mississippi, somewhat previous to that date. It is more than possible that some other unknown and unheralded adventurer had been there before either of these historic personalities and gone much farther than they. It is a well-known fact among explorers and those who really know that field that it is not always the individual who gains the honor of discovery who was actually the first to accomplish the deed. And they were bold men, those seventeenth-century French adventurers in America; they got along remarkably well with the Indians; and some of the unknowns may have traveled far up the Missouri, into the haunts of the grizzly bear, long before we realize or the all-too-inadequate records show. It may have been a Jesuit priest or a hard-bitten *coureur de bois*. Who knows?

What is evidently the earliest recorded information about the grizzly by an English explorer is found in the journal of an adventurous young man by the name of Henry Kelsey. The unimpeachable records of the Hudson's Bay Company inform us that "Henry Kelsey entered the service of Hudson's Bay Company on 14 April 1684, as an apprentice for four years [for the company's fur-trading enterprise in Arctic America], at the end of which service he was to receive £8 and 'two shuts of apparel.' "[32] We also learn from the same source that "he was above the usual age of 14 years, although in 1688 [after serving the prescribed first four years in the Hudson's Bay country] he was still referred to in the Company's records as 'the boy Henry Kelsey,' " and that he was "a very active lad, delighted much in Indian's company." Elsewhere these records make the extremely important statement that "poor and semi-educated as he [Henry Kelsey] was, he was the discoverer of the Canadian prairie."

After careful study of the records and all the related facts, including the young explorer's own journal, Charles Napier Bell, president of the Historical and Scientific Society of Manitoba, made this statement: "There can be no doubt whatever but that Kelsey, on the 20th of August, 1691, was the first white man to see the bison in what is now the Canadian West. He also likely for the first time in history places on record a description of the grizzly bear of Northwest Canada."[33] This was more than 114 years before that date of May 5, 1805, when the Lewis and Clark expedition collected their specimen of the grizzly bear in what is now northeastern Montana and which provided the necessary data on which the scientific description of the species was later established.

Aside from its importance in the history of the grizzly, here is a little-known but well-authenticated story that for sheer daring and antecedency alone rivals anything in the annals of that glamorous "Company of Adventurers of England Trading in Hudson's Bay"; and it is one of the most unusual in the whole history of exploration of the interior of our continent.

It was not until as recently as 1926 that the story of Henry Kelsey attracted the attention of historians; and the well-documented account was jointly published in 1929 as *The Kelsey Papers* by the Public Archives of Canada and the Public Records Office of Northern Ireland.[34]

Henry Kelsey was presumably born in England in 1670, the same year in which Charles II, King of England, granted the charter to his cousin, Prince Rupert, the Duke of Cumberland, and seventeen other noblemen and gentlemen, marking the beginning of the Hudson's Bay Company and leading to the ultimate acquisition of all Canada as part of the British Empire. Kelsey was barely into his teens when he joined the company and was immediately sent to Hudson's Bay. In spite of his lack of background, and being an apprentice was little more than being a slave to his superiors, he had a natural adaptitude for the peculiar circumstances which surrounded his new life in the Arctic wilderness. This is indicated by the frequency with which the lad's name appears in the company's official records and the fact that he went on to occupy the organization's highest office. A recorded company authorization of 1689 reads: "That the boy Henry Kelsey be sent [from York Fort] to Churchill River with Thomas Savage, because we are informed he is a very active lad delighted much in Indian's company, being never better pleased than when he is traveling amongst them. . . ."³⁵

Kelsey made numerous trips deep into the territory that stretched as an unknown wilderness to the westward from Hudson's Bay. The longest and most important of these journeys, and the one on which he discovered the western prairies, the bison, and the grizzly bear, was begun at York Fort on Hudson's Bay on 12 June 1690. He was then only twenty years old; he apparently traveled alone, by canoe and by foot; went as far westward as the present Province of Alberta, and did not return until the fall of 1692.

The journal of this trip is written in a strange sort of verse; and for the date of "ye 20th August [1691]" we find the following entry:

To day we pitcht to ye outermost Edge of ye woods this plain affords Nothing but short Round sticky grass & Buffillo & a great sort of Bear wch is Bigger than any white Bear & is Neither White nor Black But silver hair'd like our English Rabbit. . . .

A September entry gives another interesting side light on the grizzly and its habitat at that time. After passing through an area of woodlands of "small nutts wth little cherryes very good . . . till you leave ye woods behind," he goes on to record:

> "And then you have beast of severall kind
> The one is a black a Buffillo great
> Another is an outgrown Bear wch. is good meat
> His skin to gett I have used all ye ways I can
> He is mans food & he makes food of man
> His hide they would not me it preserve
> But said it was a god & they should Starve
> This plain affords nothing but Beast & grass. . . ."

There is no doubt whatever that these are references to the grizzly bear, and here we have the earliest known specific account of this animal recorded in the English language. These facts have been carefully checked and authenticated by the

EARLIEST REFERENCE TO THE GRIZZLY

The manuscript of Henry Kelsey, written in 1690, contains the earliest known reference in the English language to the grizzly bear. The above photostat of the original is accompanied by a "translation."

> And then you have beast of severall kind
> The one is a black a Buffillo great
> Another is an outgrown Bear wch is good meat
> $\qquad\qquad\qquad\qquad\qquad$ ways
> His skin to gett I have used all y^e ~~means~~ I can
> He is mans food & he makes food of man
> His hide they would not me it preserve
> But said it was a god & they should Starve

various scholarly gentlemen referred to in the accompanying footnotes.

It should be added as a closing comment that Henry Kelsey became the British governor in Hudson's Bay in 1718, which high post he held for four years. On 1 September 1722 he sailed for England, where he died in 1729.

To tabulate all of the early references, specific and speculative, relating to the grizzly would serve but little constructive contribution to the purpose of this book. A good many of these are confined to a line or few and are of marked similarity, such as Baron Lahontan's report on his travels and gathered information in his *Memoir on the Fur-Trade in Canada* (1703): "The Reddish Bears are mischievous Creatures, for they fall fiercely upon the Huntsmen, whereas the black ones fly from 'em."[36]

What Pierre François Xavier de Charlevoix has to say, however, is of importance, for it is the earliest comprehensive report on the bear-hunting activities among the western Indians and the interesting ceremonial and other related aspects of the natives' hunting activities. This early French Jesuit, traveler and historian, made a trip in 1720–1722 along the Great Lakes and down the Mississippi. This was on his second trip to America, having previously spent four years as a "professor" at Quebec, and in the interim he had been a professor of *belles lettres* in France.

The *Journal of a Voyage to North America*, by Charlevoix,[37] has been translated and quoted from by a considerable number of writers, historians, and scholars.[38] The present writer has chosen to use the translation which was made a part of Thomas Pennant's important work, *Arctic Zoology*, published in London in 1784. This is one of the earliest authoritative discourses on the zoology of North America, and Pennant was one of the first naturalists to specifically designate the grizzly bear as a species. His material on the bears was drawn principally from Charlevoix, Hearne, and Andrew Graham, "long a resident of Hudson's Bay." In an effort to retain a semblance of proper chronological sequence, the quotes directly credited to Charlevoix, which are included in Pennant's later account of the "grizzly bears" of North America, are here given:

"The chase of these animals is a matter of first importance, and never undertaken without abundance of ceremony. A principle warrior first gives a general invitation to all the hunters. This is followed by a most serious fast of eight days, a total abstinence from all kinds of food; notwithstanding which, they pass the day in continual song. This they do to invoke the spirits of the woods to direct them to the place where there is abundance of bears. They even cut the flesh in diverse parts of their own bodies, to render the spirits more propitious. They also address themselves to the manes of the beasts slain in preceding chases, as if it were to direct them in their dreams to plenty of game. One dreamer alone cannot determine the place of the chase, for numbers must concur; but, as they tell each other their dreams, they never fail to agree; whether that may arise from complaisance, or by a real agreement in the dreams from their thoughts being perpetually turned on the same thing.

"The chief of the hunt now gives a great feast, at which no one dares to appear without bathing. At this entertainment they eat with great moderation, contrary to their usual custom. The master of the feast alone touches nothing; but is employed in relating to the guests ancient tales of the wonderful feats in former chases; and fresh invocations to the manes of the deceased bears conclude the whole. Then they sally forth amidst the acclamations of the village, equipped as if for war, and painted black. Every able hunter is on a level with a great warrior; but he must have killed his dozen great beasts before his character is established; after which his alliance is as much courted as that of the most valliant captain.

"They now procede on their way in a direct line; neither rivers, marshes, or any other impediments, stop their course; driving before them all the beasts which they find in their way. When they arrive in the hunting-ground, they surround as large a place as their company will admit, and then contract their circle; searching, as they contract, every hollow tree, and every place fit for the retreat of the bear; and continue the same practice till the time of the chase is expired.

"As soon as the bear is killed, a hunter puts into its mouth a lighted pipe of tobacco, and, blowing into it, fills the throat with the smoke, conjuring the spirit of the animal not to resent what they are going to do to its body; nor to render their future chases unsuccessful. As the beast makes no reply, they cut out the string of the tongue, and throw it into the fire: if it crackles and runs in, which it is almost sure to do, they accept it as a good omen; if not, they consider that the spirit of the beast is not appeased, and that the chase of the next year will be unfortunate.

[There is no description of the actual combat involved with the bears, although it is easy to imagine this when we consider the Indians' only weapons were flint-pointed arrows and spears and stone axes—against a beast which has often proved disastrous to modern hunters armed with powerful repeating rifles.]

"The hunters live well during the chase, on provisions which they bring with them. They return home with great pride and self-sufficiency; for to kill a bear forms the character of a complete man. They again give a great entertainment, and now make a point to leave nothing. The feast is dedicated to a certain genius, perhaps that of Gluttony, whose resentment they dread, if they do not eat every morsel, and even sup up the very melted grease in which the meat was dressed. They sometimes eat till they burst, or bring on themselves some violent disorders. The first course is the greatest bear they have killed, without even taking out the entrals, or taking off the skin, contenting themselves with singing the skin."[39]

In the original French version Charlevoix also tells of the use of dogs by the Indians in their hunting: "The Indians always carry a great number of dogs with them in their huntings; these are the only domestic animals they breed, and that too only for hunting: they appear to be all of one species, with upright ears, and a long snout like that of a wolf . . . and excellent hunters they make."[40]

In his 1769–1772 journey from Prince of Wales's Fort on Hudson's Bay across northwestern Canada to the Arctic Ocean that indomitable English explorer Samuel Hearne "saw the skin of an enormous grizzled Bear at the tents of the Esquimaux at the Copper River; and many of them are said to breed not very remote from that part."[41] His journal for the date of July

73

1771 (while on the Copper-mine River) states: "The place where we lay that night, is not far from Grizzled Bear Hill; which takes its name from the number of those animals that are frequently known to resort thither for the purpose of bringing forth their young in a cave that is found there . . . [I saw] many hills and dry ridges on the East side of the march which was turned over like ploughed land by these animals, in searching for ground squirrels, perhaps mice, which constitute a favorite part of their food. It is surprising to see the extent of their researches in quest of those animals, and still more to view the enormous stones rolled out of their beds by the bears on those occasions." Whether or not this refers to the barren ground bear or one of the more truly classified grizzlies is of little importance in this respect, as they all come under the same general classification.

Another significant early reference is found in Edward Umfreville's account of his 1783–1787 travels in the region to the west of Hudson's Bay. Attempting something of a delineation of that country's natural history, he has this to say: "Bears are of three kinds;—the black, the red, and the grizzle Bear. The former is the least offensive, and, when taken young, the most docile and susceptible of kind usage. As to the other kinds, their nature is savage and ferocious, their power is dangerous, and their haunts to be guarded against. The numbers of maimed Indians to be seen in this country exhibit a melancholy proof of their power over the human species. A Canadian last summer had his arm lascerated in a dreadful manner by one of these destructive animals; yet if a man is mounted upon a good horse, he may attack one with success; nor will they always fall on a person unprovoked. They feed on berries, roots and flesh. In summer they travel about, but in winter they live in a state of inanimation in some recesses under the ground, and sustain nature by sucking their paws."[42] This is one of the earliest references to bears "sucking their paws" during the period of hibernation—a false idea, widely adopted through many generations of misinformed journalists and storytellers.

Chapter VII

LEWIS AND CLARK BLAZED A TRAIL

WE have come to regard the Lewis and Clark Expedition of 1804–1806 as the discovering point from which most all things are measured, relating to the exploration and development of our spreading empire across the western wilderness. There is no denying the historical importance of this journey under the command of Captains Meriwether Lewis and William Clark, both at the time serving as officers in the Army of the United States, from the vicinity of St. Louis on the Mississippi, to the headwaters of the Missouri River and across the Rocky Mountains to the mouth of the Columbia River on the Pacific Ocean, thence back to their original starting point. The actual travel by land and water, including the various side trips, amounted to about one third the circumference of the earth.

Much of the country through which this expedition passed had long been known, in a crude and cursory way, by the hardy French and English adventurers of the fur trade and by a few adventurous Yankees; but no expedition into the continental wilderness of North America fulfilled such a profound mission in the destiny of this continent, and one of the scientific by-products constitutes a most important page in the story of the grizzly bear.

Thomas Jefferson was deeply interested in natural history

and all the allied sciences, as well as the future expansion and development of the new nation of which he was the second president, and Captain Lewis, his private secretary, had been designated as coleader of the expedition to see that all his official as well as unofficial interests should be carried out. This undertaking set the pattern for expeditions as we know them today, with objectives of acquiring scientific knowledge, along with the geographic investigations.

Lewis and Clark have been credited with "discovering" the grizzly bear; and, while this is an anachronism of credit, they were the first to bring serious attention to this animal and the whole natural history of our West, based on firsthand collected material, and the first fine specimen they obtained provided the basis for the scientific description of this animal in the permanent record.

Because of the importance of the Lewis and Clark journal of their expedition, it has been deemed expedient to include here those parts which are most pertinent to the subject of this book. The quotes and footnote references, unless otherwise indicated, have been made from the Elliot Coues edition, as this compilation includes not only a direct transcript of the authors' original manuscript but additional related information drawn from the field notes of the explorers and from other sources, and it is generally accepted as the best reference work. The inside bracket annotations are by McCracken.

The first reference to the grizzly bear in the Lewis and Clark journal[43] is recorded for the date of August 31, 1804. It was incidental to a meeting with a large body of Yankton Sioux (Dakota) Indians at the expedition's camping place on the Missouri River, which Coues establishes as "In Knox County, Nebraska, about the 900th river-mile point [from their starting point near St. Louis], and opposite the lower one of two islands to be found on later maps by the name of Buffalo."[44] About 200 men of the Yanktons, from their homes on the Jaques, Des Moines, and Sioux rivers, visited the explorers camp in a body; and "some of them wore a kind of necklace of *white bear's claws* three inches long, closely strung together round their necks."[45] The common name for the grizzly bear among the Sioux (Dakota) was *"matohota,"* which properly translated means "gray bear." The name of "white bear," which is frequently used in the Lewis and Clark journal, may be the result of inaccurate translation, which is easily understandable; and this may explain the use of the name "white bear" in the writings of other early travelers and historians.

The Lewis and Clark Expedition spent the winter of 1804–5 among the Mandan Indians. These winter quarters on the upper Missouri River became known as Fort Mandan, a familiar stopping place for many early travelers into the great Northwest. It was here that George Catlin, the great pioneer artist, spent the winter of 1832–33. Today it is the site of the town of Mandan, opposite Bismarck, North Dakota.

In the early spring the expedition continued on their way, and the first grizzly collected was on April 29, 1805.[46] It was on the bank of the Missouri, a few miles above the mouth of the Yellowstone River, shortly after crossing the present boundary line of North Dakota into what is now the state of Montana. This is prairie, not mountain country. The journal for the date on which this incident occurred reads:

"We proceded early, with a moderate wind. Captain Lewis, who was on shore with one hunter met about eight o'clock two white bears. Of the strength and ferocity of this animal the Indians had given us dreadful accounts. They never attack him but in parties of eight or more persons, and even then are often defeated with a loss of one or more of their party. Having no weapons but bows and arrows, and the bad guns with which the traders supply them, they are obliged to approach very near to the bear; as no wound except through the head or heart is mortal, they frequently fall a sacrifice if they miss their airm. [It should be noted here that white traders were already operating in the country. One of these, met on November 1, 1804, was a Mr. Hugh McCracken.[47] It should also be remem-

bered that this was the period of single-shot flintlock guns.]
He [the grizzly] rather attacks than avoids a man, and such is
the terror which he has inspired, that the Indians who go in
quest of him paint themselves and perform all the superstitious
rites customary when they make war on a neighboring nation.
Hitherto those bears we had seen did not appear desirous of
encountering us; but although to a skillful rifleman the danger
is very much diminished, yet the white bear is still a terrible
animal.

"On approaching these two, both Captain Lewis and the
hunter fired, and each wounded the bear. One of them made
his escape; the other turned upon Captain Lewis and pursued
him seventy or eighty yeards, but being badly wounded the
bear could not run so fast as to prevent him from reloading his
[muzzle-loaded] piece, which he again aimed at him; and a
third shot from the hunter brought him down. He was a male,
not quite full grown, and weighed about 300 pounds. The legs
are somewhat longer than those of the black bear, and the
talons and tusks much larger and longer. The testicles are also
placed much farther forward and suspended in separate
pouches from two to four inches asunder, while those of the
black bear are situated back between the thighs and in a single
pouch, like those of the dog. [No mention is made of *os penis*,
which they undoubtedly observed.] Its color is yellowish
brown; the eyes are small, black, and piercing; the front of the
forelegs near the feet is unusually black, and the fur is finer,
thicker, and deeper than that of the black bear. Add to which,
it is a more furious animal, and very remarkable for the wounds
which it will bear without dying."[48] This is the first concise
account of a firsthand encounter and description of a grizzly
bear, in the Lewis and Clark journal.

Immediately following is a brief but interesting verbal vignette of the animal wildlife of that district at the time of the
visit: "We are surrounded with deer, elk, buffalo, antelopes,
and their companions the wolves, which have become more
numerous and make great ravages among them."

It was on May 5, 1805, that the Lewis and Clark Expedition collected the particular grizzly which became the "type specimen" on which was based the accepted classification and naming of this animal, and all related varieties, in scientific nomenclature by George Ord—which will be dealt with in a later chapter.

The location where this bear was taken has been generally given as "near the mouth of Poplar River"—called by them Porcupine River, but not the Porcupine of today, which is about fifty miles farther west. Examination of the original journal indicates the spot was a short distance east of the present Wolf Creek and not far from the present town of Wolf Point.

Here is the account as recorded in the original journal:

"Captain Clark and one of the hunters [Drewyer] met this evening the largest brown bear [grizzly] we have seen. [In the journal there is no consistency in use of a name for this bear.] As they fired he did not attempt to attack, but fled with a most tremendous roar; and such was his extraordinary tenacity of life that, although five balls passed through his lungs and he had five other wounds, he swam more than half way across the river [Missouri] to a sand-bar, and survived twenty minutes. He weighed between 500 and 600 pounds at least, and measured 8 feet 7½ inches from the nose to the extremity of the hind feet; 5 feet 10½ inches around the breast; 3 feet 11 inches around the neck; 1 foot 11 inches round the middle of the foreleg; and his talons, five on each foot, were 4⅜ inches in length. [The estimated weight given, for a bear of this size, seems to be a conservative one, although most writers and hunters, even to the present day, have greatly exaggerated the guessed weight of these bears.] This [animal] differs from the common black bear in having its talons much longer and more blunt; its tail shorter; its hair of a reddish or bay brown, longer and finer, and more abundant [this was in the spring, when the hair is longest and inclined to be somewhat faded in color]; his liver, lungs, and heart much larger, even in proportion to his size, the heart being equal to that of a large ox; his maw ten times larger; his testicles pendant from the belly and in separate pouches four inches apart. Besides fish and flesh, he feeds on roots and every kind of wild fruit."[49]

The encounters with these bears by members of the expedition not only provide interesting high lights in their adventures, and side lights on the character of the grizzlies at this early period, but it is gratifying to note with what care and detail they recorded the facts which have a scientific bearing on their observations.

Under date of May 11, 1805, another encounter relates that "About five in the afternoon one of our men [Bratton] . . . came running to the boats with loud cries, and every symptom of terror and distress. For some time after we had taken him on board he was so much out of breath as to be unable to describe the cause of his anxiety; but he at length told us that about a mile and a half below he had shot a brown bear [grizzly], which immediately turned and was in close pursuit of him; but the bear being badly wounded could not overtake him. Captain Lewis, with seven men immediately went in search of him; having found his track they followed him by the blood for a mile, found him concealed in some thick brushwood, and shot him with two balls through the skull. Though somewhat smaller than that killed a few days ago, he was a monster animal, and a most terrible enemy. Our man had shot him through the center of the lungs; yet he had pursued him furiously for half a mile, then returned more than twice that distance, and with his talons prepared himself a bed in the earth two feet deep and five feet long; he was perfectly alive when they found him; which was at least two hours after he had received the wound. The wonderful power of life which these animals possess renders them dreadful; their very track in the mud or sand, which we have sometimes found 11 inches long and 7¼ wide, exclusive of the talons, is alarming; and we would rather encounter two Indians than meet a single brown bear."[50]

A footnote appended by Coues states: "The grizzly bears have by this time won the respect of the party. Captain Lewis records at this date [in his unpublished field notes] a very prudent and reasonable resolve: 'I most generally went along, armed with my rifle and espontoon [a military half-pike]; thus I feel myself more than a match for a brown bear, provided I get him in open woods or near the water; but feel myself a little diffident with respect to an attack in the open plains. I have therefore come to a resolution to act on the defensive only, should I meet these gentlemen in the open country.' "[51]

The grizzlies encountered by members of the Lewis and Clark Expedition showed a marked and consistent aggressiveness—long fostered by the rather feeble opposition of arrows and stone axes in the hands of the only challenging enemy their species had ever known. In nearly every instance the bears made a fight of it. On the evening of May 14 (1805) six of the expedition's good hunters undertook to kill a large bear observed a short distance from the river. Stalking to within about forty paces of the animal, "four of the hunters now fired, and each lodged a ball in his body, two of them directly through the lungs. The furious animal sprang up and ran open-mouthed upon them; as he came near, the two hunters who had reserved their fire gave him two wounds, one of which, breaking his shoulder, retarded his motion for a moment; but before they could reload he was so near they were obliged to run to the river, and before they reached it he had almost overtaken them. Two jumped into the canoe, the other four separated, and concealing themselves in the willows, fired as fast as each could reload. They struck him several times, but instead of weakening the monster, each shot seemed only to direct him toward the hunter; till at last he pursued two of them so closely that they threw aside their guns and pouches, and jumped down a perpendicular bank of 20 feet into the river. The bear sprang after them and was within a few feet of the hindmost, when one of the hunters on shore shot him in the head and finally killed him."[52]

On June 12 Captain Lewis, accompanied by some of his hunters, went out "to kill something for breakfast" and bagged two large grizzlies. They also saw "wolves, antelopes, mule-deer, and vast herds of buffalo." They got "a beautiful view of the Rocky Mountains," covered with snow, and toward which the expedition was moving.

Two days later Captain Lewis had a rather narrow escape from one of these bears. It was the day after they had discovered the Great Falls of the Missouri, and the coleader of the expedition was proceeding on foot farther upstream to explore the upper falls and rapids, to find the best way to get past the obstruction. Coming upon a herd of at least a thousand buffalo, the captain shot one of these animals for supper. He had, however, "forgotten to reload his rifle and was intently watching to see the buffalo fall, when he beheld a large brown bear which was stealing on him unperceived, and was already within 20 steps. In the first moment of surprise he lifted his rifle, but remembering instantly that it was not charged, and that he had no time to reload, he felt there was no safety but flight. It was in the open level plain—not a brush nor a tree within 300 yards, the bank of the river sloping and not more than three feet high, so that there was no possible mode of concealment. Captain Lewis therefore thought of retreating in a quick walk, as fast as the bear advanced, toward the nearest tree; but as he turned, the bear ran open-mouthed and at full speed upon him. Captain Lewis ran about 80 yards, but finding that the animal gained on him fast, it flashed on his mind that, by getting into the water to such a depth that the bear would be obliged to attack him while swimming, there was still some chance of his life; he therefore turned short, plunged into the river about waist deep, and facing about presented the point of his espontoon. The bear arrived at the water's edge within about twenty feet of him; but as soon as he put himself in this posture of defense, the bear seemed frightened, and wheeling about, retreated with as much precipitation as he had pursued."[53]

Just above the junction of the Medicine and Missouri rivers, at the Great Falls, the expedition camped on the left bank, opposite to three islands in the middle of the river, to which they gave the name of "White Bear Islands, from observing some of those animals upon them . . . One of the men [Willard] . . . being attacked by a white bear, was closely pursued to within forty paces of the camp, and narrowly escaped being caught. . . ."[54] This same bear, a very short time later, attacked another member by the name of Colter, who had gone out alone and was compelled to seek refuge in the river.

Five days later, on June 25, another of the members, J. Fields, came upon three grizzlies a short distance above the falls and was attacked by one of these, narrowly escaping from serious injury. On the twenty-seventh, while portaging the baggage around the Great Falls, Drewyer and J. Fields were attacked by a very large bear after having climbed a tree, the animal being shot while it stood directly below, glaring up at them.

The expedition journal for the following day carries the information that "The white bears have now become exceedingly troublesome; they constantly infest our camp during the night, and though they have not attacked us, as our dog which patrols all night gives us notice of their approach, yet we are obliged to sleep with our guns by our sides for fear of accident, and we cannot send one man alone to any distance, particularly if he has to pass through brushwood. We saw two of them today. . . ."[55] Just above the Great Falls another camp was named Whitebear Camp; and there is another reference to the effect that "the bears, which have annoyed us very much of late, were prowling about our camp all last night." There are other accounts of members of the expedition being attacked by the bears.

In the chapter which is devoted to botany and zoology the Lewis and Clark journal gives the following consensus of opinion which had been gained from their observations: "First the brown, white, or grisly bear, which seems to be of the

same family, with an accidental variation of color only, inhabits the timbered parts of the Rocky Mountains. These are
rarely found on the westerly side [of the Rocky Mountains],
and are more common below the Rocky mountains, on the
plains or on their borders, amidst copses of brush and under-
wood, and near the water-courses. We were unable to learn
that they inhabit at all the wooded country bordering on the
coast as far in the interior as the [Cascade] range of mountains,
which passes the Columbia [River] between the Great Falls
and the rapids [Cascades] of that river."[56] This information
was set down after the expedition had crossed the Rockies and
had the benefit of considerable experience and observation of
the grizzly bears on the western side of the mountains.

Coues appends an important footnote to the above: "The
grizzly bear is the most notable discovery made in zoology by
Lewis and Clark. Their accounts are very full, as we have
already seen. . . . This bear was found to be so numerous and
so fierce, especially in the Upper Missouri region, as to more
than once endanger the lives of the party, and form an im-
pediment to the progress of the Expedition. Our authors carefully distinguish the grizzly, in all its color-variations, from the
black bear (*Ursus americanus*); and they are at pains to describe it minutely and repeatedly, laying special stress, for
specific characters, upon its great size in all its dimensions, its
general build and the form of the feet and claws, the peculiarity of the scrotum, together with the inability of this species
to climb trees, its great ferocity, and its remarkable tenacity of
life. Their remarks are for the most part judicious and pertinent, establishing the species as a distinct form from the black
bear; and have been confirmed by subsequent investigators.
The differences had long been known to the Indians, and are
correctly set forth."[57]

One further reference from this source is certainly worthy
of being made, for it records some opinions of the Indians
indigenous to the western side of the Rocky Mountains,
around the upper Clearwater River, in the Bitterroot Moun-

tains of present Idaho. The memorandum is under the journal's date for May 31, 1806, and reads in part: "Two men visited the Indian village, where they purchased a dressed bear-skin, of a uniform pale reddish-brown color, which the Indians called *yackah*, in contradiction to *hohhost*, or white bear. This remark induced us to inquire more particularly into their opinions as to the several species of bears; we therefore produced all the skins of that animal which we had killed at this place, and also one very nearly white which we had purchased. The natives immediately classed the white, the deep and the pale grizzly red, the grizzly dark brown—in short, all those with the extremities of the hair of a white or frosty color, without regard to the color of the ground of the foil, under the name of *hohhost*. They assured us that they were all of the same species with the white bear; that they associated together, had longer nails than the others, and never climbed trees . . . This distinction of the Indians seems to be well founded, and we are inclined to believe: 1st, that the white, grizzly, etc., bear of this neighborhood forms a distinct species which, more-over, is the same with that of the same color on the upper part of the Missouri, where the other species is not found; 2nd, that the black, reddish-brown, etc., is a second species, equally distinct from the white bear of this country. . . ."[58]

From the unusual amount of detailed information in the Lewis and Clark journal it is easily understood why their published account should so strongly influence and be so widely copied by so many writers, whose works of fact and fiction followed in the natural sequence of documentation and glamorization of our wild West.

Chapter VIII

A NEW SPECIES IS CHRISTENED

Use of the name "grizzly" has heretofore been used for the sake of simplicity, for this hairy monarch of the western wilderness was not known to the old-time Indians by that name. He had remained something of an orphan, so far as name and accredited family relationships were concerned. In the journals of the various early travelers, as well as among the frontiersmen who came in contact with this animal, the terms "grizzly," "grisly," "gray bear," "white bear," and an assortment of local cognomens were used without any particular authority or source of origin. These names were all quite natural ones. The word "grizzly," according to the Century dictionary, comes from the Old French word *grisel*, which was used to designate anything that was "somewhat gray or grayish" in color. The word "grisly" is derived from the Anglo-Saxon "grislic," meaning "horrible . . . as a monster, demon, or specter." The first is characteristic of the animal's appearance, while the second is representative of its temperament. The designations "gray bear" and "white bear" are quite likely translations of Indian common names in use when Europeans established an identification for these bears.

There is always an unwritten manual to every frontier country, which is imparted from one traveler to another and one indigenous generation to another. Such things as rivers, mountains, lakes, and animals frequently get their permanent names from such origins. The naturalists are, however, much more meticulous and more highly respectful of protocol in the establishing of scientific nomenclature.

The specimens brought back by the Lewis and Clark Expedition, with all the attendant body measurements and various other details to supplement the skins, provided the naturalists with the necessary prerequisites to describe the grizzly bear as a species. At almost the same time scientists had been afforded the opportunity of observing two live specimens of the grizzly. These were cubs brought back by the great explorer, Lieutenant Zebulon Pike, who afterward was made a general and who in 1806 had commanded an overland expedition that crossed the continent to the southwest, into Old Mexico, and gave a new historic interest to the Santa Fe Trail. The cubs were displayed in heavily iron-barred cages at Peale's Philadelphia Museum. Here is an interesting contemporary description which reflects the popular opinion of what were evidently the first live animals of this species ever displayed in a public zoo in the United States:

"When first received they were quite small, but speedily gave indications of that ferocity for which this species is so remarkable. As they increase in size they become exceedingly dangerous, seizing and tearing to pieces every animal they could lay hold of, and expressing eagerness to get at those accidentally brought within sight of their cages, by grasping the iron bars with their paws and shaking them violently, to the great terror of spectators, who felt insecure while witnessing such display of their strength . . . They were still cubs, and very little more than half-grown, when their ferocity became so alarming as to excite continual apprehension lest they should escape, and they were killed, in order to prevent such an event."[59]

In a letter addressed to His Excellency, Thomas Jefferson, President of the United States, and dated Washington, February 3, 1808, Zeb Pike gives the following information regarding these young grizzlies:

Sir:—I have the honor of receiving your note last evening, and in reply to the inquiry of Mr. Peale, can only give the following notes:

The bears were taken by an Indian in the mountains which divides the western branches of the Rio Del Norte and some small rivers, which discharge their waters into the east side of the Gulf of California, near the dividing line between the provinces of Biscay and Sonora. We happened at the time to be marching along at the foot of those mountains, and fell in with the Indian who had them, when I conceived the idea of bringing them to the United States, for your Excellency. Although then more than 1600 miles from our frontier post, Natchitoches, I purchased them from the savage, and for three or four days my men carried them in their laps on horseback. As they would eat nothing but milk, they were in danger of starvation. I then got a cage prepared for both, which was carried on a mule, lashed between two packs, but always ordered them to be let out the moment we halted, and not shut up again until we prepared to march. By this treatment they became extremely docile when at liberty, following my men, whom they learned to distinguish from the Spanish dragoons, by their feeding them, and encamping with them, like dogs through our camp, the small villages and forts when we halted. When well supplied with sustenance they would play like young puppies with each other and the soldiers, but the instant they were shut up and placed on the mule, they became cross, as the jostling of the animal knocked them against each other, and they were sometimes left exposed to the scorching heat of a vertical sun for a day without food or a drop of water, in which case they would worry, and tear each other, until nature was exhausted, and they could neither fight nor howl any longer. They will be one year old on the first of next month—March 1808—and, as I am informed, they frequently arrive at the weight of eight hundred pounds. . . .

With sentiments of the highest respect and esteem,
Your obedient servant,   (signed) Z. M. Pike.

DeWitt Clinton had gathered together the loose ends of scattered information regarding the grizzly bear and undertaken to give them scientific significance, as already indicated in this book. His discourse is the earliest approach to a thesis on the subject, falling barely short of establishing a classification in permanent nomenclature. It is, therefore, a part of the record; and further details regarding it will be found in the Appendix of this present book. It is easily recognized, however, how strongly DeWitt Clinton drew his information from the Lewis and Clark journal, which was published the same year of 1814, although it seems quite evident that the facts were previously available.

There was at the time, and still is, a well-established rule that the name first given to a new species by its scientific classifier shall be retained; and it is also customary to add to the Latin name of any such new animal the name of the scientist who first formally describes and names it. There are a considerable number of other naturalists, both contemporary and through the succeeding years, who more or less seriously described the grizzly bear and suggested names for it. Some of these accepted the name *Ursus ferox* DeWitt Clinton, while others gave credit to *Ursus cinereus* Richard Harlan and *Ursus canadensis* Harlan Smith.[60] To set down all of those here would only add a considerable amount of repetition and possible confusion. It probably suffices to say here that the accepted common name of this animal became "grizzly bear" and that the accepted scientific classification has become known as *Ursus horribilis* Ord. Just how George Ord came to be the recognized classifier is a very important as well as interesting part of the record.

George Ord's classification and naming of the grizzly bear is included in his "Zoology of North America," which was published as part of the second (American) edition of what is popularly referred to as *Gutherie's Geography*.[61] Ord listed a total of thirty-three genera of North American mammals, from monkeys to whales, and his classifications are considered one of the most important contributions to the scientific nomenclature of our culture. They have won for that comparatively unknown naturalist the characterization of "Father of North American Zoology." His work, published in the almost obscurity of that second edition of *Gutherie's Geography*, is universally recognized as the first and the most comprehensive and systematic original work on the zoology of America by an American—and for almost a full century it stood as the most accurate which had been published. Until quite recently, however, *only one copy* of the book *was known to survive*, and this was George Ord's own copy—which has since disappeared![62]

In 1893 the only known copy of this work, with the author's own added marginal notes, was owned by Dr. J. Soles Cohen, of Philadelphia, Pennsylvania—since known as the "Cohen Copy." Through the instrumentality of Samuel N. Rhoads, of the Academy of Natural Sciences, Philadelphia, and the co-operation of the owner, this monumental work by George Ord was privately reprinted, on New Year's Day, 1894, at Haddonfield, New Jersey,[63] and there was a somewhat abridged edition of only the zoological list similarly printed in October of the same year. The first mentioned reprint has since become a rarity.

Because of the importance of Ord's "Zoology" as part of the record relating to the grizzly bear, all that he had to say regarding this particular animal is reprinted in full as a part of the Appendix of this present book. The quotes are taken from a copy of the original Rhoads's reprint which is in this writer's personal library.

It was not, however, until 103 years after the publication of Ord's "Zoology" that a definite classification of the grizzly bears was accomplished, by Dr. C. Hart Merriam, of the U. S. Biological Survey.

In the meantime, however, like the Indians who fought bravely and desperately to protect and preserve the homeland with which a benevolent nature had blessed them, and the buffalo which the invading white man slaughtered with wanton abandon, the grizzly faced a similar fate of destruction and extinction as a species throughout the broad expanse of its range in the United States.

Chapter IX

A GREAT CREATURE MEETS ITS NEMESIS

THE Indian and the grizzly lived for many centuries in a state of primeval feud. The tribes who inhabited the Western Plains and Rocky Mountains had long depended on hunting as the principal means of providing the necessities of life. There was very little or no agriculture in their pre-white man curriculum of existence, and these nomadic hunters had followed the buffalo herds and lived on the abundance of other varieties of big game, such as elk, antelope, mountain sheep, and deer, as well as the bear. Their weapons had been relatively inadequate. The flint-tipped or even the metal-pointed arrow or spear was hardly a devastating accessory to the chase of these animals. By the natural processes of long dependency, however, the Indian had learned to use the bow and arrow with remarkable efficiency; and through the natural and realistic necessities of survival they had developed a high perfection of stealth, stamina, personal bravery, and knowledge of the habits and peculiarities of game, which combined to make these red men probably the best hunters on earth.

The Indian's arrow was a short-range weapon, although it was more effective than generally believed. Our early pioneers, who were armed only with muzzle-loading single-shot guns, were at first inclined to hold the arrow in some degree of disrespect—until they had the misfortune of suffering its execution. Kit Carson, the great frontier scout, is credited with once remarking that he never realized how fine a weapon the bow and arrow really was until he had them used against him in the darkness of a wilderness night. What the Indian lacked in material potentials of offensive combat, whether it was a human enemy or the more dangerous grizzly bear, was amply compensated for by his skillful and intelligent mastery of the crafts and strategy of stalking, ambush, marksmanship, attack, and escape. These were all integral factors in the code of primitive survival.

The red man excelled in all the qualifications important to wilderness life. General Randolph B. Marcy, in his book *Thirty Years of Army Life on the Border* (1866), gives the following interesting side light on this: "I know of nothing in the woodsman's education of so much importance, or so difficult to acquire, as the art of trailing or tracking men and animals. To become an adept in this art requires the constant practice of years, and with some [white] men a life-time does not suffice to learn it. Almost all the Indians whom I have met are proficient in this species of knowledge, the faculty for acquiring which appears to be innate with them. I have seen very few white men who were good trailers, and practice did not seem very materially to improve their faculties in this regard; they have not the same acute perceptions for these things as the Indian. . . . An Indian, on coming to a trail, will generally tell at a glance its age, by what particular tribe it was made, the number of the party, and many things connected with it, astonishing to the uninitiated." (P. 292.)

In the same book General Marcy strongly attests to the effectiveness of the Indian's bow and arrow. In the following instance this well-informed authority quotes the Hon. H. H. Sibley, of Minnesota, who was himself an accomplished sportsman and intimately acquainted with the subject upon which they both agreed: "The bow and arrow, in experienced hands, constitute quite as efficient a weapon in the chase of the buffalo, as the firearm [of that early period of which they wrote],

WHEN EPHRAIM ROAMED THE PLAINS
Brigadier General Randolph B. Marcy chasing a grizzly on horseback.
From a drawing by Frederic Remington

for the greater rapidity with which the discharges are made, and the almost equal certainty of execution. The force with which an arrow is propelled from a bow, wielded by an Indian of far less than the ordinary physical strength of a white man, is amazing. It is generally imbedded to the feathers in the buffalo, and sometimes even protrudes on the opposite side. It is reported among the Dakota or Sioux Indians, and generally credited to them, that one of their chiefs, *Wah-ne-tah* by name, who was remarkable for his strength and activity up to the close of his life, and who was equally renowned as both hunter and warrior, on one occasion discharged an arrow with sufficient force to pass clear through the body of a female buffalo and kill the calf by her side." (Pp. 344–45.)

In the above citation the authors were dealing specifically with buffalo hunting, although the hide and body of that animal was almost as tough and difficult to penetrate as that of the grizzly bear. The latter was extremely more dangerous when wounded. Another important fact pointed out is the great rapidity in which the discharges could be made by the Indian with his bow and arrow. The white man's muzzle-loading gun required the time-consuming necessity of reloading after every shot, and there was the added hazard of "keeping one's powder dry." Damp powder, which was all too frequently a serious problem, made these white man's weapons of little more value than a club. The Indian had the advantage of being able to fire many well-aimed arrows in the same period of time that a white man might be getting ready for a second shot. The red knights of the prairies sometimes carried as many as a hundred arrows, and they were capable of shooting them with accuracy, even from the back of a racing horse, with such rapidity that two or more of the shafts were in flight at the same time. George Catlin, in his book on the North American Indians (London, 1841, p. 230), relates watching the Mandans practicing their "game of arrows," in which each Indian would stand holding a bunch of arrows in his left hand and undertake to have the most arrows in the air that was possible at the same time. Having eight arrows up at once was apparently not exceptional.

One should not entertain the idea that the Indian of pre-white-man era and the years that shortly followed was the only aggressor in his war with the grizzly. The statements of highly reliable documentarians strongly indicate that the great bears of that period frequently took the unprovoked initiative against individuals and sometimes whole camps or villages of the red men. It was by no means a one-sided feud. George Bird Grinnell, one of the most respected authorities on the western Indians, whose knowledge of these people was founded on long and intimate personal association with them, has the following to say in his two-volume work, *The Chey-*

enne Indians: "Stories are told of man-eating grizzly bears, that habitually preyed on the people, lying in wait for and capturing them, and even driving large camps away from favorite camping places. Such stories go back to a time before the coming of the whites, for the acquisition of horses and iron-pointed arrows tended to put the Indian more nearly on an equality with his brute enemy, than he was when the red man traveled afoot and his weapons were of stone. In primitive times every advantage was with the bear. It was swift of foot, enduring, and hard to kill. Its tough muscles, heavy fur, strong hide, and thick coating of fat were hardly to be pierced by the primitive arrow."[64]

Similar indications of this characteristic of the grizzly to make unprovoked attacks have been previously cited and others will follow. This was not restricted to any particular area. In the early days it was as apt to be encountered on the Mexican border as it was in Montana or Oregon. Three further citations are given here, two of these dealing with the territory of New Mexico in the Southwest. "We found the grizzly bear abundant," writes C. B. R. Kennerly in his *Report of Explorations and Surveys.*[65] "When impelled by hunger they become very fierce and, descending into the valleys, frightening off the *pastores,* who, in their terror, abandoned their flocks to these huge monsters." Vernon Bailey, the eminent naturalist and at the time senior biologist of the Division of Biological Investigations, U. S. Biological Survey, has the following to say in his *Mammals of New Mexico:* "Evidently they [the Mount Taylor grizzly of the Zuni country] became stock-killing animals at an early date, and as the country filled up with domestic herds they wrought their own destruction by setting the hand of every man in self-defense against them."[66] It should be remembered, in connection with this last reference, that the Spanish conquistadors introduced cattle raising in our present Southwest as early as around 1560 to 1600.

Turning to the Canadian West, we find the following additional information by the eminent British naturalist, John Richardson, who accompanied the Franklin Expedition, in his book *Fauna Boreali Americana,* which was published in London in 1829. In his chapter on the "Grisly Bear—*Ursus ferox* Lewis and Clark," Dr. Richardson has this to say: "The following story is well authenticated. A party of voyagers, who had been employed all day in tracking a canoe up the Saskatchewan, had seated themselves in the twilight by a fire, and were busy in preparing their supper, when a large Grisly Bear sprung over their canoe that was tilted behind them, and seizing one of the party by the shoulder carried him off. The rest fled in terror with the exception of a métis, named Bourassa, who, grasping his gun, followed the Bear as it was retreating leisurely, with its prey. He called to his unfortunate comrade that he was afraid of hitting him if he fired at the Bear, but the later entreated him to fire immediately, without hesitation, as the Bear was squeezing him to death. On this he took a deliberate aim, and discharged his piece into the body of the Bear, which instantly dropped its prey to pursue Bourassa. He escaped with difficulty, and the bear ultimately retreated to a thicket, where it is supposed to have died; but the curiosity of the party not being a match for their fears, the fact of its decease was not ascertained. The man who was rescued had his arm fractured, and was otherwise severely bitten by the Bear, but finally recovered. I have seen Bourasso, and can add that the account which he gives is fully credited by the traders resident in that part of the country, who are best qualified to judge of its truth from the knowledge of the parties. I have been told that there is a man now living in the neighborhood of Edmonton-house, who was attacked by a Grisly Bear, which sprung out of a thicket, and with one stroke of its paw completely scalped him, laying bare the skull, and bringing the skin of the forehead down over the eyes. Assistance coming up, the Bear made off without doing him further injury, but the scalp not being replaced, the poor man has lost his sight, although he thinks that his eyes are uninjured." (P. 27.)

Instances such as these appear quite frequently in the writings of highly reputable travelers through various parts of the grizzly country in the early days.

Little wonder is it that all the Indians had such a respectful opinion of these animals. It was further heightened by the red man's basic precept of great pride in his accomplishments of personal prowess and bravery, and the symbols thereof were a fetish to him. The scalps of his defeated enemies were worn with as high a dignity of self-respect as the present-day soldier wears his decorations for personal valor, along with his service ribbons. There is but little fundamental difference. In the same manner the red man hung the long brown claws of the grizzly around his neck. The most illustrious chief or warrior could display no personal decoration that was more highly respected; and no honorable person ever wore such a necklace of claws that had not been taken by his own hands—any more than a present-day soldier would wear any medal for bravery which was not his personal privilege to display.

The following incident is related by John M. Murphy in his book *Sporting Adventures in the Far West*:[67]

"All the members of the tribe celebrated the victory over a grizzly bear by a feast on the body, and by indulging in dances; while the slayers related their deeds with the extravagant language of their race. This daring act made them famous at once and they were conceded to be the highest type of warriors. From that day forth they always wore a necklace of the claws of the bear as proof of their bravery and importance. . . .

"I remember distinctly with what, to me, seemed ludicrous dignity or gravity, a Sioux chief once pointed out a string of ugly looking claws that hung around his neck, and then to the anklets of the same material that encircled his blanket-clad legs, and in which heroic tone he assured me that he had killed their former owner himself, and was now considered to be unrivalled as a brave. He thought that if the Great Father in Washington knew that he was so great a person he would send him pleanty of meat, flour, tea, coffee, and sugar, and keep him from the necessity of going out buffalo hunting to keep his family from starvation. He asked me to tell the Great Father in Washington who he really was, and what were his wants. When I volunteered to do so, on condition that he give me the interesting necklace of grizzly claws that he wore, my offer was rejected at once. He said he would not part with them on any account; adding that he would much rather part with his favorite wife." These comments are infected with a certain amount of *lèse-majesté* on the part of Mr. Murphy, although they nevertheless indicate the importance which the Indian invested in the wearing of the claws of the grizzly.

Some of the tribesmen of our Old West did not hunt the grizzly, for reasons that were directly associated with ancestral worship of this animal. Some ill-informed writers, who did not know the whole story, have interpreted situations of this sort to declare that the Indian was afraid of the grizzly. While the red men of those early days were human, even as you and I, their philosophy did not tolerate fear of any kind. This fact was well known and has been amply attested to by many an American scout and experienced soldier of the Indian-fighting days on the Western Plains. It cannot be said that the Indian was afraid of the grizzly any more than our own mountain men and hunters of that period can be accused of being afraid of either the grizzly or the Indian. Aside from any restrictions due to the red man's ancestral worship, there is a great difference between *fear* and *intelligent respect* or *wary caution*—a difference which is not always recognizable by those who have not had sufficient personal experience with real danger.

Previous to about 1850 the principal weapon in the hands of our frontiersmen was the muzzle-loading, single-shot gun. This made exciting and dangerous days for the grizzly hunters. To dwell briefly on the history of firearms, the famed *Kentucky Rifle* made its appearance about 1725. Most of these early flintlock weapons were made around Lancaster, Pennsylvania. They got their name from the region where they first found popular use—just as "Panama hats" were made in Ecuador for use in Panama during the building of the canal.

The long-barreled, flintlock American rifle was a mighty good weapon for its day, and our backwoods colonists learned how to use them with great efficiency. During the Revolutionary War this fact became quite well known, as far away as the courts of England. They helped to shape the course of history. They later became the principal defender and provender of the men who led our western course of empire. Their barrels generally ran thirty-six to forty-eight inches in length, which was good for accuracy but a disadvantage to the western frontiersmen who had to carry them on horseback or for handling in the thick timber or underbrush where the beaver trappers frequently had to depend on quick use of them. The authority Townsend Whelen gives the following estimation of the potential use of these guns: "A skilled user of a Kentucky Rifle could measure and empty a charge of powder into the barrel, insert the lead ball and patch, and ram them down, replace the ramrod under the barrel, place a few grains of powder in the pan of the flintlock, and be ready to fire in about thirty seconds."[68] Whelen also had this to say about their use: "He might, with some luck, hit a small target 150 yards away, but would seldom try beyond 100 yards, and found from experience that between 60 and 100 yards was the best range."

Most of these early "pea rifles" used bullets that ran about seventy to the pound, with the total amount of lead and powder being the equivalent to less than that contained in the early models of a 30–30 caliber cartridge. The average sportsman of today would consider it little short of personal suicide to tackle a grizzly with the most *modern* type of *repeating* rifle of this caliber—although some Indians in western Canada and Alaska still continue to use such a weapon, even smaller ones.

The inadequacy of the early small-bore, single-shot muzzle-loading rifle, and the inefficiency of the flintlock method of ignition, for use against such game as buffalo and grizzly, was quickly realized, although it was not until "the late 1840's that there was evolved . . . the short, heavy-calibre plains rifle . . . of rugged construction . . . and capable of accurately delivering a heavy ball with great shocking power at [comparatively] long range."[69] There was also a demand for a gun that could be loaded with greater rapidity and less hazard than the muzzle-loader, which resulted in several crude types of breech-loaders.

In spite of the vastly improved muzzle-loading single-shot guns, the grizzly bear did not meet its equalizer until the large-caliber, breech-loading *Sharps* rifle came into use in the West. The 1848 model of this famous gun accompanied practically every wagon train that went westward across the plains in the 1850s and every upriver boat on the Missouri and other western tributaries of the Mississippi. The first of these weapons used a linen or paper cartridge embodying both powder and lead bullet, which was inserted into the receiver, and the sharp metal edge of the breechblock sheared off the rear end of the cartridge as it was brought back into firing position, thus exposing the powder, which was then ignited by a percussion cap. The *Colt* repeating firearm, adapted to both revolver and rifle, was patented in England in 1835 and in the United States the following year, but this was still a muzzle-loading gun. There were also other breech-loading rifles, some of which got out into the West somewhat earlier than the *Sharps;* but it was the latter that really put thunder and lightning into the hands of those who carried forward the western warfare against both man and beast. This, and the highly improved repeating, metal-cartridge rifles which shortly followed, in the hands of the white man, proved to be the fatal nemesis of the Indian, the buffalo, and the grizzly bear. None of them submitted with any sudden dispassion or loss of character, and the chronicles of these fights and fighters constitute some of the most exciting episodes in frontier history.

Chapter X

THEY WERE MANY AND MIGHTY

GRIZZLIES were more abundant at the beginning of our pioneering days than might be suspected. Excerpts from the Lewis and Clark journal have already given an indication of the frequency with which these animals were to be met with on the Upper Missouri and its tributaries and in the Rocky Mountains of the Northwest. This was typical of most all the area from Canada to Mexico and from the plains to the Pacific Coast. They were, of course, more numerous in some sections than others, depending on the natural characteristics of the terrain and such other factors as water and food in season.

We have come to think of the grizzly as principally an inhabitant of the high valleys and basins of the Rocky Mountains, although it was less than a hundred years ago when these great bears were frequently found considerable distances out on the Plains. Even then their normal habitat was the more timbered high hills and mountains, although the easy and abundant food provided by the large herds of buffalo lured many of these bears to become nomads of the open Plains. Theodore Roosevelt, from his vast store of knowledge of our western game, had the following to say regarding the grizzly: "In the old days . . . he wandered at will over the Plains . . . roving hither and thither in burly self-confidence

. . . searching for roots, digging up gophers, or perhaps following the great buffalo herds to prey on some unwary straggler which he was able to catch at a disadvantage in a washout. . . . Old hunters, survivors of the long-vanished ages when the vast herds thronged the high plains and were followed by the wild Indian tribes, and by bands of whites who were scarcely less savage, have told me that they often met [grizzly] bears under such circumstances. . . ."[70] Later in the same account Roosevelt remarks: "The bison was the most easily approached of all game, and the great bear could often get near some outlying straggler, in its quest after stray cows, yearlings, or calves. In default of a favorable chance to make a prey of one of these weaker members of the herd, it did not hesitate to attack the mighty bulls themselves; and perhaps the grandest sight which it was ever the good fortune of the early hunters to witness was one of these rare battles between a hungry grisly and a powerful buffalo bull."[71]

Of the territory somewhat farther south, the frequently quoted General Marcy gives us a similar estimation from his long personal experience: "In 1858 these animals [grizzlies] were abundant about the headwaters of the Arkansas and Platte Rivers [in what is now southern Wyoming and the state of Colorado], and they were often seen in the vicinity of Pike's Peak [around Colorado Springs] and the present site of Denver City. . . . The Black Hills, in the neighborhood of Fort Laramie, I should regard as the most likely place for finding the animal now [1866]."[72]

Swinging on down into the Southwest, we have the following information from the research of Vernon Bailey, senior biologist of the Biological Survey: "Grizzly bears were once so numerous [in New Mexico] as to be a serious menace to human life and domestic stock."[73] Bailey also gives the further and more specific data on the subject: "In the foothills and valley country around the Magollan Mountains, in 1852 [grizzly] bears were reported common in the open country by J. H. Clark and other collectors, even in the Rio Grande

Valley of southern New Mexico. In his journal notes of December 3, 1824, in the Rio Grande Valley below Socorro, James Ohio Pattie records 'great numbers of bears, deer, and turkeys—a bear having chased one of our men into camp; and we killed it.' Again, on October 28, 1826, while in the Rio Grande Valley above El Paso, he says: 'At a very short distance from The Pass I began to come into contact with great bears and other wild animals. In one instance a bear, exceedingly hungry, as I supposed, came upon my horses as I was resting them at midday and made at one of them. I repaid him for his impudence by shooting him through the brain.' "[74]

It is evident that grizzlies were once equally, if not more, plentiful in the coastal areas along the Pacific, particularly in California where the salubrious climate was conducive to developing bears of unusual size and pugnaciousness. Although these mighty animals have been entirely extinct in that state for more than thirty years, they were once easily found even in close vicinity to the city of San Francisco, as well as present Hollywood. "On the 10th of April [1806]," writes G. H. Langsdorf in his *Voyages and Travels*,[75] "he [Don Luis Arguello] sent out eight soldiers on horseback to catch a live bear to fight with a wild bull at the Presidio. They returned on the evening of the same day with a large dark-brown bear, taken by means of ropes and slings. He lay upon an ox-hide stretched over branches of trees bound together, and had been drawn on this for some miles by a pair of oxen. He had been muzzled, and his paws were tied fast together. This confinement, together with the way he had been dragged, and his rage, had heated him exceedingly. . . ." Considering the length of time it must have required the "soldiers" to rope and hog-tie a grown grizzly, then to prepare the described means of hauling the beast back to the Presidio, plus the slow moving pace of oxen, and the limited direction in which it had been possible for them to travel by land, it seems quite certain that this grizzly was found within a short distance of the present

city of San Francisco, possibly within the area of the munici-
pality.

Even as late as the early 1860s the grizzlies were presumed
to be such a menace to farmers and stock raisers in the Sacramento Valley and other similar areas in California that "a
bounty of Ten Dollars was given by the State for each grizzly
scalp, and several hunters each got more than a hundred scalps
in one year."[76] Thus the grizzly bear became officially designated as a *predatory animal*, with a monetary premium put on
his scalp, for the encouragement of his wholesale destruction
—a policy which was adopted, officially or otherwise, throughout his entire natural range in the United States and to this
day persists in some areas where but a few individuals of the
species still linger on the brink of total extermination. Not
even the rattlesnake has had such a determined and widespread
campaign of destruction waged against them as a species.

For the present our principal concern is evidence of the
former abundance of these animals; and the following quotation is taken from the last-cited source, which appeared in
Outing Magazine in the issue of November 1902: "A party
of five professional hunters spent a whole year in hunting for
grizzlies in Oregon in 1848, and they brought to Sutter's Fort
at Sacramento over 700 pelts."[77]

The question naturally comes to mind as to just how many
grizzlies there actually were, in total number, scattered over
their entire range in the West at the beginning of our pioneer
period—say in 1850, or a little more than a hundred years ago.
Any figure arrived at can at best be little more than something
between an estimate and a wild guess. The number of buffalo
on the Western Plains has been estimated, by reliable authorities, from 50,000,000 to as high as 125,000,000. The buffalo's
natural habitat was the open country and he was inclined to
travel in mass concentrations, moving north or south with the
seasons; and the total range of these bovines covered less total
area than the range of the grizzly bear. The latter was also by

nature a furtive creature, being inclined even in the early days to do most of his traveling and hunting at night, and during the daytime kept out of sight in rough or timbered retreats. Also, being dangerous and of little or no value as fur or food, the majority of the early travelers were more inclined to stay out of his way than they were to go looking for him. The journals of these men, and even the recorded accounts of hunters, give us only a clue to general abundance. There is some help to be found in the estimated census undertaken in recent years by several of the state and the U.S. Government game and wildlife agencies in their respective areas, although even these may be misleading. However, based on all available information bearing on the subject, this writer would hazard the estimate that there were at least 100,000 grizzly bears in the United States, roaming the Rocky Mountain and adjacent regions and the area westward to the Pacific Coast, in the year 1850. That is really a lot of grizzly bears, although it is apt to be an underestimate of the actual number.

That the physical prowess of these creatures was prodigious there can be no doubt. In his full prime he has long been recognized by scientists as the largest and most powerful of all the present-day creatures on this or any other continent, and this record goes back 200,000 years or more. He is also one of the most agile and dexterous of the larger mammals. Add to this his intelligence and well-known pugnacious disposition, and you have a primeval beast of brawn and dangerousness, probably unrivaled as far back as there is any history of man on this earth.

Our pioneer white hunters who went after the great silvery-coated bears of the West made it a combination which could only result in excitement and frequent mayhem. For these men, particularly those who went across the Great Plains in the 1820s to 1850s, were a hardy breed of adventurer. They had to be to survive. A good many of them had acquired their sinew-and-guts in the Appalachians and the country westward to the Mississippi, where they had ample opportunity to learn their lessons in frontier existence from family training, first-hand experience, and a full realization of such important matters as complete self-dependence and that the price of imprudence, error, or weakness might easily be tragedy. Plowing fields, milking cows, and raising pigs was not to their taste. Hunting and trapping and a free life in the wild out of doors was much more to their liking, and the prospect of rich rewards from many large bundles of beaver skins and other fur was the added magic lodestar that lured them into the long journey westward.

These early western adventurers were mostly young men, some still in their teens, but some of these mere boys were destined to make history—like the runaway boy who joined one of the Santa Fe caravans and was known as Kit Carson. They were not exactly an angelic fraternity, although a few, like Jedediah Smith, were deeply imbued with the tenets of the Christian faith and maintained that faith throughout their life; while there were still others, like Bill Williams, who began his career as a missionary to the Indians, only to forsake his alliance with God to become a wayward knight-errant of the mountain men and the free trappers. But whether or not these men had been whelped as sons of the eastern frontier, or as shoemakers' apprentices, or ministers' sons, carpenters, store clerks, runaways from eastern schools or jails, or just kids with a blind yen for wild adventure, the Old West had a realistic faculty of reducing all to the common denomination of self-survival. Those who remained long enough to become a part of this new country were amalgamated into a new and distinct breed of American—one of the hardiest, toughest, and most wilderness-wise breed the white race has produced.

To have said less, about either the grizzlies or the white pioneers who invaded their country, would only have been to understate the case. Nor does this writer want to underestimate the Indian as a hunter; but he lacked the ruthless sweep and abandon of his white counterparts. After all, the Indians had been hunting the buffalo for several thousands of years, and the white hunters virtually exterminated the vast herds within the very brief space of a few years. There is nothing praiseworthy in this accomplishment. It is merely cited as a criterion of the character and characteristics of the white men who pioneered our conquest of the West.

An enlightening vignette is given by the previously quoted General Marcy, a contemporary who was well acquainted with these whites who roamed the wilderness in small parties or alone: "With the speed of a horse and the watchfulness of a wolf or antelope, whose faculties are sharpened by necessity; who, when they got short of provisions look for something to eat, and found it in the water, in the ground, or on the surface; whose bill of fare ranges from grass-seeds, nuts, roots, grasshoppers, lizards, and rattlesnakes, up to antelope, deer, elk, bear and buffalo—and they have a continent to roam over. They will be neither suppressed, caught, conquered, overawed, or reduced to famine."[78]

They subsisted principally from hunting, and there was little else but fur as a source of income. Hunting the grizzly was by no means remunerative. The hide was not worth skinning off, let alone the trouble of drying or packing to the nearest trading place; and neither was the meat worth the effort, or the risk, with the plenitude and ease with which one could get other varieties of far more palatable and harmless game. Going after Old Ephraim, with a single-shot muzzle-loading "pea rifle," was largely a matter of unadulterated adventure. It was thrust upon some, but others took it up with an enthusiasm that was almost an obsession—like gambling or drinking whisky, or like a dog that never learns a lesson from getting his face full of porcupine quills. The frequent hazard of being charged did not deter them, nor the fact that the odds were against them. They had but one physical advantage in the event of a critical emergency—they could climb trees and the big grizzlies could not—and many a bearded and buckskin-clad frontiersman found that he could make an undignified but effective escape like a monkey-up-a-tree, with far greater speed and dexterity than he had ever believed possible. Sometimes there was no suitable tree close enough. The only alternative to being severely worked over with teeth and claws was to fight it out with a knife. Instances in which wounded grizzlies were actually killed with a knife are surprisingly frequent, as are also the number of hunters who were maimed or killed.

It is very ironical that so many lone white men have penetrated and become intimately familiar with the "unknown" areas well in advance of the more professional men who led elaborate expeditions and reaped the long-lasting credits. Those solitary pre-vanguards of what we call the civilized world frequently take native wives and literally become members of the tribe and have exciting experiences and learn important things which often remain unwritten and lost to the record. This was true of our Old West. There were many trappers, fur traders, and just plain adventurers who lived in the tepees of the tribes into which they were adopted, and raised families, long before the rivers, lakes, and mountains were visited by those who became famous as their discoverers. These plebeian pioneers were not historians. Many could not even write their own names. A considerable number were killed, in one way or another, within a relatively short time. Stanley Vestal, in his book *Mountain Men*, tells us that, "Counting all the mountain men together—both free trappers and engagees of the various companies in the field [in the mid-1820s]—there were not a thousand men in the Rockies. Of these, one died a violent death every ten or twelve days, as a matter of course."[79] Those who survived were frequently silent and evasive about their adventures—taking with them into the grave most or all of their recollections and what they had learned. We can only imagine at their exploits and wish they might be included in books such as this. There were some, of course, who undertook to write the accounts of their experiences and others whose stories, or parts thereof, have gotten into print in one way or another and in varying degrees of authenticity. There were also, fortunately, a few whose journals of serious intent have provided the basis for fine accounts of those exciting days. The honest experiences of some were of such unusual character that even the fiction writers have hardly dared to use them in their stories.

Chapter XI

RESPECTED BY THE GREAT

AMONG all the colorful characters who made frontier history in our Old West there is probably no more illustrious triumvirate than Jedediah Smith, Jim Bridger, and Kit Carson. Their adventurous careers were contemporary and quite similar, although their personalities were very different. They all figured prominently in the exploration and conquest of the western wilderness, and their experiences with grizzly bears were among their narrowest and most exciting escapes.

It might be said, in the greatest of brevity, that Jed Smith was religious, Jim Bridger was boisterous, Kit Carson was serious, and all were very brave men. There was eleven years difference in their ages. The first two went West with the same outfit, and Carson followed four years later. They were all engaged in the fur trade as trappers and traders, as well as being hunters, Indian fighters, and pathfinders for those who followed.

Jed Smith and Jim Bridger both joined that historic Henry-Ashley Expedition which went up the Missouri River in the spring of 1822, to set a new pattern for the lucrative fur industry, and which resulted in creating the audacious "Mountain Men" of the Rockies. Jim, although he had barely entered into his nineteenth year, went with the Major Andrew Henry party, and Jed followed close behind with the party under the command of William H. Ashley. The latter group got into serious trouble when about eight hundred hostile Indians made a surprise attack, killing thirteen of Ashley's men, wounding a dozen others, and taking all their horses. Smith was one of two volunteers who undertook the desperate dash, in the best of present-day movie style, to get through the Indian country and bring back Major Henry's men barely in time to save their comrades from complete catastrophe. It was then that Jed Smith and Jim Bridger were together baptized into the harsh realities of frontier existence.

The Henry-Ashley men had become organized on the Upper Missouri and were spreading out into the surrounding country the following year of 1823 when our two neophytes got mixed up with grizzly-bear incidents which are classics of their kind. Bridger's indoctrination into the dangerous proclivities of Old Ephraim came first. He is by no means the hero of the story. In fact, his biographers seem to have passed it over rather lightly, forgiving the part he played on the excuses of youth, the influence of an older and less courageous companion, and desperate circumstances. The real gallant of the whole affair was another, and it has come down to us as the tragic saga of Hugh Glass—an "old man" in his fifties. The story has been variously told. There has even been a lengthy poem written about it.[80] The first published account, in considerable length and detail, appeared in the St. Louis newspaper *Missouri Intelligence*, on June 18, 1825, and several other versions are to be found in J. Cecil Alter's book *Jim Bridger*.[81]

It seems that Hugh Glass went out looking for trouble with a grizzly bear while the party was traveling in search of beaver-trapping territory, and he became involved in more than he had expected. Just what happened is retold here in the plebeian prose of another member of the party. The following quotation is taken from the original journal of James Clyman, which was in the Huntington Library when transcribed by Charles L. Camp for his book on this American frontiersman.[82] The narration is told very briefly and provides much for the imagination to feed upon:

"Hugh Glass . . . met with a large grissly Bear which he shot and wounded the bear as is usual attacked Glass he attempted to climb a tree but the bear caught him and hauled to the ground tearing and lacerating his body in fearful rate by this time several men were in close gun shot but could not shoot for fear of hitting Glass at length the beare appeared to be satisfied and turned to leave when 2 or 3 men fired the bear turned immediately on Glass and give him a second mutilation. on turning again several more men shot him when for a third time he pounced on Glass and fell dead over his body. . . ."

But this is only part of the story. Hugh Glass was not killed; but he had been so badly bitten, bone-broken, and torn apart by the grizzly that he was not only unable to travel, but it was impossible even to move him. After sewing him up with mending thread and otherwise ministering to their half-dead companion as best they could, it was finally decided to leave the unfortunate victim to his fate—in the same manner that Indians abandoned those who were too badly wounded or too aged to continue on a journey. Major Henry, who was in charge of this party, asked for volunteers to stay behind with Glass. This was no idle request, for there were Indians around, who had already decided that white men's scalps were very desirable trophies; and even to rejoin their companions under the most favorable of circumstances, in this vast wilderness, would be a difficult undertaking. After considerable silence on the part of everyone the youthful Jim Bridger agreed to remain, and shortly afterward, on the promise of a few extra dollars of pay, he was joined by a man named Fitzgerald.

According to the *Missouri Intelligence* account the two Good Samaritans stayed with Hugh Glass for five days, "when, despairing of his recovery, and at the same time seeing no prospects of immediate death, they cruelly abandoned him, taking with them his rifle and all his accoutrements [as well as his horse], so that he was left without means of defense, subsistence, or shelter. . . ." Upon rejoining their companies they reported that "Glass had died of his wounds and they had buried him in the best manner possible. . . ."[83]

There is still more to the story—which has been variously recounted. With the triple breath of death blowing coldly upon his soul, he survived his mutilations, broken bones and starvation, and the hazard of helplessly being scalped by Indians. He regained enough strength to bathe his own wounds with cold water; and he finally set out to return to Fort Kiowa, a post on the Missouri River, southeast of the present city of Pierre, South Dakota—a distance of about a hundred miles. It has been claimed that he "crawled" most of that distance! "With inconceivable hardships and distress," the 1825 newspaper account continues, "he at last reached Fort Kiowa." And after further recovery he set out *up the river*, to find the men who had abandoned him.

It is only natural that Hugh Glass should have carried a heavy load of vengeance in his heart, particularly against Jim Bridger and Fitzgerald. There is pretty good evidence that when he finally came face to face with Bridger that young man gazed blankly into the open gates of Eternity. In the meantime, however, Glass's desire for revenge had lost its cutting edge. After staring at the scared youngster for a few interminable moments he probably said: *"Where the hell is my horse and gun?"* Such was the metal in which these men were cast. They both trod on along the western trails to become famous in the best traditions of the Mountain Men.

The experience certainly must have made a deep and lasting impression on Jim Bridger. In any event, there are no books filled with glowing accounts in which he went looking for future trouble with grizzly bears. In Shannon Garst's recent book, *Jim Bridger—Greatest of the Mountain Men* (1952), the Hugh Glass incident is modestly presented, and that's about all. J. Cecil Alter, in recounting Captain Raynold's expedition in the valley of the Big Horn in 1859, quotes that "Bears are very numerous, more than a dozen having been seen in the course of the day's march, and one, a yearling cub, was brought down by Bridger's rifle." (P. 344.) Alter tells of other grizzlies being shot by members of parties which Bridger served as guide. On the Powder River Expedition of 1865, in the Big Horn Mountains, a large one was killed after having its "hide perforated with twenty-three balls." (P. 413.) On this same expedition, on the Tongue River, on August 28 "four of the Omaha [Indian] scouts went a short distance from the camp and met a grizzly which they very imprudently fired upon. The grizzly closed upon them, killing one of the scouts and fearfully mangling two others before a relief party could drive away the bear." (Pp. 415–16.) Jim Bridger certainly had plenty of opportunities to become involved in many exciting episodes with grizzly bears. If such was the case, the record is sadly deceiving—but he did live to ripe old age.

Jedediah Smith was not so fortunate as Jim Bridger. He came to the West from poor parents, with thirteen brothers and sisters, and had little to go on beyond a strong ambition, great personal courage, and a deep faith in God. But Jed Smith rose rapidly to a business partnership with Ashley, one of the most powerful figures in the fur industry of that era, and afterward headed his own organization in the fur trade. Far more important were his accomplishments in the field of exploration. Stanley Vestal called him "the greatest pathfinder. . . . He ranks with Lewis and Clark: in fact, he surpasses them. . . . They traced a single route to the Western Ocean; Smith found three. No man living in his time was his equal in first-hand knowledge of the Far West."[84]

Jed Smith came about as near being killed by a grizzly bear as it seems possible to survive such an experience. This came so early in his short but illustrious career that it has an added historic significance. The incident is not only a classic example of personal courage and fortitude on the part of the victim but also an example of the devastating aggressiveness of these

bears. Jed had been put in charge of one of the first small parties that was sent out from Fort Kiowa in the spring of 1823.
They had passed the Black Hills and were near one of the
forks of the Cheyenne River.[85] James Clyman was a member
of this party, and an account of what happened is found in his
journal, from which the previously cited Hugh Glass incident
has already been quoted. It is given here in all that same
plebeian prose and stark realism—certainly one of the classics
of its kind:

"While passing through a Brushy bottom a large Grssely
came down the valley we being in single file men on foot
leading pack horses he struck us about the center then turning ran parallel to our line Capt Smith being in the advance
he ran to the open ground and as he emerged from the thicket
he and the bear met face to face Grissly did not hesitate a
moment but sprung on the Capt taking him by the head
first pitching sprawling on the earth he have him a grab by
the middle fortunately catching by the ball pouch and Butcher
Knife which he broke but breaking several of his ribs and cutting his head badly none of us having any surgical Knowledge
what was to be done one Said come take hold and he would
say why not you so it went around I asked the Capt what
was best he said one or 2 go for water and if you have a
needle and thread git it out and sew up my wounds around my
head which was bleeding freely I got a pair of scissors and
cut off his hair and then began my first job of dressing
wounds Upon examination I found the bear had taken nearly
all his head in his capacious mouth close to the left eye on one
side and close to his right ear on the other and laid the skull
bare to near the crown of the head leaving a white streak
where his teeth passed one of his ears was torn from his head
out to the outer rim after stitching all the other wounds in
the best way I was capable and according to the captains directions the ear being the last I told him I could do nothing for
his Eare. O you must try to stitch up some way or other he
said then I put in my needle stitching it through and through

and over and over laying the lacerated parts together as nice as I could with my hands water was found in about a mille when we all moved down and encamped the captain being able to mount his horse and ride to camp whare we pitched a tent the only one we had and made him as comfortable as circumstances would permit. This gave us a lisson on the character of the grissly Beare which we did not forget."[86]

No human could go through such an experience without retaining a deep respect for the cause of his scars. While Jed Smith could not have lived the life he did without having additional encounters of one sort or another with these bears, he certainly did not take up grizzly hunting as a sporting pastime or otherwise. There is no discredit in this. It is doubtful if Jed could have avoided that almost fatal encounter, even if he had been the smartest bear hunter in the West. The attack was sudden, bold, and evidently unprovoked, a good example of the bold aggressiveness of these animals before they learned to respect men with high-powered repeating rifles; and the fact that Jed Smith evaded having any future trouble with them is a testimony to his serious attitude toward the more businesslike aspects of the fur trade, an important phase of which was to explore new territory and new routes to bigger and richer fields for the harvest. He was killed by Comanche Indians when still a young man of only thirty-two.

The third of this triumvirate of great American western pioneers was Christopher "Kit" Carson. Trapper, hunter, Indian fighter, guide, and in all the sterling qualities of a frontiersman he has few if any superiors. Clarence A. Vandiveer, one of the highly regarded historians of the fur trade, says that "Kit Carson was by far the greatest of all the Rocky Mountain Men . . . excepting perhaps the veteran explorer, Jedediah S. Smith."[87] Theodore Roosevelt acclaimed him "the best, the bravest, the most modest of them all . . .";[88] and Buffalo Bill Cody named his only son and greatest pride Kit Carson Cody, because of the deep and long-cherished admiration in which he held this great American frontiersman. Among his own kind he won for himself the enviable title "Nestor [wisest] of the Rocky Mountain Men," and the Indians called him "Monarch of the Plains."[89]

No one ever questioned the courage of Kit Carson or his wise judgment in matters relating to life in the wilderness he knew so well. Born in Kentucky on December 24, 1809, and said to be a grandson of Daniel Boone,[90] he went West on the Santa Fe Trail in 1826, while still in his sixteenth year.[91] When he died in Colorado, in his fifty-eighth year, he left behind a long trail that had taken him through about every wild section of the Western Plains and mountains. He wandered back and forth across the Rockies and knew the three forks of the Missouri, the Big Snake, the Green, the Colorado, the Platte, the Yellowstone, the Columbia, and most of the other rivers and all of the mountains of the West. The exploits of Kit Carson had become traditions long before his career came to an end. His first biography, authorized from facts supplied by himself, was written by Dr. DeWitt Clinton Peters and published in 1853,[92] fifteen years before his death.

Kit got mixed up with two grizzlies that made what appears to be an unprovoked attack while he was out alone hunting other game. It was after he had spent the summer of 1833 on the Laramie River. Dr. Peters' narrative is garnished with a liberal amount of layman's journalism, some details of which are in error, although the account is undoubtedly based on facts supplied by Carson himself. It is quoted here directly from the original work, although this writer has deleted most of the innocent fallacies.

While out procuring meat for camp, Kit shot an elk with his muzzle-loader; and he hardly had time to observe the effects when the echo of the blast "was broken in upon and completely lost in the terrific roar from the woods directly behind him . . . and he instantly saw two huge and terribly angry grizzly bears. As his eyes first rested upon the unwelcome guests, they were bounding towards him, their eyes flashing fiery passion, their pearly teeth glittering with eagerness to mangle his flesh, and their monster fore-arms, hung with sharp, bony claws, ready and anxious to hug his body in a close and most loving embrace. There was not much time . . . In fact, one instant spent in thought then would have proved his death warrant without hope of reprieve. Messrs. Bruin evidently considered their domain most unjustly intruded upon. . . .

"Dropping his rifle, the little leaden bullet of which would now have been worth to him its weight in gold . . . he bounded from his position . . . The tree! he hoped and prayed, as he fairly flew over the ground with the bears hot in chase . . . Grasping a lower limb he swung his body up into the first tier of branches just as the passing Bruin brushed against one of his legs . . . Instantly drawing his keen-edged hunting knife, he cut away for dear life at a thick short branch. The knife and his energy conquered the cutting . . . a few sharp raps made with the severed branch upon the nose of the bears that were now endeavoring to ascend the tree . . . caused them to retreat.

"This scene . . . kept Mr. Carson and Messrs. Bruin actively busy for sometime . . . They had the daring trespasser in their domain up a tree and almost in their reach; and to keep out of the way of their uncomely claws, Kit was obliged to gather himself up in the smallest possible space and cling to the topmost boughs.

"The bears now allowed themselves a short reprieve . . . Then they renewed their endeavors to force the hunter from his resting place. Mounted on their hind paws they would reach for him; but the blows with the stick, applied freely to their noses, would make them desist. In vain did they exhaust every means to force the man to descend . . . Together the bears made a desperate effort to tear Kit from the tree. . . .

"Then finally one at a time they departed; but it was not until they had been out of sight and hearing for some time that Kit considered it safe to venture down from the tree;

when he hastened to regain and immediately reload his rifle."
(Pp. 82–85.)

The mere fact that Kit Carson made an unceremonious retreat and tree-climbing escape from those two attacking
grizzlies, and that he refrained from playing the part of a
buckskin-clad gladiator, by standing his ground and fighting
it out with his keen-edged hunting knife as some of the later
and more reckless adventurers chose to do, was just plain good
judgment.

The foregoing, however, is the only narrative of an exciting
encounter with the grizzly which is included in Dr. Peters'
biography of Kit Carson—although most of his experiences
were in localities where these animals were found in their
greatest abundance. Even in the instances when grizzlies were
killed by government exploring parties, which he later served
as guide, Kit Carson's name does not figure in the glamorous
manner which might be expected. There are a good many instances when he displayed an unusual degree of self-confidence
in taking the calculated risks of shooting it out or being scalped
and pincushioned by Indians; but the grizzly bear exploits are
noticeably absent. He apparently considered the lack of profit
and vainglory, which were the rewards, of insufficient incentive for him to get tangled up with these dangerous beasts.

Most good folks are far too often inclined to measure the
importance of an adventurer or explorer by the amount of
catastrophes he has narrowly escaped in a wild career. This
is a false evaluation. Mishaps, which make the most exciting
stories, are invariably the result of incompetence or poor judgment. The really smart individuals are those who avoid that
sort of thing—although gambling, in one form or another, is a
human weakness common to most men, particularly that virile
breed of men who pioneered the West in the early days. Any
man who went hunting the grizzly with a muzzle-loading
single-shot gun, and a hand knife to back it up, no matter how
strong and skillful he might be, was gambling with high odds
against him—but there were plenty who did.

Chapter XII

THE AMERICAN KING OF BEASTS

By nature's own prescription the grizzly was a killer and flesh eater, in spite of his omnivorous appetite. He knew no natural enemy who seriously challenged his despotic rulership among the wild creatures of this continent.

Theodore Roosevelt was once asked what was the most aggressively dangerous animal in North America, and he is credited with having made the rather surprising reply that in his opinion it was "a mean Texas longhorn steer." The eminent authority was not attempting to be facetious, and he undoubtedly had in mind the danger of an unprovoked attack. It is true that a mean old steer, and sometimes a bad-tempered domestic bull, may be far more apt to make a purely impulsive charge upon a passive visitor than even a grizzly bear would do. Going a bit further, by these same liberal standards of evaluation, the most dangerously destructive creature that ever lived on this fair continent of ours, taken collectively as a species, certainly is the white man of our western pioneer era—the men who slaughtered the great herds of buffalo, virtually exterminated the grizzly bears throughout most of their native haunts, and destroyed the culture of a great, proud race of their fellow men, in such a very brief period of history. The record seems to support strongly the fact that it was the white man who was really the bravest, boldest, and most dangerous of all—the real American *king of beasts!*

The grizzly was not a malignant man-killer. That he was guilty of occasionally staining his chops with the taste of human conquest, resulting from unprovoked aggression, is beyond doubt; but he was not, as a species, a confirmed diabolist. He had never really had to fight to survive, and his character had been developed to disdain rather than defy. Even in those early days when he first came to know the predatory white man, his practices of mayhem were generally inspired by circumstances which would make justifiable homicide a proper verdict if the affair had been between man and man. It was more often than not a case of meeting an enemy in a counter-attack, rather than seeking whomsoever he might tear to pieces and devour. The pioneer trappers and others who avoided putting themselves in belligerent relations with the grizzly seldom got into serious difficulties with him. But there have been a lot of white hunters who have gone looking for trouble with these great bears; and, while the mortality has been pretty high on both sides, the grizzly here met his undeniable superior. In fact, these bears have fared even worse than either the buffalo or the Indian.

While the white man depended on superiority of weapons and numbers, he cannot be denied a magnificent personal courage and fortitude. One of the great examples of this is when a grizzly bear was met in hand-to-claw combat. This writer has killed thirteen of these animals and acted as guide when twelve others were killed; and, while I suffered not a single scratch, I gained a very healthy respect for these powerful creatures, which rapidly increased with each new experience. I got the idea that it would be nothing less than inescapable suicide to attempt to finish off even a small and badly wounded grizzly with a hand knife—but there are a good many instances in which this was actually accomplished.

Killing the black bear with a knife became the paragon of perfection in the sportsman's code of accomplishment among certain overzealous devotees in the Deep South prior to the Civil War. Many a lusty plantation owner and canebrake character had his pack of bear dogs and frequently followed them for the exciting moments of the kill. A considerable number of these resorted to the knife, to give their Nimrodian egos an extra stimulant of satisfaction. Probably the most enviable record in this field is that of General Wade Hampton, a plantation gentleman, who served as a cavalry commander of the Confederacy and was governor of South Carolina during the Reconstruction Period. According to Theodore Roosevelt, he participated in the killing of about 500 black bears, slaying thirty or forty of these with a knife . . . although his entire pack of about forty hunting dogs, probably the best in the country, was not capable of killing one large bear without assistance.[93] Then there was that remarkable backwoodsman and homespun political leader, Davy Crockett, who ended his days by a hero's death in the ruins of the Alamo. His blackbear scalps also ran into the hundreds, possibly exceeding those credited to Wade Hampton, and he too dispatched a good many by the dramatic method of *cold steel, with blade as slick as silk*. There was, of course, a vast margin of difference between a black bear and a grizzly.

Even a young member of Old Ephraim's tribe was capable of making a mighty exciting hand-to-claw fight. This is evidenced by a foursome in which two very experienced trappers and hunters undertook to polish off a pair of young grizzlies in strictly gladiatorial manner—and almost came out second best. The human participants were Jim Baker and Tim Goodale, who accompanied General Marcy as guides on his government expedition across the Rocky Mountains from Fort Bridger to New Mexico, during the winter of 1857–58. Jim Baker had previously served General Frémont in a similar capacity, second only to the great Kit Carson. Jim and Tim had a long experience behind them, having hunted and trapped together, and shared a lot of exciting danger, including the deaths of a good many grizzly bears. On one occasion, while they were trapping the headwaters of Grand River, they came upon two young grizzlies and decided to "pitch in and sculp the varmints with their knives"—just for the hell of it. General Marcy describes the incident as it was told to him by Jim Baker.

"They laid aside their rifles and 'went in,' Baker attacking one and his companion (Tim Goodale) the other. He says the bears immediately raised themselves upon their haunches, and were ready for the encounter. He ran around, endeavoring to get an opportunity to give a blow from behind with his long knife; but the young brute was too quick for him, and turned as he passed around so as always to confront him face to face. He knew if he came within reach of his paws that, although young, the bear could inflict a formidable blow; moreover, he felt great apprehension lest the piteous howls set up would bring the infuriated dam to their rescue, when their own chances of escape would be small. These thoughts made him extremely nervous. And anxious to terminate the combat as soon as possible. He made many desperate lunges at the bear, but the animal invariably warded them off with his fore paws like a pugilist, and protected his body at the expense of several severe cuts upon his legs. This, however, only served to exasperate him, and at length the bear took the offensive, and, with mouth frothing in rage, he bounded toward Baker, who grappled with him and gave him a death-wound under the ribs.

"While all of this was going on his companion had been furiously fighting with the other bear, and by this time had become greatly exhausted, and the odds were turning decidedly against him. He entreated Baker to come to his assistance at once, which he did; but, much to his astonishment, as soon as Baker entered the second contest his companion ran off, leaving him to fight the battle alone. He was, however, again victorious, and soon had the satisfaction of seeing his two antagonists stretched out lifeless before him; but he firmly resolved never again to make war on a bear with a hunting knife, saying he would 'never fight narry 'nother grizzly without a good shootin-iron in his paws.' "[94]

It is only natural that the hand knife should figure in many of the most critical of early encounters with grizzlies. Every hunter and trapper carried a well-sharpened blade on his belt, for it was an absolute necessity in skinning, as well as other routine purposes; and in the days of single-shot rifles it was the principal auxiliary weapon. The pistol did not become a popular adjunct of masculine accoutrement until later. The only trouble is that so few of the hunters who stood their ground and faced the grizzly with a knife lived to tell about it, although it seems highly doubtful if more bears than men survived these mortal combats. "In a very exceptional instance," wrote Theodore Roosevelt, "men of extraordinary prowess with a knife have succeeded in beating off a [grizzly] bear, and even in mortally wounding it, but in most cases of a single-handed struggle, at close quarters with a grisly bent on mischief, means death."[95]

Among the most rugged and audacious of the pioneers were the métis, the French and Scotch half-breeds of Western Canada along the eastern margin of the Rockies. Their pattern of existence was much more rigorous than farther south. The winters were long and bitterly cold; the country was rough for traveling; the game frequently migrated, leaving whole regions in the shadow of starvation; and it was often difficult to obtain trading-post powder and balls for their antiquated guns. These men had to be fine hunters. Noted for their thrift in the use of ammunition, they were adept in the art of *"close-um"* in stalking game, in the belief that one shot at very close range is worth several at a distance. They were also particularly skillful in using a sharp knife.

There were some great bear hunters among these people. Such names as the three Testawits brothers, François, Jean-Baptiste, and Duncan, Wahscoppi, Moskoskolah, Annosi, Bourassa, and a good many others became traditional in the countries of the North Saskatchewan, Athabaska, Slave and the Peace. With old .28-bore and like weapons, operated by the untrustworthiness of flint and percussion caps, they had their own technique in slaying the mighty grizzly. First, they would "make a little talk with him," as they stealthily stalked very close and hoped that he would charge. When the bear came rushing in, with one-way intent to tear the hunter into small pieces, they would calmly throw him their fur cap, or a mitten, or even a moose-skin jacket, which would generally cause the beast to stop for a quick bite or slap at the thing; and in that moment the shot would be sent with deadly accuracy into the top or the ear of the lowered head. Sometimes, however, the bear did not stop before or after the one and only shot, and then they used the knife. Making due allowance for the extra touches which time so frequently adds to traditions, there is little doubt that a good many of these Canadian mixed-bloods finished off their grizzlies with the knife, and they proudly brought home the claw hands, which their admiring women sewed together, palm to palm, and made into fire bags as long-enduring reminders of a well-deserved renown.[96]

One of the classic incidents in which a grizzly was attacked and killed entirely with a *blade of cold steel,* before a considerable gallery of eyewitnesses, has the historic figure of General "Stonewall" Jackson as its hero. This was in the days before that gallant southerner had become renowned as one of the ablest of the Confederate cavalry leaders. At the time he was a young officer in the Mounted Rifle Regiment, later known as the 3rd United States Cavalry, on duty in the Indian warfare in the West. Theodore Roosevelt, another famous cavalryman to whom the general was known as "Red," tells the story:

"It was some years before the Civil War, and the regiment was on duty in the Southwest, then the debatable land of Comanche and Apache. While on a scout after hostile Indians, the troops in their march roused a large grisly which sped across the plain in front of them. . . . Orders had been issued against firing at game, because of the nearness of the Indians.

Young Jackson was a man of great strength, a keen swordsman, who always kept the finest edge on his blade, and he was on a swift and mettled Kentucky horse, which luckily had but one eye. Riding at full speed he soon overtook the quarry. As the horse's hoofs sounded nearer, the grim bear ceased its flight, and wheeling round stood at bay, raising itself on its hind legs and threatening its pursuer with bared fangs and spread claws. Carefully riding his horse so that its blind side should be toward the monster, the cavalryman swept by at a run, handling his steed with such daring skill that he just cleared the blow of the dreaded forepaw, while with one mighty sabre stroke he cleft the bear's skull, slaying the grinning beast as it stood upright."[97]

It is hardly necessary to emphasize the courage required to meet the charge of a full-grown grizzly in a hand-to-claw combat with a hunting knife and the unusual fortitude which some of these men displayed under these circumstances. Two other incidents, which involved more or less well-known Americans, will serve as examples of such encounters. Both took place in Southern California, and they are from the reminiscences of Major Horace Bell.[98] The first involved Colonel William Butts, who had previously served as an officer in the U.S. Army and later was senior editor of the Los Angeles newspaper *Southern Californian*. He had a reputation for courting danger whenever adventure came within his reach. Such an opportunity was presented by the reports of an immense grizzly that was making repeated and devastating raids upon the domestic stock of ranchers in San Luis Obispo County. It was claimed that this renegade bear had carried away a full-grown cow. The colonel got together a party and they went up to one of the ranches for the purpose of ending the career of this fearsome beast. Here is Major Bell's account of what happened:

After some searching, "the grizzly was found on the edge of the plain near a chaparral, and was immediately attacked by the hunters, who lodged several balls in its body, with which it escaped. The party commensed to beat the bush to get the bear out, and against the remonstrances of all, Butts followed the bear's trail into the thicket. The trail soon entered the dry, gravelly bed of an arrayo and was easily followed. Butts had tracked the bear for about half a mile when he lost the trail. He stopped to deliberate, and was standing only a few feet from where the bear had lain down in the thicket. With a growl it sprang out upon him so suddenly that he had no chance of using his Jaeger, but as he went down under the ponderous weight of the bear he managed to get his hunting knife out of its scabbard, and then the mortal strife commensed. Later Butts declared that he never lost his presence of mind, but endeavored to stab the bear in its vital parts, and time after time he thrust the eight-inch blade to the hilt in the bear's body, as it stood over him biting and tearing him with its claws. Butts said 'the last sensation I had was the brute dragging itself over me, and its entrals trailing across my face.'

"A half hour later the two combatants were found—the bear dead, Butts torn into pieces and also apparently dead. The bones of his face were so crushed that he was disfigured; the bones of his left arm and right leg were fractured in several places; some of his ribs were crushed in, and his body and legs were very badly cut into strips. But he was still alive.

"It turned out that the bear had been severely wounded by the shots fired into it, but not mortally; that Butts' knife had twice penetrated the lungs and once entered the heart, and that an incision was made in the stomach nearly a foot long.

"A litter was hastily constructed and poor Butts was carefully carried to the ranch, a surgeon sent for, and then some of the party with some Indians and a Mexican cart and oxen went for the bear, which, after an immense amount of difficulty, transported it to the ranch." (Pp. 253–54.)

Major Bell gives the weight of this bear as "2100 pounds avoirdupois—almost incredible to believe." He does not say whether this was estimated or actual weight. It was probably the former. There is something about a grizzly that makes its size appear to increase in proportion to the spectacular aspects of the encounter, although this one certainly must have been a very large bear. The fact that Colonel Butts recovered sufficiently to be editor of an important newspaper is sufficient testimony to his personal fortitude.

The other incident took place in one of the canyons near Santa Monica, presumably the Malibu, which was also known as the Malaga. The central figure in this even more dramatic encounter was Andy Sublette, one of the brothers of that famous family of pioneers who made history in the early days of the fur trade on the Upper Missouri, the Platte, and the Rocky Mountains. The Sublettes were instrumental in founding Fort Laramie, from which stronghold they ran their lucrative fur-trading empire and dictated war or peace as their fancy or profits required. After selling their interests to the American Fur Company, Andy settled in Los Angeles—where he was highly regarded as "a natural born gentleman, with manners as refined, gentle and polished as though he had never been beyond the confines of the most cultivated society."[99] But under the skin he had an adventurous spirit and a deep fascination for hunting grizzlies. Second only, if not equal, to this was an intense affection for his favorite hunting companion, a dog by the name of *"Old Buck."* They both share the spotlight in their final hunt together, and here is Major Bell's account of it:

"Andy Sublette . . . had only recovered from severe injuries received in an encounter with a bear at Elizabeth Lake, when in company with Jim Thompson he went on another bear hunt, that was to be his last. Somehow Andy became separated from the party, and found a grizzly which he shot; but before he could reload, the fierce brute was upon him. Poor Andy! it was his last fight, and gallantly did he maintain his renoun. His faithful dog, *Old Buck*, was with him, and the two fought, Andy with his knife and *Old Buck* with the weapons furnished by Nature; and together they gained the victory over the mountain king. When Thompson found them the bear lay dead, Andy was insensible and *Old Buck*, lacerated in a shocking manner, was licking the blood from his master's face. Tenderly the two, man and dog, were brought to the city, and comfortably lodged and cared for in the Padilla Building, later the U.S. Hotel corner. For many days the struggle between life and death was fierce. Sometimes Andy would get the better of the Grim Destroyer, only to be again driven to the wall. *Old Buck* was as tenderly cared for as was his gallant master. Jim Thompson, with his great good heart, watched night and day by the bedside of the two, while others stood ready to assist. *Old Buck* lay on a nice pallet at the side of his master's bed. When Andy in his delirium would imagine himself still fighting the bear, he would cry out *'seize him, Buck!'*, *'at him, old fellow!'*, *'we'll get 'im yet!'*, and other like expressions; at which *Old Buck* would raise his forepaw onto the side of the bed and give a soft and bewildered growl.

"Finally death came out first best, and poor Andy Sublette was one of the first to be interred in the Fort Hill Cemetery. *Old Buck*, still in a very bad way himself, rode in the wagon that took Andy to his last resting place—he and Jim Thompson being chief mourners. About every *gringo* in town turned out at Andy's funeral . . . and it is safe to aver that there was not a person who left that graveyard with tearless eyes, on account not just of the loss of a gallant man, a friend and a Christian neighbor, but for the doleful distress of poor *Old Buck*, who utterly refused to be comforted or to be removed from beside his dead master's grave. So there he was left to exhaust his grief, which we all thought he would do in a little while. Twice, and sometimes three times a day, Jim Thompson and other kind-hearted friends would take *Buck* food and drink, and tried in vain to induce him to leave the grave. The faithful old dog refused to be comforted, refused to eat or drink; and on the third day he died. He was buried at the feet of his friend and master."[100]

The records are quite liberally splattered with the red-hued accounts of other American pioneers in the West who stood and fought it out with grizzlies. It was more often than not at a very high price. "One of the most complete wrecks of humanity I ever saw was a man whom a grizzly, in the last moments of his life, had gotten into his embrace," wrote Colonel Richard I. Dodge; and after relating the incident he had this to say about the survivor: "When I saw him he was apparently in good health, but could not use or even move his right arm or either leg. He gave me the particulars of his fight and described his wounds with great animation and gusto, smoking his pipe the while."[101] This is typical of these men of the days of the Old West; and as we now look back, across the rich tranquillity of cultivated states, crossed in every direction by busy highways and dotted with prosperous towns and cities, some may see only foolhardy bits of wild adventure in their stories. Certainly the worst of Indian warfare did not leave such reminders of deeds of daring and fortitude. And, whether these grizzly-bear hunters were just a bit foolhardy or remarkably brave, there is probably no stronger symbol of the American spirit than these men who tamed our West and turned the tide of history from wilderness to prosperous and powerful commonwealth. Fortunately that spirit has not entirely died. It is something healthy for us to look back upon—something that will stand us in good stead in the troubled world in which we live today.

Chapter XIII

WILD SPORT IN OLD CALIFORNIA

THE Spanish colonial occupation of California developed a culture which had many aspects of the motherland and some peculiarly its own. It was even quite different from that in Mexico, from where it had been transplanted; and this had been growing in its own way for a considerable time before the sunny lands beyond the Rockies were taken into the spreading empire of the United States. The Californians had inherited the sanguineous interests traditional to their race—in which such things as bullfights and cockfights were like strong wine to their fiery spirits. But these Californians added a new dissipation for their bravado. This was the bear-and-bull fights, which became popular entertainment on religious fete days and other auspicious occasions. But they were considerably more than just that, for the method by which the bears were captured created one of the most exciting sports their race had ever enjoyed.

Grizzlies were used in the bear-and-bull fights. The bigger and fiercer they were the better. Grizzlies were plentiful in California; and it was found that lassoing these dangerous beasts from horseback, and all the incidental maneuvers of using only ropes and bare hands to bring them in alive, provided an ultimate in thrills and skills. Horsemanship and use of the lasso were accomplishments of great pride to the gentlemen *vaqueros* of old California, and roping grizzly bears for the fiesta fights became their sport of sports. This practice persisted for some years after California became a full-fledged state of the Union on September 9, 1850. A bear-and-bull fight was held at the mission in the vicinity of Los Angeles as late as 1857, the grizzlies being roped by *vaqueros* in San Fernando (Los Angeles County).[102] Another recorded event of the same kind was held there in 1854,[103] and there were a number of others held in San Diego, Monterey, San Francisco, and elsewhere, some at even later dates. One of the last of these was held at San Fernando Mission in the 1860s.

The *reatas* used for roping grizzlies had to be strong ones and were made with special care. They were generally made of oxhide, which was first dried in the sun and then soaked in water until the skin began to have a bad odor. Strips of about half an inch in width were then cut, and usually four of these were tightly braided together to make the finished product.

Roping grizzlies was often practiced by the ordinary *vaqueros*, although it was generally left to the grandees of the community when an important *fiesta* was involved. The party usually consisted of four men, who were called *lazadores*. With due ceremony they would assemble on their finest horses, both rider and mount decorated with rich vestments and trappings of embroidery and silver. Then they would dash away with all the verve and pomp of a matador riding to the *plaza de toros*. It was seldom necessary to go very far. "In the early 1850's grizzly bears were more plentiful in Southern California than pigs," wrote Major Bell in his *Reminiscences;* "they were, in fact, so numerous in certain localities, as Malibu, La Laguna de Chico, Lopez and other places, as to make the rearing of cattle impossible." (P. 250.)

When a grizzly was located by the venturesome sportsmen, their first objective would be to get him out in the open where the *reatas* could be used to advantage. This was sometimes difficult to accomplish, for the bear's natural impulse was to get into the thickest chaparral or roughest rocky retreat he could reach. The *lazadores* were fine horsemen and their mounts were equally smart at this sort of thing; but in thick or rough cover the bear could move with far greater speed, and sometimes a sudden charge would prove disastrous to both rider and horse. This, however, was only part of the game, and eventually this grizzly or another was driven out into sufficiently open ground to have a lasso sent flying through the air. Sometimes the loop caught the beast around the neck, although a more desirable catch was by one of the forepaws. This was a critical moment and required very expert horsemanship. Finding himself thus caught, the grizzly would invariably launch into an instantaneous and vicious counterattack, roaring with all his might. It also required a remarkable display of the training and power of the rider over his mount, for there is nothing on earth which horses fear more than a bear. One slight whiff and the average horse lunges into a state of panic almost beyond control. In my own experience in riding through bear country I have repeatedly been almost thrown and came to the conclusion that a horse is the best bear dog on earth. But the fine mounts of these Spanish-Californians were so completely under the control of the rider that they seldom disobeyed the slightest pressure of the rein or a knee pressed against their side. Blowing trumpet blasts from their nostrils and with eyes popping in their sockets, the horses would lurch to the commands, the next objective being to jerk down the bear before it could charge in and grab the horse and rider. Quick action was also required on the part of the other *lazadores*, for a grizzly with only one lasso cinched upon him was an extremely dangerous proposition. Sometimes with two ropes attached it was almost impossible to hold a full-grown bear. Three or four hardly made it a safe pastime.

Grizzlies are noted for doing the unexpected. There are accounts in which, when a bear was caught about the neck by only one rope, he just sat on his haunches and began hauling in the line with his paws and teeth, like a fisherman pulling in a hand line. Unless another lasso was quickly brought to bear upon the animal from the opposite direction, the lone rider might have to drop his rope and escape. Occasionally grizzlies were roped that weighed close to two thousand pounds and possibly even more. This was no child's play or sport for an amateur.

As the other horsemen closed in, their objective was to get lassos attached to at least one front leg and a hind one. In this manner it was possible for the combined strength of the horses to stretch out the beast. Even under the best of circumstances a big grizzly required rather desperate efforts to hold in check; and the noise he made, added to that of horses and riders, was something to make the most staid heart pound like an Indian war drum. The only advantage of a rope around the animal's neck was to choke off his breath—a slow process which only aggravated him all the more.

With all four *reatas* securely attached, the *lazadores* would yell in triumph, as the horses pulled desperately in different directions and the powerful beast writhed and fought the tough ropes with teeth and claws in a noisy, fearful manner. The earth was torn up and dust rose in clouds about them. It was never over quickly, nor was it a one-sided contest. The tide might turn at any moment. Sometimes a big bear got away, even when four lassos were secured to him, and occasionally a horse or *lazador* was killed.

Then came the really ticklish part. When the quarry was moderately subdued, they would endeavor to get him stretched out on his back. With his *reata* securely fastened to the saddle, and his horse braced solidly against it, one of the best of the men would slip to the ground and move in with an extra *reata* in his hand or teeth. Cautiously approaching the grizzly, he would get a noose around the animal's two forepaws. This accomplished, he would get the loose end around the bear's neck and then draw it tightly. It took considerable courage, skill, and strength, for the man's approach invariably set off new violence on the part of the bear. This done, however, and another *lazador* would dismount to assist in the final hog-tying. When all four legs were securely lashed down, they would undertake to bind his jaws together. Sometimes this was undertaken first, rather than left to the last. When all was secure, however, the rope around his neck was removed, so the animal could breathe freely—and the *lazadores* congratulated each other for a day of fine sport.

The well-tied grizzly was then transported into the city or wherever the fight was to be held. Less venturesome attendants followed the *lazadores* with a pair of bullocks to take care of this, while the gentlemen sportsmen rode gaily back to some appropriate place to toast each other's bravery. The whole hide of a big steer, laid over a drag of tree branches, provided a simple means of transportation. The bear was usually kept securely tied until the time of the fight, although the animals were generally not captured more than a day or two in advance—so they would be strong and vigorous for the spectacle.

It was not always for the bear-and-bull fights on fiesta days that the *lazadores* rode out to rope grizzlies in old California. Nor did it always require the birthday of a saint or some like occasion for a celebration at the mission. The fights were frequently staged for their sheer unholy excitement or for profits other than to the church. After the coming of the Americans these fights were occasionally staged entirely for the dollars in profit which their ballyhoo could put in the pockets of the promoters. Even all these combined were hardly sufficient to provide the thrill-loving Spanish gentlemen of the land with all the practice they required, and they often indulged in this dangerous sport just for the sheer excitement of it. Reports of a particularly destructive bear that was making persistent raids on any rancher's stock were always a sufficient incentive to send them forth on a roping mission. The only difference in the whole procedure was that, when the grizzly was completely tied claw-and-jaw, the helpless beast was dispatched on the spot with the thrust of a knife or a lance.

Roping a grizzly, whether for a holy fiesta or the unholy promotion of profit, required a highly specialized skill, as well as a lust for thrills. In later years the feat was occasionally accomplished by cowboys on the Western Plains, although they rarely went so far as to hog-tie the critters by hand as the *lazadores* did. There were rare occasions, in California, when newly arrived Americans made the mistake of attempting the feat. General Marcy relates one such incident, the result of which was fortunately more comedy than tragedy.[104]

The would-be gringo *lazador* was a naval officer with an unusual flare for adventurous excitement. He probably supported the idea that an American could do anything that a Spanish-Californian could do—which included roping a grizzly in particular. The gentleman from back East, by long and constant practice, became quite proficient in the use of the lasso, and he was apparently a good rider. So confident did he become that he employed a guide and set out into the mountains of Southern California with the firm resolve of roping "a few grizzlies before night."

There was no difficulty in finding a prospective trophy. It proved to be a very large bear "whose terrific aspect amazed him not a little." He had come out with a firm determination, however, in strong opposition to the advice of both friends and the guide; and, taking lasso in hand, he sent his fast horse dashing in pursuit. Instead of retreating, as expected, the mighty beast deliberately reared up on his bulky haunches, facing his bold adversary. The young naval officer whirled his rope in an expert manner and sent it artistically through the air to fall about the big bear's neck; then the horse was turned and the rope snapped taut. Instead of being able to choke the beast and drag him off in triumph, however, the horse was brought to an abrupt stop, and the bear just sat there, scrutinizing the rope with mingled anger and disdain. As the tightened noose began to choke the bear, he gave it several violent slaps with first one paw and then the other. Finding this did not relieve him of the annoyance, and glaring at the audacious rider and his mount, the grizzly began pulling in the rope, hand over hand, or rather paw over paw. The officer redoubled the application of whip and spurs, but it was all of no avail. In spite of all the frantic efforts of the horse they began to lose ground. The bear was now making a frightful noise as its jaws snapped repeatedly upon the lasso, and the gringo *lazador* found himself being dragged inch by inch toward the frightful monster. He yelled for the guide to come to his assistance. The latter responded promptly. He rode up abruptly and with one quick slash of his knife cut the lasso. Then he rode away—probably cursing the gringo under his breath. The young naval officer, however, joined him without condemnation or protest, and, when asked if he wouldn't like to find a smaller bear to start on, the ambitious sportsman announced that "he believed he would rope no more grizzlies that day." It is not stated whether he ever tried again or if he realized how really lucky he had been.

Bear-and-bull fights were occasionally staged in the 1850s around some of the more prosperous of the gold camps, where the heterogeneous rabble of miners had money to spend, there wasn't very much in the way of entertainment, and popular interests ran strongly toward the bawdy and sensational. Here the fights took on many of the aspects of pugilistic promotions of the bare-knuckle days. One of the most vivid eyewitness descriptions of one of these contests is by an Englishman, J. D. Borthwick, the account of whose three years of wandering through California from 1851 to 1853 was published in London in 1857.[105]

This fight was staged in the flourishing mining camp of Moquelumne Hill, not very far from the town of Placerville in Eldorado County. The population was described as "a mixture of equal proportions of French, Mexicans, and Americans, with a few stray Chinamen, Chileans, and suchlike"; and the town itself, "with the exception of two or three wooden stores and gambling saloons, was all of canvas. Many of the houses were merely skeletons clothed in dirty rags of canvas, and it was not difficult to tell what part of the population they belonged to, even had there not been crowds of lazy Mexicans vegetating about the doors. The Indians, who were pretty numerous about here, seemed to be a slightly superior race to those farther north . . . they apparently had more money, and consequently must have had more energy to dig it. They were also great gamblers . . . at which the Mexicans fleeced them of all their cash . . . their presence not compatible with that of a civilized community. . . ."

At the time of Mr. Borthwick's visit, in April of 1853, the town and all the approaching roads and trails for some distance around were liberally posted with placards announcing the big fight. These were stuck to trees and rocks and wherever they might be seen to attract attention. They loudly smacked of the typical ballyhoo so familiar to American promotions intended to excite the interest of paying customers. Here is how they read:

WAR! WAR!! WAR!!!

the celebrated Bull-killing Bear,

GENERAL SCOTT,

will fight a Bull on Sunday the 15th inst., at 2 P.M., at Moquelumne Hill

The Bear will be chained with a twenty-foot chain in the middle of the arena. The Bull will be perfectly wild, young, of the Spanish breed, and the best that can be found in the country. The Bull's horns will be of their natural length, and *not sawed off to prevent accidents.* The Bull will be quite free in the arena, and not hampered in any way whatever.

The proprietors who were promoting the fight then went on to state that they had nothing to do with the humbugging which had characterized the last such fight, and gave the most confident assurances that their public would on this extraordinary occasion witness the most exhilarating and splendid exhibition of incited mayhem ever seen in the country. That the ballyhoo was not entirely without merit can best be appreciated by Mr. Borthwick's own description of what he witnessed as one of those who attended:

"On Sunday the 15th, I found myself walking up toward the arena, among the crowd of miners and others of all nations, to witness the performance of the redoubted General Scott.

"The amphitheatre was a roughly but strongly built wooden structure, uncovered of course; and the outer enclosure, which was of boards about ten feet high, was a hundred feet in diameter, and enclosed by a very strong five-barred fence. From the top of this rose tiers of seats, occupying the space between the arena and the outside enclosure.

"As the appointed hour drew near, the company continued to arrive till the whole place was crowded; while, to beguile the time till the business of the day should commence, two fiddlers—a white man and a gentleman of colour—performed a variety of appropriate airs.

"The scene was gay and brilliant, and was one which would have made a crowded opera-house appear gloomy and dull by comparison. The shelving bank of human beings which encircled the place was like a mass of bright flowers. The most conspicuous objects were the shirts of the miners, red, white, and blue being the fashionable colours, among which appeared bronzed and bearded faces under hats of every hue; revolvers and silver-handled bowie-knives glanced in the bright sunshine; and among the crowd were numbers of gay Mexican blankets, and red and blue French bonnets; while here and there the fair sex was represented by a few Mexican women in snowy-white dresses, puffing their cigaritos in delightful anticipation of the exciting scene which was to be enacted. Over the heads of the highest circle of spectators was seen mountain beyond mountain fading away in the distance; and on the green turf

Famous Indian chiefs wore a necklace of grizzly claws with even greater pride than the scalps of their human enemies. From McKenney and Hall, *History of the Indian Tribes of North America* (Philadelphia: E. C. Biddle, 1836).

Theodore Roosevelt's first grizzly. The hunter, rancher, Rough Rider, and future president was one of the foremost authorities on the bears of North America. From Roosevelt, *Hunting Trips of a Ranchman* (New York: G.P. Putnam's Sons, 1885).

Bear at elk carcass. From *Hunting Trips of a Ranchman.*

The hide of one of the largest grizzlies ever killed, this sixteen-hundred-pound Alaskan brown bear was shot by the author on the Alaska Peninsula in 1916. The hide measured eleven feet four inches in length and ten feet six inches spread from claw to claw. Photo by E. B. B. Warren, courtesy Marjorie Goppert.

Hind and forefoot of a rather small grizzly from southwestern Yukon Territory. Photo by E. B. B. Warren, courtesy of Marjorie Goppert.

An unidentified woman poses with a fallen grizzly. Author photo, courtesy of Marjorie Goppert.

Wahb, Ernest Thompson Seton's fabled Yellowstone grizzly. From Seton, *The Biography of a Grizzly* (New York: The Century Company, 1899).

The grizzly survives today on several ecological "islands" in the lower forty-eight states, most notably the Greater Yellowstone Ecosystem, where this bear was recently photographed. *National Park Service photo.*

of the arena lay the great center of attraction, the hero of the day, General Scott.

"He was, however, not yet exposed to public gaze, but was confined in his cage, a heavy wooden box lined with iron, with open iron bars on one side, which for the present was boarded over. From the centre of the arena a chain led into the cage, and at the end of it no doubt the bear was to be found. Beneath the scaffolding on which sat the spectators were two pens, each containing a very handsome bull, showing evident signs of indignation at his confinement. Here also was the bar, without which no place of public amusement would be complete.

"There was much excitement among the crowd at the result of the battle, as the bear had already killed several bulls; but an idea prevailed that in former fights the bulls had not had fair play, being tied by a rope to the bear, and having the tips of their horns sawed off. But on this occasion the bull was to have every advantage . . . and he certainly had the good wishes of the spectators, though the bear was considered such a successful and experienced bull-fighter that the betting was all in his favor. . . .

"At last, after a final tattoo had been beaten on a gong to make the stragglers hurry up the hill, preparations were made for beginning the fight.

"The bear made his appearance before the public in a very bearish manner. His cage . . . was dragged out of the ring, when, as his chain only allowed him to come within a foot or two of the fence, the General was rolled upon the ground in a heap. . . . He floundered half-way round the ring at the length of his chain, and commenced to tear up the earth with his fore-paws. He was a grizzly bear of pretty large size, weighing about twelve-hundred pounds.

"The next thing to be done was to introduce the bull. The bars between his pen and the arena were removed. . . . But he did not seem to like the prospect, and was not disposed to move till pretty sharply poked from behind, when, making a furious dash at the red flag which was being waved in front of the gate, he found himself in the ring face to face with General Scott.

"The General, in the meantime, had scraped a hole for himself two or three inches deep, in which he was lying down. This, I was told by those who had seen his performance before, was his usual fighting attitude.

"The bull was a very beautiful animal, of dark purple colour marked with white. His horns were regular and sharp, and his coat was as smooth and glossy as a racer's. He stood for a moment taking a survey of the bear, the ring, and the crowds of people; but not liking the appearance of things in general, he wheeled round, and made a splendid dash at the bars, which had already been put up between him and his pen, smashing through them with as much ease as the man in the circus leaps through a hoop of brown paper. . . . Again persuaded to enter the arena . . . he had made up his mind to fight; and after looking steadily at the bear for a few minutes as if taking aim at him, he put down his head and charged furiously across the arena. The bear received him crouching down, and though one could hear the bump of the bull's head and horns upon his ribs, he was quick enough to seize the bull by the nose before he could retreat. This spirited commencement of the battle was hailed with uproarious applause. . . .

"In the mean time, the bear, lying on his back, held the bull's nose firmly between his teeth, and embraced him round the neck with his fore-paws, while the bull made the most of his opportunities in stamping on the bear with his hind-feet. At last the General became exasperated at such treatment, and shook the bull savagely by the nose, when a promiscuous scuffle ensued, which resulted in the bear throwing his antagonist to the ground with his fore-paws.

"For this feat the bear was cheered immensely, and it was thought he would make short work of him; but apparently wild beasts do not tear each other to pieces so easily as is generally supposed . . . and the bull soon regained his feet, and, disengaging himself, retired to the other side of the ring, while the bear again crouched down in his hole.

"After standing a few minutes, steadily eyeing the General, the bull made another rush at him. Again poor bruin's ribs resounded, but again he took the bull's nose into chancery. The bull, however, quickly disengaged himself, and was making off, when the General, not wishing to part with him so soon, seized his hind-foot between his teeth, and, holding on by his paws as well, was thus dragged round the ring before he quitted his hold.

"This round terminated with shouts of delight from the excited spectators, and it was thought the bull might have a chance after all. He had been severely punished, however; his nose and lips were a mass of bloody shreds, and he lay down to recover himself. But he was not allowed to rest very long, being poked up with sticks by men outside, which made him very savage. He made several feints to charge them through the bars. . . . He was eventually worked up to such a state of fury as to make another charge at the bear. The result was much the same as before, only that when the bull managed to get up after being thrown, the bear still had hold of the skin of his neck.

"In the next round both parties fought more savagely than ever, and the advantage was rather in favor of the bear: the bull seemed to be quite used up, and to have lost all chance of victory.

"The conductor of the performances then mounted the barrier, and, addressing the crowd, asked them if the bull had not had fair play, which was unanimously allowed. He then stated that for two hundred dollars he would let in the other bull, and the three should fight it out till one or all were killed.

"This proposal was received with loud cheers, and two or three men going round with hats soon collected the required amount. The people were intensely excited and delighted with the sport. A man sitting next me, who was a connoisseur in bear-fights, and passionately fond of the amusement, informed me that this was 'the finest fight ever fit in the country'.

"The second bull was equally handsome as the first, and in as good condition. On entering the arena, he seemed to understand the state of affairs at once. Glancing from the bear to the other bull standing at the opposite side of the arena, with drooping head and bloody nose, he seemed to divine at once that the bear was their common enemy, and rushed at him full tilt. The bear, as usual, pinned him by the nose; but this bull did not take such treatment so quietly as the other: struggling violently, he soon freed himself, and, wheeling round he caught the bear on the hind-quarters and knocked him over; while the other bull, who had been quietly watching the proceedings, thought this a good opportunity to pitch in also, and rushing up, he gave the bear a dig in the ribs on the other side before he had time to recover himself. . . .

"After another round or two with the fresh bull, it was evident he was no match for the bear, and it was agreed to conclude the performance. The bulls were then shot to put them out of pain, and the company dispersed, all apparently satisfied that it had been a very splendid fight."

As something of a postscript to the account, it is stated that the great bullfighting grizzly General Scott was killed in the next battle he fought, a few weeks afterward.

In those earlier days of the Spanish era, before the bear-and-bull fights became the promotions of money-making Americans, the animals were generally tied together by a rope attached to a front leg of each. In most cases it was the bull that charged first, frequently running its horns deeply into the body of its adversary, and occasionally this first violent thrust would result in the death of the bear, although the latter was the final victor in most of the contests. If a grizzly was equal to the occasion, fresh bulls would be put in as long as he could stand up and fight them; and there are records of bears that tore to pieces as many as five or six bulls in an afternoon's entertainment. There are also instances on record in which spectators became so excited during the fights that they fell into the arena and were likewise torn into a horrible mass by an enraged grizzly.

The roping of these dangerous ursines and bear-and-bull fights were typical of California in the Spanish colonial era. There are a number of records, however, which give substantial proof that the cowboys who herded cattle on the open range along the mountainous margin of the Plains occasionally undertook to capture a grizzly with their lariats. These men were certainly as capable with a saddle under their seat and a rope in their hand, and they were in no manner lacking in reckless bravado, but they did not have that same ancestral instinct of a bullfighter, and there is no extensive proof that they ever took the sport to heart with affection or finesse.

A few attempts at bear-and-bull fights were undertaken east of the Rockies, although they fell far short of becoming a popular pastime. One such spectacle was promoted at Helena, Montana, in the fall of 1868, as indicated in the following account which appeared in the *Helena Weekly Herald* for the date of Thursday, October 8, of that year:

"An old hunter and trapper, now operating on the Missouri river, in the vicinity of Sun river, has succeeded in caging a grizzly of enormous size. The monster devours elk and antelope most voraciously, and accepts the situation as coolly as could be expected. A citizen, well known to pugilistic fame, has made arrangements to have him brought to Helena for an encounter with a wild bull. Heavy timbers are now being procured for the construction of a strong twenty-foot square pen, and seats will be provided for the accommodation of an audience of fifteen hundred. This promises to be the most exciting affair of the kind that ever took place in Montana."[106]

The foregoing was supplied to this writer by Miss Virginia Walton, of the Library, Historical Society of Montana, where a diligent but unsuccessful search was made to find some further information about the actual fight. Perhaps the plan did not seem so feasible, once it was being pursued!

Chapter XIV

FABULOUS MR. "GRIZZLY" ADAMS

In the fall of 1856 a tall, rawboned man with a long gray beard and garbed in well-worn buckskins was occasionally seen passing through the streets of San Francisco, accompanied by one or more large grizzly bears. They went along with this strange character like well-mannered dogs, and all oblivious to the staring populace who hurriedly got a safe distance away. The folks around San Francisco in those days knew what a grizzly bear was, and they were accustomed to picturesque personalities from the mountains and the plains. The town had mothered a lot of frontier flotsam and jetsam, buckskin princes and pirates of the western fur trade, motley emigrants of the wagon trains and ships from round the Horn, wild spenders from the gold mines, tarnished tin horns, sharpsters and purveyors of whisky and women, and a lot more who had been attracted like flies to the boom town on the sunny California coast. But here was something so different that it amazed even them.

The man's name was James Capen Adams and he lived with his grizzly bears and a lot of other wild animals in a basement on Clay Street. He called his place "The Mountaineer Museum." He had come in from the mountains only because of ill-health, largely the result of injuries suffered in killing other grizzlies and other wild animals with a knife; and the great shaggy beasts which followed him through the streets and shared his living quarters had been his companions and helpers in an amazing series of adventures.

A newspaperman, Theodore H. Hittell, who was on the staff of the *Daily Evening Bulletin*, became deeply interested in the old bear hunter and between July 1857 and December 1859 got from him the story of his unique experiences. The book was first published in San Francisco in 1860, under the title *The Adventures of James Capen Adams, Mountaineer and Bear Hunter*, by Theodore H. Hittell.[107] The illustrations were drawn by Charles Nahl, the accomplished California artist, who evidently made the portrayals of Adams and his grizzlies from life. Incidentally, the official Bear Flag of the State of California is derived from the painting of a grizzly by this same artist,[108] which evidently represents one of Adams's bears; and Hittell's story of the old bear hunter's career has become recognized by many as one of the great classics of its kind.

Born in Medway, Massachusetts, October 20, 1807, Adams was raised in the shoemaker trade. Being of an adventurous nature, the lad discarded his apprentice pegging awl and hired himself to a company of showmen as a collector of wild animals. Shortly afterward he became an apprentice trainer of dangerous beasts for exhibition purposes. In the latter capacity he was seriously injured while working in a cage with a large Bengal tiger. For a long period it was doubtful if he would ever completely recover, but, able to use his hands, he returned to the shoemaker trade. After another fifteen years, however, he joined the gold stampede to California, making the journey across the Great Plains with one of the covered-wagon caravans.

No book such as the present one could be complete without including something of this fabulous hunter. The original story is particularly rich in both adventure and wilderness lore of the mountains of the Far West, in the days when vast areas were practically unknown except to Indians and a few trappers. There is only room here, however, for the high spots of this unusual man's remarkable experiences with grizzly bears.

James Capen Adams arrived in California in the fall of 1849. He was then forty-two years old. After three years of shifting from one misfortune to another he became "disgusted with the world and . . . took the road toward the wildest and most unfrequented parts of the Sierra Nevada, resolved to make the wilderness my home, and wild beasts my companions." He started out alone, in an old wagon drawn by two oxen; and his worldly possessions were little more than a Kentucky rifle that used 30 balls to the pound, a Tennessee rifle that used 60, a revolving pistol, and several bowie knives. But within him was a "buoyant and hopeful spirit . . . to become part of the vast landscape, a kind of demigod in the glorious and magnificent creation . . . as happy as a king." Thus Adams established himself "on a northern branch of the Merced River, twenty or thirty miles northeast of the famous *Yo-Semite*, and a hundred and sixty miles east of San Francisco . . . in the favorite haunts of the grizzly bear, the monarch of American beasts."

In the spring of 1853 Adams turned to capturing wild animals in a peculiar but serious manner. To work in wilder country he made an overland trip northward through California, across Oregon, and into the country north of the big bend of the Columbia River in Washington. He was accompanied by two faithful Sierra Indians, Tuolumne and Stanislaus, and a young Texan named Sykesey. In a beautiful valley of the mountains, far from civilization, they built large wooden pens, like small log cabins, and began capturing panthers, wolves, and bears, which were taken to their camp alive, to be tied up to the nearby trees.

The project—a strange one for that era—was just getting well under way when Adams located the den of a big old grizzly with two yearling cubs and determined "to slay this dam, and make myself master of her offspring. . . ." He went

"GRIZZLY" ADAMS AND BEN FRANKLIN

The fabulous frontiersman with one of the "tame" grizzlies that traveled with him through the western wilderness.

after them alone. The old one was dispatched without undue difficulty. But when he undertook to capture the yearlings with a lasso, they turned upon him like inspired tyrants and he "was compelled, for my personal safety, to betake myself to a tree, and was glad to find one to climb." They tried to climb up after him, and it was necessary to pound their paws to keep them down. When they finally returned to their dead mother, Adams was able to escape.

After several days of strenuous effort, and the use of horses hired from a neighboring Indian chief, the young grizzlies were eventually roped and brought into camp. His companions got one, a male, and Adams captured the other one, a female. "She is the prettiest little animal in all the country," he avowed, and "such was the manner in which my bear, Lady Washington, one of the companions of my future-hunting life, was captured. From that time until this [when the account of his experiences was taken down by Hittell], she has always been with me; and often shared my dangers and privations, borne my burdens, and partaken of my meals." Thus begins one of the strangest stories in western lore.

At the start it took considerable courage, a stout cudgel, patience, and some personal injuries for Adams to convince young Lady Washington what was expected of her. As Adams related: "It would, indeed, be difficult to describe her violence, the snarls she uttered, and the frothing anger she exhibited . . . until she acknowledged herself well corrected . . . and became a most faithful and affectionate servant." He trained her to carry a pack on her back. "I talked to her, tried to make her understand what was wanted, and reproved her with a stick." Then he began taking her along when he went out to build traps and to hunt other bears, and "she followed like a dog, during the whole day remaining at my side, partaking of my lunch at noon."

Their first encounter with another grizzly, at close quarters, provided a tense situation. While stalking quietly through a dense thicket to get close enough to some deer to shoot one with his pistol, the only weapon he was carrying, "suddenly Lady Washington gave a snort and chattered her teeth. I wheeled around, and directly behind the Lady, in full sight, standing upon his hind legs and wickedly surveying us, stood a savage old grizzly. That he had hostile intentions, all his actions clearly showed; and there I was, almost without arms, and with the Lady as well as myself to take care of. In the emergency, I seized the chain with which the Lady was usually tied, and which was now wrapped around her neck, and unwound it as noiselessly as possible. I was then about to move to a tree, when the enemy dropped upon all fours, came a little nearer, and rose again. . . . I stood still, with my pistol in hand; and thus we eyed each other. But seeing his indecision, I resolved to turn it to my advantage; and suddenly discharging the pistol, rattling the iron chain, and at the same time yelling with all my might, I had the gratification of seeing the enemy turn tail and run. . . . It seemed as if a thousand devils had sprung up all at once and the old bear tore through the bushes as if each particular one was after him. Such was the first instance in which Lady Washington stood side by side with me in the hour of danger and dire alarm; and from that time, I felt for her an affection which I have seldom given any human being."

Almost daily Adams and his companions tended their traps and hunted. Many were the bear, panther, wolves, and other animals they captured; they shot other grizzlies and various game; and many were the exciting experiences they had. On one occasion another white hunter who joined them for a day of sport was caught by a grizzly that "with one tearing grasp, ripped through his breast, and drew out the heart, liver, stomach and intestines. . . ." And five days after burying this member of the party the rest shot four grizzlies that were found together. By this time around the camp was tied a veritable menagerie of wild animals—gray and black wolves; black, brown, and grizzly bears; large and small panthers, as well as smaller and less dangerous animals.

At the end of the summer Adams set out for Portland, about three hundred miles distant through the wilderness, to ship the strange cargo by boat to his brother in Boston. He hired thirty additional horses and six Indians for the overland journey; and not only were the horses heavily loaded with hides and improvised boxes containing live young bear cubs, wolves, and other animals, as well as bags of dried meat to feed the menagerie, but they also led a motley herd of animals that walked, including six large bears, four wolves, four deer, four antelope, two elk, and an Indian dog. Most of the way there was little more than old Indian trails to follow, and at times these were lost.

After numerous vicissitudes in getting the caravan over mountains and across rivers, Portland was reached and the summer's accumulation of beasts was put aboard the sailing bark *Mary Ann*, bound round the Horn for Boston; that is, "all except my favorite, Lady Washington, to whom I had become so attached that I could not think of parting with her." Then Adams, with his two faithful Indians and the Lady, continued on the long overland journey back to his California home on the headwaters of the Tuolumne River in the high Sierras.

But the adventures of James Capen Adams and Lady Washington had only begun. They spent the winter together in his cabin. The Lady now weighed about three hundred pounds. "She accompanied me to the scenes of my labors, stayed by me while I worked, and followed me when I hunted . . . she was faithful and devoted . . . the Lady could truly be pronounced second to none of all the creatures over which the Creator appointed man to be lord and master." When they went hunting too far from home to return at night, she carried their camp equipment on her back; they shared together the evening meal and fire; they slept side by side; and she transported home the game he shot. He sometimes even hitched her to a sledge to drag loads of firewood through the snow.

In the spring of 1854 Adams made a trip into Yosemite Valley, taking along Lady Washington and a greyhound dog. He was accompanied on this hunting expedition by Tuolumne the Indian and a white hunter by the name of Solon. It was on this venture that Adams acquired the grizzly "Ben Franklin," the story of which rivals that of Lady Washington.

Camped at the head of the Merced River, all the party began hunting bears, panthers, wolves, and deer, which were to be found in abundance—although most of the grizzlies were left to Adams. Soon the den of a monster she-bear with newborn cubs was found in a deep canyon densely grown up with chaparral, thorn bushes, pine, and cedar. Adams determined to kill the dam and capture the cubs and set out alone to do so.

For three days and nights he waited, hiding in the thicket in front of the den. He could occasionally hear the young cubs inside, but the old one would not come out. Finally he fired off his rifle; and, this failing, he crept up to the very mouth of the cave and yelled inside. "A moment afterward there was a booming in the den, like the puffing and snorting of an engine in a tunnel, and the enraged animal rushed out, growling and snapping, as if she could belch forth the fire of a volcano. She rose upon her hind legs, and exhibited a monster form. . . . I fired; and dropping the rifle, drew my pistol in one hand and knife in the other . . . The bear staggered and fell backward, and began pawing and biting the ground . . . and so anxious was I to complete the task, that I commenced leaping over the bushes to plunge my knife in her heart; when, gathering her savage strength, she rose, and with one last desperate effort sprang towards me . . . I discharged the six shots of my revolver . . . which laid her still for a moment; when, leaping forward, I plunged my knife to her vitals. Again she tried to rise . . . but could not."

Going into the dark recess of the cave, Adams found two beautiful little cubs, only about a week old. Their eyes were still closed. They were both males. He carried them back to the camp inside his buckskin shirt. One was given to Solon, and the other he decided to keep for himself, naming the little fellow "Ben Franklin." As the greyhound had recently given birth to puppies, all but one of the litter were disposed of, and the mother was induced to accept the two baby grizzlies in their place.

By the time the party returned to the headwaters of the Tuolumne the cubs were doing fine and Adams had become very attached to little Ben Franklin. He had decided to raise him as a companion for Lady Washington.

About the middle of April of the same year Adams started on another hunting expedition, over the Sierras and into the Rocky Mountains. This was a longer and more difficult journey than the one up into Washington—"over deserts, totally unknown mountains, and through countries of Indians often hostile to white blood." He took along Lady Washington, Ben Franklin, and the latter's foster brother, the young greyhound which had been raised with him, also the two Indians, Stanislaus and Tuolumne, and a white man named Gray. They traveled with an old wagon drawn by two oxen, with a pair of mules hitched ahead. To get over the Sierras they followed the Emigration Road, used by the gold seekers who had come across the Plains.

Everything went as well as might be expected until they got over the Humboldt Mountains and out on the two-hundred-mile trip across the desert of the Great Basin. Here they all came very near perishing from thirst and exhaustion. Ben Franklin's feet became so sore from the sharp rocks and hot sand that Adams had to make moccasins for his feet. But finally they reached the Rockies. They had hunted everywhere they could along the way, and already young Ben Franklin had shown remarkable progress toward becoming a companion and aid to his master, along with Lady Washington. Adams had several exciting encounters with grizzlies, occasionally using his knife in the final dramatic moments. His accounts of these adventures are not only thrilling but spiced with rich bits of natural history; and the most remarkable feature of it all is the part which the two tamed grizzlies played in this unusual saga of the wilderness.

They went into Salt Lake City on the Fourth of July (1854) to sell the hides and young animals they had captured, later moving on a short distance past Fort Bridger, where a hunting camp was established, to sell meat to the emigrants traveling along the road.

It was here that one of the most extraordinary episodes occurred. Lady Washington had a romance with a bold Beau Brummel who came right into the hunting camp in the darkness of night. Realizing that a tête-à-tête was the sole purpose of the nocturnal visitor, Adams would not permit any interference. On three consecutive nights the big grizzly came to call. The surprising part is that Lady Washington did not break away from her man-made little world.

Shortly afterward Adams was seriously mauled by a grizzly dam who had two cubs with her. While endeavoring to finish off the old one with a knife, he was struck down and badly bitten. Lying perfectly still in the bear's clutches, he waited until she went back to the cubs. Then, getting to his feet, he drew his pistol; but, as the bear was evidently dying, he just waited for her to expire.

Returning to his home in the Sierras in the fall, Adams set out to capture a full-grown grizzly. A large and heavy log trap was built, and finally a monster bear walked into it: "the largest specimen of the grizzly, perhaps, that was ever taken alive." The giant bear almost tore the trap apart, and Adams was compelled to stand by night and day for more than a week, using an iron bar and firebrands to keep him from escaping. It was nearly two months before this grizzly could be transferred into a movable cage and transported back to the camp. Adams named this one "Samson" and estimated his weight at over fifteen hundred pounds.

Adams made other trips, high-lighted with exciting and unusual experiences, in conquest of California grizzlies, with plenty of panthers and other game for variety. On several occasions Lady Washington and Ben Franklin fought with tooth and claw to assist their master in his struggles to finish off other grizzlies with his knife. They all carried severe scars of battle. In one of these fights Adams had his scalp almost torn from his head.

It was on one of these hunting expeditions that the anticipated addition to the family arrived. The Lady gave birth to a pretty little cub: "which gave unmistakable evidence of having the blood of the Rocky Mountain bear in its composition." This little fellow thrived well and grew up to be the one known as "Fremont."

Finally fever and the effects of many injuries suffered in fights with grizzlies and other dangerous game brought such serious illness upon James Capen Adams that he was compelled to give up hunting. Taking his animals with him, he went to San Jose, where he first began exhibiting them to the public. Then he went to Santa Clara and on to San Francisco. It was in the early part of October 1856 that he established his "museum" in the basement on Clay Street and Theodore H. Hittell got his story. Adams had with him at this time: "Lady Washington, Ben Franklin,—noble Ben, and his foster-brother Rambler. The monster who rattles his chain in the cage, and fairly shakes the building, is Samson; and the white coated rogue by the side of the Indian dog is Funny Joe. The black and cinnamon bears, the panthers, wolves, foxes, wild cats, elks, and other animals ranged around." All of these had been captured, mostly with his own hands, by the dreamy-eyed old man with the profuse beard and garbed in fringed buckskins that were soiled and worn from long, hard wear in the mountains. And, of all the creatures in that basement, James Capen Adams was certainly the strangest.

Ben Franklin died in the "museum" on January 17, 1858. The San Francisco *Evening Bulletin* ran a lengthy obituary story under the heading "Death of a Distinguished Native Californian."

On January 7, 1860, Adams took his animals aboard the

clipper ship *Golden Fleece,* bound around Cape Horn for New York City.

The next thing we find about Adams and his animals is an announcement in the *New York Clipper,* a weekly paper published in New York City and devoted to theatrical and sports news, in the issue of Saturday, April 28, 1860:

"Barnum, of the Museum, and J. M. Nixon, of Niblo's Garden, have entered into a joint engagement with Mr. J. C. Adams, the 'Old Hunter of '49', for the exhibition of the '*California Menagerie*', which they will open on the 30th, at the corner of Thirteenth Street and Fourth Avenue. All sorts of animals seem to be comprised in the 'company', and those among our fellow citizens who are partial to 'roaring' amusements will doubtless then be on hand."

On May 5 another popular New York theatrical and sports paper, *Wilkes' Spirit of the Times,* carried a lengthy advertisement of the "*California Menagerie,*" featuring "J. C. Adams, The Old California Trapper of '49" and the exhibition of his "wonderful collection of Wild Animals of the Pacific and The Far West! Captured and Trained by him during a Hunting Expedition of over Four Years in the regions of the Rocky Mountains!" In typical P. T. Barnum technique it heralded the affair as "The most curious, unique, and interesting MUSEUM OF ANIMATED NATURE *ever presented to the Public.*" The advertisement also announced that "On Monday, A GRAND CARAVAN PROCESSION with Splendid Band Chariot and Car; ADAMS, THE TRAINER, will appear on the car, with his PACK BEAR, accounted the same as on his journey in the mountains. . . . The Procession will start from Thirteenth Street at 10 o'clock, proceed down Broadway to Park, up Chatham-street and Third Avenue to Union Square, and thence to the place of exhibition."

Thus the strange story of James Capen Adams continues. He and the wild animals which had been captured by his own hands in the mountains of the faraway West come to Manhattan, and, with his faithful grizzly companion Lady Washington still at his side, they parade together down Broadway.

In a review on the "California Menagerie" the *New York Clipper* in its issue of May 19 referred to it as *"A-dams great show"*; and in a lengthy editorial in the issue of June 23, *Wilkes' Spirit of the Times* had the following to say: "Shall We Have Zoological Gardens?—We trust the project for the establishment of zoological gardens in Central Park of this metropolis will be persecuted with vigor. . . . No gathering exists of the beasts and birds of our own native land. . . . Just look at the collection made by the old Rocky Mountain hunter, ADAMS, and then see what might be done with means and science. He has gotten together some eight or nine varieties of the American bear, from the monstrous grizzly of the size of an ox down to the little golden bear. . . . Let us have the Zoological Gardens in Central Park with as little delay as possible." Again, in the issue of June 30, the *New York Clipper* carried the following comment: "A highly interesting and instructive exhibition is that of 'Adams' California Menagerie', now located at 13th Street east of Broadway. The performances of the animals are unique, and we are glad to learn that their stay here, now some weeks, has been remunerative to the proprietor as well as instructive and entertaining to the visitors."

Adams had been seriously ill since leaving California. It is said that one of the wounds on his head had been torn open afresh during a severe struggle with one of his animals on shipboard while making the rough passage around Cape Horn. After eight weeks on Broadway, however, he made a new contract with Barnum to join his circus for a summer tour through the New England states. Upon completion of this engagement Adams retired to Neponset, a small town near Boston, where relatives lived—immediately became confined to bed and within a few days he died.

"I have looked on death in many forms, and trust that I can meet it whenever it comes, with a stout heart and steady nerves," are the words with which James Capen Adams closed his personal story just prior to leaving San Francisco as an ill and badly scarred old man. "If I could choose, I would wish, since it was my destiny to become a mountaineer and grizzly bear hunter of California, to finish my career in the Sierra Nevada. There would I fain lay down with the Lady, Ben, and Rambler at my side; there, surely, I could find rest through the long future, among the eternal rocks and evergreen pines."

Surely James Capen Adams fulfilled an extraordinary career and was certainly the most unusual bear hunter who ever lived.

Chapter XV

"GOOD GRIZZLY: DEAD GRIZZLY!"

THE grizzly and the Indian have had a lot in common. Their *pied-à-terre* had become firmly planted in America long before the first white man set foot on this continent. They had a certain synonymity of character and faced a similar fate—marked for racial destruction by the same natural enemy who chose to make their native land his own. Just as the cry of our frontier fighting army of the West became *"The only good Indian is a dead Indian,"* the cattle- and stockmen adopted a similar war cry against every grizzly bear that breathed. The only difference is that the determination of the white man to exterminate the grizzly has been retained more persistently and carried a great deal closer to an ultimate and complete conclusion.

The most potential contributing factor in the destruction of the grizzly in the United States was the introduction of domestic cattle and farm stock into the grassy mountain valleys and more open ranges west of the Great Plains. The cattle industry was one of the important cornerstones upon which our western empire was built. It found its beginning in much the same manner as the horse became part of the western American scene. The early Spanish conquistadors who pushed northward from Mexico in the mid-sixteenth and seventeenth centuries, to explore and take possession of the new domain, invariably drove with them suitable numbers of cattle and other domestic stock. These provided a source of food during the journey, and, wherever they established themselves, the propagation of these animals became part of their pioneering projects. In one way or another, while these elaborate expeditions were en route and after the frontier settlements were established, some of the cattle escaped into the vast surrounding wilderness, just as the horses got away. They found a natural habitat that was highly suitable to their requirements, and they immediately began to multiply. According to the Tenth Census of the United States *Report Upon the Statistics of Agriculture* (1880), there were 100,000 head of cattle in Texas by 1830; there were 330,000 head in 1850; and the official estimate for 1860 was 3,535,768. The vast majority of these roamed free and wild, although a small fraction of them had always been more or less in the hands of pioneer cattle raisers.

Grizzlies were abundant in most areas of the Southwest and they quite naturally cultivated a taste for beef. Cattle were slow-moving creatures, as compared to the native animals, and the young ones and cows fell easy prey to the carnivorous bears. They were not particular whether the stock was in a wild herd or the more docile property of a pioneer rancher.

Up North, however, the rapid settlement of the country gave a new aspect to the embryo cattle industry down on the Mexican border. Along the river routes and overland trails westward from the Upper Mississippi the forts and supply stations were developing into towns, and there was a healthy demand for beef, at a price which offered a handsome profit. The men of the Southwest were a hardy lot and they did not lose much time in setting about to take advantage of this situation. They started rounding up the wild cattle with a new zest. As early as 1837–38 a herd of several hundred unbranded longhorns were driven overland from the Rio Grande country. Thus began the great cattle industry of the West.

The native Indian inhabitants of the Southwest had always

considered the grizzly a natural enemy to their existence, and this attitude received well-founded support among the European pioneers who settled in the country. Everyone became aware of the stock-killing activities of the big bears, and the new interest in cattle as a remunerative enterprise put a new emphasis on the bear situation. According to Vernon Bailey, "the destruction of these grizzlies was absolutely necessary before the stock business of the region could be maintained on a profitable basis."[109] The problem was taken so seriously in some areas that the ranchers combined their efforts and carried on an organized campaign to exterminate the ursine vandals. Thus the grizzly became marked as the first and foremost predatory enemy of the cattlemen—an unfortunate imputation which was destined to follow the stock industry as closely as the lariat and the branding iron and to survive as long as there was a grizzly left in the country.

In the slaughter of the buffalo there was some semblance of practical purpose, for their hides and meat or merely their tongues were used; and such other things as cutting down every tree in a forest had the useful purpose of building homes and stores; but the grizzlies were hunted, killed, and left to rot like the lowest of criminals.

Various contributing factors accumulated against Old Ephraim as the cattle industry developed and spread through most of his range. The numbers of bear hunters became vastly increased with the great improvement of high-powered repeating rifles; the use of packs of trained hunting dogs made it much easier to find the quarry and a great deal safer to kill him; and the rapidly spreading settlement of the fertile land constricted the range of these animals and depleted the other game which for centuries had provided a source of supply for his natural appetite for meat. No longer was it safe for him to wander freely out into the open country; and, even if he did, the herds of buffalo were gone and there was little but domestic stock to feed upon. Being a furtive creature, he retired to the rough retreats in the mountains, where food of any kind was sometimes scarce. Being highly intelligent in such matters as nature had made important to him, there is little doubt that he acquired an increasingly wary respect for this new human enemy which so seriously threatened his power and very existence.

The stockmen pressed further and further their war of attrition. Cash bounties for the random killing of any grizzly were offered by cattle and sheep growers associations, as well as local and state governments; the use of poison and sufficiently heavy steel traps was introduced; and these animals also became the paramount trophy of many ambitious sportsmen. All these factors, aided by modern firearms, dogs, poison, and traps, spelled out the destruction of the grizzly. His stand was heroic, but the odds were overwhelmingly against him.

There was a lot of difference from the black bear that went beyond the matters of color and size. These ebony relatives of Old Ephraim had always been looked upon with a certain amount of disdain by Indian and white hunters alike. Their dispositions were as far apart as a siesta is from a midwinter hibernation sleep. In some sections the blacks and their color phases of brown and cinnamon grew as big as some of the grizzlies—600 pounds or more—but they were looked upon like fat old women. No one ever told of a black bear charging a hunter, even when they were wounded. Unlike the grizzlies, they were able to climb trees; and, faint hearts that they were, they generally went scurrying away and climbing up among the branches whenever pressed by even a mongrel dog. They occasionally made a midnight raid upon a sheep or a farmer's pigpen, but even this was considered more the act of a juvenile delinquent than the unforgivable deed of the hardened criminal. Their greatest asset, however, in this great transition from wilderness to rural domestication, was an ability to adapt themselves to the new environment. They were not handicapped by the haughty and irreconcilable pride of Old Ephraim and were content to hide in the swampy and scrawny badlands unfit for the white men's acquisition. In many areas and states where the mighty grizzly has entirely disappeared the lowly black bear is still to be found in considerable numbers.

There is an interesting parallel to be found in the relative situation of the wolf and the coyote, in which the big bold canine killer, who once followed the buffalo herds to pull down the weak and wounded stragglers, has become entirely a historic memory, and the lowly coyotes still howl in chorus in the moonlight and are content to steal the farmers' chickens for big excitement.

Still another parallel, in the effete East, is the moose and the white-tailed deer. When the white man began settling along the Hudson River, it is said, there were more moose in what is now the state of New York than there were deer. The largest of the antlered ungulates has long been a thing of the past, while the almost effeminate deer are today something of a nuisance to the gardened estates of fashionable Westchester, almost within sight of the tall buildings of metropolitan Manhattan.

As the settlement of the West progressed, the hunting of grizzlies settled into four general methods: still-hunting, with dogs, steel traps, and poison.

Still-hunting has always been the most highly accredited practice of the Nimrods. It is what fly-fishing is to the fresh-water fishermen. The stealthy and silent matching of wits with wild game in their own native haunts has always appealed to the best sporting instincts of man; and, while it gives the animal more of a chance, the motive is more personal vanity of accomplishment than any feeling of altruism. Among bona fide sportsmen there is a high degree of fair play—just as the best of game-bird hunters disdain to shoot at a sitting target—although it is not the sportsmen who deplete a species.

Grizzlies were never plentiful in the same sense as other game. Even in the best of territories they were never found "in herds" like elk, deer, mountain sheep, and the like. On rare occasions they might be found in numbers up to half a dozen or more, collected at some particularly good feeding place; it was not uncommon to find an old female traveling with two or three of her own two-year-old offspring, or in the mating season two or more males might be found courting a single lady grizzly, but they generally traveled alone. Their normal habit was to spend the day bedded down in some secluded retreat or vantage point well guarded against unsuspected approach. And once a grizzly became aware of the presence of a human prowler in his immediate environs he could slip away like a ghost. Their little piglike eyes were notoriously shortsighted and feeble, but their noses were as amazingly far-ranged and keen as the eyes of the eagle. The big bears were smart too. If they found human tracks in their ranging ground, they generally moved to safer territory or waited until dark to start moving around. Even if an unsuspecting grizzly was located, it was not always easy to stalk close enough for a shot; and killing a grizzly on foot, even with a high-powered repeating rifle, was always at the risk of real danger.

In regions where the terrain was unusually rough, or the cover was so thick it made game difficult to locate, the still-hunters would frequently resort to waiting at advantageous lookout points, in the evening or early morning, to get a shot at bears coming to or leaving their feeding grounds. In the fall the berry patches were always a likely place. Or they might use some form of baiting.

When a grizzly made a kill, of some other wild animal or domestic stock, he would generally drag it to some secluded spot to enjoy the feast. Large bears have been known to transport a full-grown elk or even a hefty steer a mile or more over rough and difficult country. Their strength was amazing. They did not make such a kill every day. Sometimes it was infrequent. On such happy occasions, however, he ate very heartily; and, not being able to consume it all at one sitting, Old Ephraim gave serious attention to preserving and protecting what was left for future meals. After satisfying his immediate appetite he would cover up the cache with leaves or even parts of dead trees, sometimes digging out a shallow hole in the ground beforehand. Then he would wander away, to return for the next meal, or he might lie down near enough to protect it from trespassers.

If a still-hunter was fortunate enough to find where a grizzly had made a fresh kill, and located the cache, there was no better plan than to wait in hiding for the bear to return. This required astute judgment in selecting the right spot, from which the approaching animal would not get any warning of human scent, yet close enough to get a good shot in the gathering darkness of evening.

The grizzly was not only highly intelligent, but he was always very cautious and wary. In the days before the white man with his devastating guns the grizzly did not have any reason to be so cautious. But they learned the difference very quickly; and, like wise men, they adopted the logic of avoiding serious trouble rather than blustering boldly into it. When returning to one of their own caches they learned to approach it with the stealth of an old-time Indian creeping into the encampment of an enemy. They might even make a wide circle out around the place, to get the scent from every direction.

Even if a bear made a direct approach to a cache, the direction of the breeze might shift and the hunter would have to change his position, or the bear might come a different way than anticipated. He might not arrive until it was too dark to be seen or to risk a shot. The bear might have found the human tracks and not come at all. Waiting through the dense darkness of a whole night could be an eerie experience for even a hardened veteran. It was always possible that the bear might stumble onto the hunter and make a spontaneous charge. At the end of one long night there was the problem of waiting through another, or a third. Had the grizzly somehow become aware of the ambushed enemy and not come back at all?

Frequently hunters would provide their own bait. They might shoot an elk or other local game and leave it untouched for the bear to find. They might lead an old horse up into a canyon or other place where a grizzly was known to be working and shoot the horse at the desired location. Or, when a freshly killed cow or other domestic stock was found, the rancher or some ambitious neighbor might take up a waiting vigil for the culprit to return.

It is doubtful, however, if the grizzly would have become exterminated in all the areas where they are now nonexistent if still-hunting had been the only method of hunting.

The use of dogs gave a number of important advantages to the hunter. A dog with a good nose could follow a trail, even if it was not a hot one, until he found its maker. There was no safe retreat, day or night. The dogs would find him in the thickest underbrush or the worst jumble of rocks. They might do it in a brief time or it might take many hours, but find him they would. The hunter, or hunters, could usually follow on horseback. Once the grizzly got the alarm he would take off for the roughest retreat he knew, and he might lead the dogs on a long chase, where it was impossible for the riders to go or men to keep up on foot. The bear was in no physical danger from even a large pack of the best of dogs. Their whole purpose was to stop his flight, by darting in to bite his flanks or otherwise bring him to bay. So long as the riders kept reasonably close to the dogs, their chances were good. When the bear was stopped, and if the dogs were able to hold him, the men could leave their horses and come in for the kill.

It was not always as easy as that. Before the hunters got close enough for a shot, the bear might take off for another long dash and the men would have to return to their horses. The dogs would close in, slashing their teeth into his unprotected rear end. In this method of hunting it was not the men who braved the danger but the dogs. It was not unusual for more than one of the pack to suffer serious injury or death. All that Old Ephraim had to do was lay one claw upon a dog; and, whenever he managed to get an unfortunate dog in his clutches, it was generally torn apart in short order. Even when the hunters finally arrived on the scene there was seldom any great danger. For, if a wounded grizzly charged, the dogs would rush in and divert the attack. A good pack could find almost any bear that existed in a wide area, and the chances of his escape were pretty poor.

This writer once hunted with a very successful bear hunter in the Selkirk Mountains of British Columbia who used a dog in a rather unorthodox manner. Bear dogs are generally of the more aggressive breeds, such as airedales, hounds, and mixed breeds of other fighting varieties. But this old character used a Gordon setter. The friendly old bird dog was always by his side as they moved silently through cedars and jack pines in the little valleys up in the mountains; and the dog's highly educated nose would work on bear (and mountain lion) just as his breed are accustomed to work on quail. His eccentric master knew the country as he knew the dark corners of his own little log cabin beside the North Thompson River, with its dirt floor and dirty dishes. He also was thoroughly familiar with the habits of bears and where they were most apt to be found at any season and any time of day. Never have I known a man who could travel so silently through the woods or brush, or who was so keenly alert to the little currents of air; and his aged "bird dog" seemed to know his every thought and wish.

As a lad of only eighteen I went out with him several times. Not only did he teach me a great deal about bears, but I will never forget some of the little vignettes of impressions which have always remained so vividly in my memory. He had a habit of whispering very softly to the old dog when there was a feeling that game was close. The dog would become tense; his eyes would move quickly in acknowledgment of every softly whispered word or phrase; and he would literally tiptoe along, with his keen nose intensively guiding them in the proper direction. As they approached the day bed of a bear, the dog's head would move nervously and he would begin to stop. Then the old man would stop, and his eyes would move slowly about, from one likely spot to another, as he quietly worked the well-oiled lever of his old Winchester. Here he would take over, moving like a panther, always keeping in a position to give the best range of vision, going forward ever so slowly, until the bear made a sudden and often very noisy dash from under the screening boughs of a spruce or a dense thicket. The dog always seemed to be frightened and would dash behind his master almost before the shot was fired; and, when it was all over, he would tremble like a shivering child.

In the fall, when the berry bushes were heavy with their fruit, the old hunter would go to the best of these places. If it was in the early morning, and the breeze was in the right direction, he would go to the places where he knew the bears were in the habit of traveling from the big berry patches back to their day beds in the thick timber; and in the evening he would take his stand where they came out to feed. Finding a suitable spot, he might lie down and go to sleep, with the Gordon setter close beside him. When a bear began an approach the dog would ram his cold nose against his master's whiskered face, to arouse him and "point" the direction, well in advance of Bruin's appearance. That the plan worked was amply attested by the fact that in both fall and spring the old man's cabin usually had bearhides nailed to dry on all four sides. There were far more blacks than silvertips, although he used the same method for both.

Some grizzlies were caught in steel traps, particularly by the bounty hunters and U.S. Government predatory control men. Not a great many were taken in pen traps or deadfalls, because an infuriated bear of this variety would tear his way through the side of most any ordinary wall of logs, and it took a mighty hefty deadfall to break his back or permanently pin him down. But it was not easy to get a grizzly in a steel trap. His sense of smell and his wary intelligence were far too keen. Even when thus captured, a large grizzly could be as mean and dangerous as one infuriated by the superficial wound of a rifle ball. The forty-pound weight of a No. 6 "Great Bear Trap," with its sixteen-inch steel jaws clamped securely to one front foot, plus an eighty-pound clog in the form of a long section of tree trunk, was not always a sufficient handicap to make such encounters at all safe for the trapper. Not only would the bear walk away with trap and clog, to the accompaniment of a rapidly developing state of bad temper, but he might charge with such speed and vengeance that the lone trapper ran a serious risk of being killed. Sometimes they escaped completely, eventually getting rid of the heavy trap by chewing off their own toes, as other trapped animals frequently do, or through other more natural processes.

The use of poison became a rather popular practice of stockmen and ranchers who could not afford the time or might not have the personal inclination to go after a grizzly with a rifle. When a freshly killed cow, sheep, pig, or horse was found, a liberal amount of strychnine was applied; and if the bear returned for another meal, which was generally the case, the poison ended his career.

Collectively, these various methods constitute the most consistent and intensive campaign that has ever been carried out for the willful extermination of a species. It extended over practically every section of the grizzly's range in the United States. Guilty or innocent, these most marvelous of America's big-game creatures are still considered a predatory criminal, without benefit of protection, even in most of the areas where only a few survivors linger on the thin brink of total extinction. The only place where they are assured a sanctuary is in our western national parks, and even these asylums offer them a sadly inadequate *pied-à-terre*, all too barren of the natural necessities which the peculiarities of this carnivorous species require; and those who from time to time wander outside face the risk of being killed as cattle thieves and criminals.

Chapter XVI

THE HAIRY OUTLAWS

THERE is hardly a section of old-time cattle country in the West, that was in the range of the grizzly, that did not have its own stories of giant outlaw bears who became famous for the number of cattle they killed and the smart manner in which they evaded the penalty of death. In some instances these cases were developed through many years and took on the aspects of dramatic legends.

The men of the cattle country in those days were not the sort who went in for pretty little fairy tales. They were a rough and hard-bitten lot. But the old grizzly was their kind of story stuff, particularly the sort with a disposition of a desperado and the sagacity of a devil. Every time he killed any of their cattle they hated his guts; but every time the posses or the hired hunters came back with only mouthfuls of complicated alibis the hatred of the folks round about had a rather respectful undertone. They knew a man when they saw evidence of one, and it was a lot better to be bad and brave than good and weak. They forgot their losses of a head of stock now and then, but they remembered and talked about each story of how the outlaw outwitted every plan and effort to fill his hairy hide full of holes. The longer these bears persisted with their depredations, and continued to get away with it, the greater grew the aura of legend around them. They frequently became known by names which in some manner characterized their individuality—such as "Old Three-Toes," "Old Club-Foot," "Old Scarface," "The Bear Cat," and the like. Sometimes ambitious hunters and trappers came from long distances, with great confidence of collecting rewards that frequently grew to as much as a thousand dollars or more. But some of these cattle-killing grizzlies evaded every well-planned effort to destroy them, in a manner that was phenomenal.

The stories of most of these outlaw bears were basically if not entirely true. Grizzlies were accused of a lot of kills, however, which they never committed. Whenever a head of stock was found dead in a rough part of the range, and there were signs that a grizzly had been feeding upon the carcass, the cattlemen quickly jumped to the conclusion that the bear had done the killing. This was frequently not the case. Cattle, as well as sheep, were continually falling victims to more natural deaths, from disease, accidents, and eating poisonous vegetation. Also, wolves and mountain lions were more habitual stock killers than ever the grizzly was. But a grizzly would never pass up a feast of meat, when it was as easily procured as finding it spread out upon his table, in most any form; and chasing away a big tawny mountain cat or a few wolves was only an extra incentive. This, incidentally, is how a lot of cattle-killing grizzlies cultivated their taste for beef or mutton. Another way was by finding stock that had been frozen to death during the winter and kept refrigerated under the snow until the bears came out of hibernation in the spring. But grizzlies with a strong taste for beef were like a lot of men with human vices—once they really got the habit, they couldn't leave the stuff alone, and they would go to desperate extremes to get it.

The cases when grizzlies became habitual cattle killers are more exceptional than the general rule. This has been well proven by careful investigations. "Perhaps ninety-nine out of every hundred grizzlies never kill stock or big game," is the conclusion reached by Enos A. Mills, the well-informed writer and naturalist of the Colorado Rockies, after thirty years of keen observation and studying these animals in their native haunts.[110] He never carried a gun, and his only interest was a serious and unbiased analysis of their temperament and char-acteristics. Few men have known the Rocky Mountain grizzly more intimately. His experience covered the period of from about 1888 to 1918 and extended over a considerable area. Mr. Mills personally investigated fourteen cases in which griz-zlies were charged with destroying cattle. In three cases no grizzly had even been at the kill. In six instances it was well established that mountain lions had made the kills; one death was due to wolves; one by poisonous plants; two were the result of stones that rolled from a landslip; and the death of one cow was undetermined. Of the eleven carcasses that had been visited by grizzlies, not a single one could be honestly charged to the condemned. The conclusion was: "The only evidence against the grizzly was entirely circumstantial; he had eaten a part of the carcass."

Not that Enos A. Mills, or any other capable investigator, ever claimed that the grizzly *never* killed domestic stock. Quite the contrary. The ratio between "outlaw killers" among grizzlies and men in the old days of our West was about the same. Those that were "bad" were generally *very* bad, but they were a comparatively small minority.

In his book *The Grizzly—Our Greatest Wild Animal*, which reports on his lifelong observation, Mills tells of several notorious cattle killers, one a Utah grizzly that "killed about one thousand head of cattle in fifteen years";[111] and, with a large reward on his head, this bear repeatedly defied every attempt made to kill him, by "hunters and trappers with rifles and traps; expeditions of men, horses, and dogs. . . . All these years he lived on as usual in his home territory, making a kill every few days, and was only seen two or three times." He tells of other similar accounts of outlaw bears, all of which "slaughtered cattle by the hundreds . . . lived with heavy prices on their heads, and for years outwitted skillful hunters and trappers, escaping the well-organized posse again and again. Knowing many of the hunters and their skillful methods, and the repeated triumphs of other grizzlies over combinations and new contrivances, I am convinced that the grizzly is an animal who reasons."

Being a natural carnivore, cattle-killing grizzlies were apt to be found wherever the species existed, particularly in localities and at times when other and easier supplies of food were scarce. Most every Rocky Mountain state and practically every region from Mexico to Canada at some time had its notorious outlaw bear. A whole book would be required to tell all the stories. Many have long been liberally festooned with the romantic tinge of legend, and the deeds of daring and sagacity of some almost defy belief.

One of these ursine desperadoes who plied his bloody trade in California is told about by Joaquin Miller in his book *True Bear Stories*. This particular grizzly inhabited one of the interior counties, where a reward for his death had remained uncollected for many years. He continued to destroy domestic stock at will, defying every effort to bring him to justice. It is a well-known fact that all living creatures in their natural wild state very rarely escape a tragic end of life, generally ending their existence on earth by being torn to pieces by some stronger predatory enemy—occasionally by their own species. If there is an exception to this harsh rule of nature, it seems to have been the grizzly bears; for they had no natural enemy except man. In any event, this renegade bear of the California mountains defied all the rules and lived on and on into the darkening shadows of senile infirmity. It was only then that the predatory white men finally closed in where the old pirate lay, nearly blind and dying of old age, and they ended his career with a hot barrage from their high-powered Winchester rifles. "It was found that he was almost toothless," writes Joaquin Miller; "his paws had been terribly mutilated by numerous steel traps, and it is said that his kingly carcass had received nearly lead enough to sink a small ship. There was no means of ascertaining his exact weight, but it was claimed that skin, bone and bullets, as he was found, he would have weighed well nigh a ton."[112]

The Biological Survey naturalist Vernon Bailey, in his *Mammals of New Mexico*, tells of some of the cattle-killing grizzlies in the Southwest. One of these had pursued a long career of notoriety in the district around Sapello Creek, north of Silver City, repeatedly escaping all efforts to apprehend him. Finally a local rancher collected a posse, and with a pack of good bear dogs they set out determined not to give up until the hairy old outlaw was killed. For nine days the dogs stayed persistently at their task of endeavoring to bring this grizzly to bay long enough for the hunters to get close enough to use their rifles. Not only did the bear defy the dogs and evade the men, but in those nine days he killed seven head of cattle, which were left to be found along the trail. Finally, however, the dogs managed to pin him down long enough for the hunters to catch up, and he was shot to death.[113] There are also other quite similar cases cited by Bailey as well as other documentarians of the Southwest, some of them persisting as recently as the summer of 1916.[114]

Among the many writers who have told about outlaw cattle-killing grizzlies, and argued their cases pro and con, is the celebrated Theodore Roosevelt. His wide firsthand experience with big game of many kinds, deep interest, and keen intelligence gives first importance to his opinions in matters of this kind. "Some [grizzlies] are confirmed game and cattle killers," he states in his book *Hunting the Grisly*; "others are not; while yet others either are or are not accordingly as the freak seizes them; and their ravages vary almost unaccountably, both with the season and the locality. Throughout 1889, for instance, no cattle, so far as I heard, were killed by bears anywhere near my ranch on the Little Missouri in western Dakota; yet I happened to know that during that same season the ravages of bears among the herds of a cowman in the Big Hole Basin, in western Montana, were very destructive."[115]

Roosevelt had serious trouble with outlaw grizzlies on his own ranch on the Little Missouri on more than one occasion. There was one big bear, which had become well known by its tracks, that suddenly took to cattle killing. "This big brute had its headquarters on some very large brush bottoms a dozen miles below my ranch house, and ranged to and from across the broken country flanking the river on each side. It began just before berry time, but continued its career of destruction long after the wild plums and even the buffalo berries had ripened. I think that what started it was a feast on a cow which had mired and died in the bed of a creek; at least it was not until after we found that it had been feeding on the carcass and had eaten every scrap, that we discovered traces of its ravages among the live stock. It seemed to attack the animals wholly regardless of their size and strength; its victims including a large bull and a beef steer, as well as cows, yearlings and gaunt, weak trail 'doughies,' which had been brought in very lately by a Texas cow-outfit. . . .

"Judging from the signs, the crafty old grisly, as cunning as he was ferocious, usually lay in wait for cattle when they came down to water, choosing some thicket or dense underbrush and twisted cottonwoods through which they had to pass. . . . When within a few feet a quick rush carried him fairly on the terrified quarry. . . . Some of his victims were slain far from the river, in winding, brushy coulies of the Bad Lands, where the broken nature of the ground rendered stalking easy. Several of the ranchmen, angered at their losses, hunted their foe eagerly, but always with ill success; until one of them put poison in a carcass, and thus at last, in ignoble fashion, slew the cattle-killer."[116]

There was another raiding bear, however, who met his nemesis in a rather unexpected manner, which Roosevelt tells about in his book *Hunting Trips of a Ranchman*. One of his friends who had a ranch in Montana had been suffering severe losses by a grizzly that repeatedly pulled down even full-grown beef steers. As usual, strenuous but unsuccessful efforts had been made to apprehend the killer. Then one day there was a new aspect to the situation. Toward evening the cowboys were attracted by the rancher's prize stallion as it came racing in toward the barns. Realizing from the horse's actions that something unusual had disturbed him, they made an investigation and found that his haunch was deeply cut with three or four gashes that appeared as if they had been made by a dull ax. They knew at once that the attack had been made by a bear, and, getting their rifles, the cowboys rode off on the back track to find out what had happened. The horse was a rather vicious range stallion, not easily frightened or put to flight. Without difficulty the men found where the horse had been attacked while grazing near a thicket, and, on further investigation, the stock-killing grizzly charged out upon the riders. There was an exciting battle, but a succession of shots from the fast-moving horses finally killed the big bear. On closer examination it was found that the grizzly's under jaw was broken and part of his face smashed in—by the stallion's sharp hoofs. This was one case in which the hairy outlaw had apparently found his intended victim a little too much for him.[117]

One of the most notorious cattle-killing grizzlies of the state of Colorado was a big, crafty bear known as "Old Mose." If the reputation with which he is credited is all true, he was quite a beast. Not only was he accused of killing around eight hundred head of cattle, together with dozens of colts and other livestock, but this grizzly had also personally killed at least five of the men who dared to challenge him in combat. It was not until April 1904 that his notorious career came to an end; and Enos A. Mills reports that his deeds of daring and destruction went back for about thirty-five years![118] His home territory covered an area of about seventy-five miles in diameter, straddling the Continental Divide, in the vicinity of Black Mountain. The stock that he killed was estimated in excess of

$30,000, and the heavy price on his head led some of the most skillful hunters and trappers to put forth their best efforts to get him. There was hardly a time when someone was not on his trail or planning some new strategy to outwit the old outlaw.

A number of times Old Mose was approached close enough to be shot. It was on these occasions that he showed his fighting spirit and killed three of the best hunters in Colorado. He was too smart to be taken by the best schemes of any of the trappers, and even poison had failed to get him. When he went on a cattle-killing raid, he did it with a vengeance, smashing down the fences that happened to stand in his way.

This bear's habits were not all bad; in fact, he seems to have had something of a sense of humor. It is claimed that on several occasions Old Mose made a silent approach to the camp of unsuspecting prospectors or campers and then went rushing in with mighty huffs and roars. It may have been to scare the intruders out of his domain, or possibly just to see them go stampeding in all directions or try to climb up into the trees like frightened monkeys, for he had never laid a little claw upon any man except those who had injured him with a rifle.

Finally, however, a large pack of well-trained hunting dogs brought the hairy old outlaw to bay, and he was killed. It is said that even after his unusually long and strenuous career his teeth were sound, his pelt was in good condition, and he gave every appearance of being in excellent condition to have gone on for several more years. What a marvelous beast he must have been!

An excellent detailed account of just how a sagacious old grizzly managed to evade and outwit the extraordinary devices of a trapper is recounted by Enos A. Mills, who was an eyewitness observer through the whole affair.[119] A thousand-dollar reward had been put on the scalp of this very active cattle-killing grizzly, and Mills went along with a trapper who felt extremely confident that he was going to collect the money. The trapper had devised a number of new ideas and tricky innovations that seemed sure to be too clever for the smart old bear.

Fortunately for the trapper the cattle were driven down out of their summer range somewhat earlier than usual, which left the grizzly without his usual food supply. The trapper had planned on this, and, taking an old cow to a selected spot, he tied her up short and then surrounded the live bait with probably the darnedest array of spring guns and carefully concealed traps that was ever contrived to get a bear. Every outlying avenue of approach was covered by a set gun, with a fine silk line attached to the trigger and stretched over the surrounding bushes and tall grass. It seemed impossible for any grizzly to get in without setting off one of the guns. The inner fortifications were equally complete and confounding, with traps concealed at every conceivable point of approach. A bear would have to have wings to get to the cow without being caught—at least that is what the trapper thought.

It snowed the first night, which was another good break. They could at least follow the bear's movements. But no bear came to test the cleverness of man. On the second night, however, he visited the intricate set. The tracks showed that the grizzly had scented the cow from a mile or more away and came straight for the bait. He had stopped short within one short step of the silk line. Probably doing some careful analyzing and debating through his educated sense of smell, the old pirate walked cautiously clear around the whole outer defense, keeping just clear of the tiny silk line. Finding no opening, *he leaped over the line!* Once inside, he cautiously approached each of the hidden traps, one after the other; and then, apparently satisfied as to the exact location of every point of danger, he killed the cow.

After feeding heartily, the bear dragged the carcass over two of the traps—as something of an added gesture of haughty disdain; and, once again leaping over the outer silk line, he wandered leisurely away down the stream that ran through the gulch.

The trapper and Mills reset the traps which had been sprung by having the carcass dragged over them, and another trap was hidden at the spot where the bear had leaped in over the set-gun line. Still another set gun was put up on the trail he had taken down the gulch.

The following night Mr. Grizzly came back all right. Once again he walked all around the outside. Whether or not he located the new trap is conjecture; but, anyhow, he leaped over the silk line at a different place. Then, again, he inspected each place where the other traps were set before enjoying another hearty feed. This time, before he left, he partly covered the remains of the carcass with a few dead logs and limbs that were available; then he leaped over the set-gun line and went down the gulch as he had on the previous visit. When he came to the new thread stretched across the trail down the gulch, he stopped, followed it to where the set gun was tied in place in the branches of a tree, walked around the dangerous device, and, returning to the trail, went on his way again.

Not only was the trapper amazed, but his pride was deeply insulted. With a new determination he built a log pen around the remnants of the carcass, using a large boulder as the back of the pen. One of the forty-pound traps was placed in the narrow entrance and another was set inside.

Nothing happened the next night, but on the one following the bear returned. He went through the same procedure; and, when he had completed the usual inspection inside, he climbed to the top of the boulder and began tearing the pen apart. Then he reached down and dragged the carcass up onto the boulder, without getting down inside. Somehow, in accomplishing this, one of the poles which had been used in the construction was thrown aside so that it fell across a line attached to one of the set guns. The sudden resounding crash of the heavy cartridge should have put to frantic flight most any wild creature, but not this hairy pirate. He methodically got down off the big boulder and walked cautiously to where the smelly contraption of destruction had been hidden in its ambush, examined it curiously, and returned to finish what good meat still remained to be eaten. When there was nothing worth tearing from the bones, the old bear walked over the line where the pole had knocked it to the ground and went away—to return no more. Thus ended another trapper's chance of collecting the thousand-dollar reward for his scalp.

Chapter XVII

STRATEGIC RETREAT, WITH DIGNITY

THE last two decades or so of the nineteenth century saw a strategic retreat of the grizzly bears and the beginning of the end for this great creature in most areas of the United States. It also saw a new type of hunter take his place on the western scene. The Old West had rapidly given way to the white man's conquest. The last of the buffalo herds had been wiped out. The days of the old-time trapper, mountain man, and much else of the rough and rugged glamour had disappeared. The last dramatic stand of the Indians, in the Badlands of South Dakota, was broken with massacre and rout. The dust of covered wagons and cattle drivers from Texas had become the smoke of steam trains on the horizon. All over the West family farms had sprung up like bright little flowers in the spring, and the "damned barbed-wire fences" marked the end of the open range. There were, of course, still sizable areas of wild country left in the hills and mountains, left dormant because it offered little or no remunerative attraction to the white settlers and industrial pioneers. Some of this was only a short horseback ride from many of the rapidly growing towns; but even this was being methodically surrounded and split by new roads and new programs of destruction.

Onto this scene came the new type of American hunter. They were head and hide hunters, primarily interested in the biggest and finest of the species, and there was no greater prize to these men than the hide of a fine old grizzly bear. They didn't give a hang for profits or even a good piece of meat. The fact that a big grizzly was a notorious cattle killer, with a high price on his head, merely made the beast more glamorous as a trophy to these men, who would travel thousands of miles just to kill such an animal.

Not that these were the first big-game-hunting "sportsmen." The lords and barons of Europe had been hanging stags' horns in their great stone castles since the medieval days of the crossbow; and a few of these sporting gentlemen had come over here during the mid-nineteenth century to shoot big game—such as the Grand Duke Alexis of Russia, for whom the United States War Department ordered General Sherman to plan and personally guide a well-staged western buffalo hunt. But in America one didn't have to be a grand duke, lord, or baron with a big stone castle to be a sportsman. In the early days of the West many a trapper or meat hunter carried in a particularly large set of antlers to fasten them up on the ridgepole of his little log dwelling, or got some friendly squaw to tan the hide of an extra-special game animal, to use it as a rug on his earthy floor or a spread for his bunk. A little later on the pioneer farmers were even more strongly inclined to keep some of the best antlers and hides of their hunts. This was the crude beginning of what was destined to become one of our popular pastimes, which only an abundant and democratic America could make possible. It was to grow into big business and be responsible for the development of the fine art of taxidermy and natural-history museum display.

The total "legal kill" of big-game animals by sportsmen in the United States, even under rigidly respected game laws, is amazing. Just as an indication of this, during the 1952–53 hunting season, in the state of Montana alone, the total reported kill of deer, elk, and antelope was 78,314. If the hunters spent an average of only fifty dollars for each head of game, which is a very reasonable assumption, the money spent would go close to four million dollars. Nor do these figures take into account the large numbers of game killed by farmers, Indians, trappers, and others who kill for meat and do not file a report with the State Game Commission.

In the early days most sports-hunters had a pretty healthy appetite for what they dignified as "trophies." Much more recently than the turn of the century the proudest result of a hunting trip for the majority was to have one's picture taken in front of the largest possible number of deer or other game hung up by their hind legs. It must be said in defense of the sportsmen, however, that they have never depleted our wild game to the extent which the local farmers and other meat hunters have; and through the years it has been the sportsmen who have been largely responsible for the enactment of game laws and various conservation measures which made possible the present state of game welfare; and they have exerted a strong influence for the establishment of game sanctuaries and other means of saving several of the species from extermination. It was only a couple of decades ago that the pronghorn antelope had become a rarity, although the rigid protection of game-law enforcement has brought these animals back to surprising abundance throughout most of the western prairie areas. Only the great grizzly bear, unfortunately, has moved steadily into the oblivion of total extinction.

No one person has done more to make Americans conscious of our great national heritage of western game animals than Theodore Roosevelt. The virile characteristics of his political career and as President of the United States have so over-shadowed his memory in the public mind that it becomes a little difficult to think of him as a grizzly-bear hunter and serious student of wild life. It is true that others spent more time in the West and killed a larger number of bears; but he had an extremely broad experience as a hunter, and very few men have had a more serious interest or better understanding of the subject. No one has written so much about our western game or brought it so forcibly to popular attention. Few knew the history and characteristics of Old Ephraim better.

Roosevelt went West in 1880—the same year that Owen Wister, Frederic Remington, Caspar Whitney, and a number of other well-known exponents of the western scene began their careers on the fading frontier. He was only twenty-one, just graduated from Harvard, where he had been active as an intercollegiate boxer in the "lightweight—135-pound limit" classification. Four years later he took up ranching on the Little Missouri in western North Dakota, shot his first grizzly that same fall (got four of them on the hunt), and began seriously writing on the subject. The grizzly was his favorite big-game animal, and his experiences and observations on them are frequently found in his writings.[120]

Nothing quite equals the getting of one's first grizzly, particularly if the hunter has read and heard and thought a lot about these dangerous creatures. I have always been glad that my own first grizzly was gotten when I was alone, under a long-drawn-out situation which afforded me a wonderful opportunity to so completely saturate my thoughts with all its exciting aspects—like the enjoyment of fine old brandy, that is much too rare and much too strong to actually drink and can only be held in the palms of one's hands as a prayer book and be quaffed in a dreamy sort of way. In this respect Roosevelt was not so fortunate as I was.

"After several days' hunting, we . . . had seen no sign of grizzly, which was the game we were especially anxious to kill; for neither Merrifield nor I had ever seen a wild bear alive," wrote T. R. in his book *Hunting Trips of a Ranchman*. (P. 328 *et seq.*) It was his first big hunting trip from the ranch on the Little Missouri, into the Big Horn Mountains in the neighboring state of Wyoming, in the fall of 1884. First he sets the stage for the death scene: "Beneath these trees we walked on a carpet of pine needles, upon which our moccasined feet made no sound. The woods seemed vast and lonely, and their silence was broken now and then by the strange noises always to be heard in the great forests, and which seem to mark the sad and everlasting unrest of the wilderness. We climbed up along the trunk of a dead tree which had toppled over until its upper branches stuck in the limb crotch of another . . . To our right the ravine sloped downward toward the valley of the Big Horn River, and far on its other side we could catch a glimpse of the great main chain of the Rockies, their snow peaks glistening crimson in the light of the setting sun. We waited quietly in the growing dusk until the pine trees in our front blended into one dark, frowning mass. We saw nothing; but the wild creatures of the forest had begun to stir abroad. The owls hooted dismally from the tops of the tall trees, and two or three times a harsh wailing cry, probably the voice of some lynx or wolverine, arose from the depths of the woods." This, in brief, was the mountain home of the grizzly and the backdrop against which Theodore Roosevelt first came face to face with Old Ephraim.

Finally the crucial moment came. "There, not ten steps off, was the great bear, slowly rising from his bed among the young spruce. He had heard us, but apparently hardly knew exactly where or what we were, for he reared up on his haunches sideways to us. Then he saw us and dropped down again on all fours, the shaggy hair on his neck and shoulders seeming to bristle as he turned toward us. As he dropped down I raised the rifle; and when I saw the top of the white bead fairly between his small, glittering eyes, I pulled the trigger. Half-rising up, the huge beast fell over on his side in the death throes, the ball having gone into his brain, striking as fairly between the eyes as if the distance had been measured by a carpenter's rule. The whole thing was over in twenty seconds of the time I caught sight of the game." This bear's weight was estimated at "above twelve hundred pounds."

Roosevelt went on to have many more experiences with grizzly bears and every other variety of game animal in our West; and he later adventured in the jungles of South America and hunted the best that Africa had to offer. His extensive personal experience was combined with a wealth of information gained from many an old-time hunter with whom he associated on his numerous trips; and it was all evaluated with the same keen intelligence which made him a president of the United States. To him the grizzly was "the King of game beasts of temperate North America . . . the mighty lord of the wilderness . . . the most dangerous to the hunter." In this respect he was confirming an often-repeated opinion; but he went considerably further than anyone else had before in characterizing Old Ephraim as a primitive personality, deserving of a deeper consideration than merely as a target for heavier and more devastating rifle ballistics. He preferred to refer to these creatures as "grisly," on the premise that "the name of this bear has reference to its character, and not its color . . . in the same sense as horrible, exactly as we speak of a 'grisly spectre,'—and not *grizzly;* but perhaps the latter spelling is too well established to be now changed."[121]

Roosevelt early recognized that they are as diversified in individual temperaments as men; and he was one of the first to advance the belief that these mighty mammals have changed their attitude toward men and become far less bold, from learning that their human enemy with a gun in his hands is an entirely different proposition than their hairy ancestors had known, when there were only primitive Indians with stone-age weapons of offense.

"My own experience with bears tends to make me lay special emphasis upon their variation in temper," he wrote in 1897, in an article on "The Bear's Disposition," for the *Book of the Boone and Crockett Club,* of which he was one of the editors.[122] "There are savage and cowardly bears, just as there are big and little ones; and sometimes these variations are very marked among bears of the same districts."

Roosevelt had a great deal more to say on these important subjects, although he never quite made a thesis of it. As early as 1885, in his *Hunting Trips of a Ranchman,* he had this to say: "Nowadays these great bears are undoubtedly much better aware of the death-dealing power of men, and, as a consequence, are much less fierce, than was the case with their forefathers, who so unhesitatingly attacked the early Western travelers and explorers. Constant contact with rifle-carrying hunters, for a period extending over many generations of bear-life, has taught the grizzly by bitter experience that man is his undoubted overlord . . . and this knowledge has become an hereditary characteristic; though if he is wounded or thinks himself cornered he will attack his foes with a headlong, reckless fury that renders him one of the most dangerous of wild-beasts." (P. 320.)

Writing in *Hunting the Grisly*, he had this further comment: "At the beginning of the present century, when white hunters first encountered the grisly, he was doubtless an exceedingly savage beast, prone to attack without provocation, and a redoubtable foe to persons armed with the clumsy, small-bore, muzzle-loading rifles of the day. But bitter experience has taught him caution. He has been hunted for sport, and hunted for his pelt, and hunted for the bounty, and hunted as a dangerous enemy to stock, until, save in the wildest districts, he has learned to be more wary than a deer, and to avoid man's presence almost as carefully as the most timid game." (Pp. 106–7.) Again, in the previously cited *Book of the Boone and Crockett Club* of 1897, he has this further to say on the subject: "Those who have lived in the Upper Missouri country nowadays know how widely the bears that still remain have altered in character from what they were as recently as the middle of the century." Later in the same article he comments upon how "extremely interesting" it was for him "to note the grotesque, half-human movements, and giant awkward strength of the great beast."

There are few if any writers, who have really known the grizzly, who have not been well aware of the keen sagacity of these animals, although it is extremely rare to find any who attribute this to anythng in the slightest degree associated with the same sort of intelligence found among humans.

Some have even excused the changed disposition of these bears to false or exaggerated reports by earlier hunters and observers, while the majority have had no serious opinion one way or the other.

The most comprehensive book that has been written about these animals is William H. Wright's volume *The Grizzly Bear*,[123] which was published in September 1909. Mr. Wright states, "I studied the grizzly to hunt him"; but, like most hunters of wide experience, he came round to a greater interest in studying these creatures rather than just killing them. What he had to say about the changing character of the grizzly is far from conclusive, although it is interesting coming from such an authority: "We are now arrived at a division of our subject where we are to meet what, at first sight, appears to be a tangle of contradictory evidence, and it behoves us to walk slowly, to preserve an open mind. . . . Were our fore-fathers wrong about the nature of the grizzly? Or has the animal radically changed in a hundred years? Personally, I believe we have to answer 'yes' to both questions; but I am convinced that the amount of alteration in the nature of the grizzly is insignificant compared to the extent to which the pre-conceptions of early hunters colored their judgment. Twenty-five years of intercourse with these bears has taught me to regard them with the most profound respect. I would no more provoke one, unarmed, or rashly venture upon any action that my experience has taught me they regard as calling for self-defense, than I would commit suicide. . . . But that they habitually seek trouble when they can avoid it, or that they ever did, I do not believe." (Pp. 229–30.) Later, however, Mr. Wright contradicts himself by stating that "to sum up, then, it seems to be beyond doubt that a century's contact with men armed with rifles has rendered the grizzly bear a more wary and cautious animal. It would, indeed, be strange if this were not so, for the grizzly is quick to learn and has had innumerable opportunities of learning; and there have been thirty or forty generations during which his indi-

vidual lessons have been moulding the instinct of the race."
(P. 246.) William H. Wright, like most writers, uses the term
"instinct" entirely as a vague term to excuse a better understanding of the motives which govern the actions of animals.

There seems to be little doubt that Old Ephraim made a
strategic retreat, in the face of an enemy which became so
strongly reinforced in numbers and power of weapons that
there was no other course to follow. Those who did not retreat
were wiped out, and the enemy continued to pursue them into
the wildest and most remote places. But there has been no loss
of dignity in the grizzly's reatreat. Never has he lost his kingly
bearing or his haughty arrogance, or the thunderous fury of
his attack when pressed a bit too hard; and never has he lost
the healthy respect of those who have known him well, in
the past or the present. Whether or not all this is the result
of an intelligence possessed by these wild creatures, of the
same or a similar nature as humans, poses a very interesting
and important question.

Chapter XVIII

FROM DESERT TO ARCTIC WASTE

THE grizzly adapted himself to virtually every geographic area of western North America, from the hot and arid desert regions of the Southwest, throughout all the various types of mountain regions from Old Mexico to the Brooks Range in upper Alaska, and far out onto the bleak and blizzard-swept tundra of the Arctic. He has been able to thrive wherever man could live and in some places where even Indians starve. He has been the most vulnerable to civilization of all our big-game creatures and now survives in a natural state only where there still remain large areas of virgin wilderness. Such sanctuaries are left only in western Canada and Alaska, and those are steadily diminishing.

Environment not only plays a vital part in the normal survival of species, but it also strongly affects their physical development and their other characteristics. Living year after year and generation after generation reflects the conditions of life. Food is often a more important factor than climate, and sometimes the character of the food is more important than the quantity. There are certain regions, for example, where an unusually high content of lime or other properties in the food eaten by deer or other ruminants develops particularly large antlers, while in other areas certain chemical deficiencies produce poorly developed teeth among humans.

These areas are not necessarily large ones. Where food is plentiful and of proper character, the animals are big and healthy, without regard to the climate. On the Alaska Peninsula, where the climate is unusually inclement throughout all seasons of the year, the persistent abundance of salmon has produced the largest bears on earth today. On the other hand, we would hardly expect to find such monstrous ursines living in the high rocky regions of the nearby mountains, where the animals must do a lot of strenuous climbing in their daily existence.

Some conditions affect animals much more quickly than others. Animals grow a heavier coat to protect them from the cold whenever the temperature requires. I once took a short-haired English bulldog on a midsummer trip to the north coast of Siberia and up into the polar ice, where we encountered considerable snow and freezing temperatures during the two months of July and August, and my canine companion "Toughy" grew a surprisingly heavy coat of hair, such as he had never had before. He lost this heavy "overcoat" when I brought him back to New York in the fall. If he had remained in the Arctic for a large portion of his life, there would probably have been far greater physical changes; and these would have increased through succeeding generations of his offspring. Many contributing factors become involved in the adaptation of animals to their environment; and it is quite natural we should find a considerable variety among the grizzly bears over such widely diversified regions from Mexico to the Arctic.

The fundamental temperaments of grizzlies are, however, pretty much the same wherever they are found. Whether they are the small, yellow-colored variety of the hot Mexican border, the larger silvertips of Montana, or the lumbering brown monarchs of the tundra regions of the Far North, there is never a chance of mistaken identity when one starts trouble with any of the members of Old Ephraim's tribe. They can all be equally dangerous, all equally different in individual character, and all equally unpredictable as to what they will do under any given circumstances.

Before going more deeply into the many varieties of grizzlies which have been established by scientific investigation, something more general should probably be given regarding these bears of the great Northwest and some of the hunting methods peculiar to the region. The most of this writer's bear-hunting experiences have been north of the U. S.-Canadian border; and, as that area offers the only reasonable opportunity for the present-day hunter to get a grizzly as a trophy, it presents an added interest.

Spreading northward from the border, nature sprawls for more than two thousand miles in a broad panorama of rugged mountains and hills, expansive forests and fast-moving rivers. This great wilderness has proved a more natural habitat for the bears than it has been for man, and it will probably provide them a sanctuary for many years to come. The terrain is rough and difficult to travel, and the winters are long and bitterly cold. Survival here is often more difficult for humans than it is for the bears, to whom travel never seems to be a hindrance even in the most abominable sort of country; and they lie comfortably tucked away in their winter beds when starvation becomes a frequent visitor to habitations of the hardy natives. That, of course, is the whole idea of hibernation—an escape from the hazards of survival when food is extremely difficult to get—but neither the red man nor the white man has ever been able to accomplish this very smart feat.

The Peace River country was long famous for its large number of bears—black, brown, cinnamon, and grizzly. It was the most-talked-about game district when I first went into the Northwest in 1913 as a teen-age young man. One of the old characters with whom I lived for a time in a little log cabin at the end of a mountain trail on the upper North Thompson had spent several years far up the Peace, and the stories he told me of that vast land of game have never been forgotten. Moose—caribou—deer—geese—cranes—swans—ducks—

grouse—fine fishing—and, best of all, the bears. Things have changed up there now, but it was a hunter's paradise for a good many years after the turn of the century.

The Hudson's Bay Company ran a big stern-wheeler river steamer up and down the stream during the summer months. She was known as the *Peace River;* and what happened as almost routine occurrence on this famous old boat is strongly remindful of earlier days on our Western Plains, when the paying passengers on the old steam trains amused themselves by shooting buffalo from the open windows as they moved slowly across the open country. Sitting on the deck of the *Peace River,* with one's feet cocked on the rail and a mug of coffee handy, the upcountry passengers amused themselves by shooting bears. They were mostly blacks and browns, to be sure, but now and then someone got a grizzly; and everyone knew there were plenty of the latter farther back in the mountains.

When the berries were ripe, the sport was best. At the beginning of each trip someone was sure to ask the boat's skipper, Captain Gullion: "How many will we see this trip, Cap?" A serious question this, which always received its due consideration before any prognostication was made. "Oh . . . eighteen, twenty, guess. . . ." But it was never the "best season" for bears, and the rattling old *Peace River* never seemed to be at the right spots at exactly the right time of day.

"When'll we see the first one, Cap?" was the second question sure to follow. "Right after supper, I guess," was Gullion's routine reply; and then, with an extra twinkle from under his bushy gray eyebrows, he was equally sure to add: "Of course . . . if you're in any hurry, guess I kin arrange matters a little earlier."

If the questioner happened to be a cheechako, making his first trip up the river, the skipper would press the matter a bit further. "All these bears up here know me pretty well, you see . . . and all I have to do is give 'em the word . . . and out they come." To the uninitiated this was always considered a bit of legpulling bunk. But those who knew would just join the skipper in a little chuckle. "Poor tenderfoot. They've got a thing or two to learn up here . . . and old Cap Gullion'll give 'em the first lesson."

The *Peace River's* skipper was a very methodical man and never in a hurry about calling out his bears to be shot at by even the most important passengers. But, when Cap left the supper table, all the old-timers left after him . . . while the less informed might loiter at the table to talk about bears over a second mug of coffee.

"*Whistle blows! Cap's calling his bears!*" Then *whang! bang!* The echo of heavy rifleshots went rolling in reverberating echoes out through the quiet of the evening. "*You got 'im, pardner!*" . . . and the clang of a signal bell brought the rattling stern-wheeler's paddles to a grinding drag. There might be other shots . . . and shouts of "*get over a boat!*" or "*stand by to pick up!*"

By this time the cheechakos knew what Cap had meant about calling his bears. They might have been too late for the first bombardment, but they'd stand wide-eyed and watch the half-breed deck hands row hurriedly ashore and drag the hulk of a bear down to the river's edge and wrestle it into the rowboat; or, if the bear had taken to the water from one of the little islands, they'd crowd to see a line made fast and stare while the capstan hoisted the dripping bear into the air and onto the deck.

The Peace River is about as wide as the Hudson in the Catskills, most of its 580 navigable miles northeast from the edge of the Canadian Rockies to Lake Athabaska; and from early summer well into the colorful fall the banks and islands are almost one continuous berry patch—from the strawberries in June to the saskatoons of September. Berries are a favorite food of all bears, for nothing quite equals them for producing all that extra fat they need for the long winter sleep. The bears came down from the hills and mountains, from as much as a hundred miles away, to feast in the land of plenty along the banks of the Peace. From early evening until the sun climbed up to shine again from the eastern sky there was hardly a sizable berry patch along this virgin river of the North that did not have a bear of some kind with his lips all stained from the sweet red juice. Their trails were beaten into the rich soil like cowpaths in an Iowa pasture, leading up to day beds in the cool shelter of the spruce and poplars; but they all came down when the heat of the day was past, some swimming out to the islands, and all intent upon the single purpose of filling their big stomachs with the luscious berries, night after night, until they were so fat it made them puff to climb the hills.

Those who have watched a big bear at work in heavily fruited berrybushes, in some remote place in the wilderness, know what an intent harvester he can be. He is a picture of blissful contentment in action, as he slouches back on his broad haunches and, with slow, methodical swings of right and left paws, gathers the berrybush tops to his mouth as a kind of cutting box, the chomping, smacking sound of his gatronomic happiness keeping him quite oblivious to all else in life. But the shrill, piercing blast of the chesty river boat's whistle, so suddenly shattering the evening quiet which hung over the Peace, and its rattling echoes bounding around against the timbered hills, was like a hundred devils swooping down to attack. It sent the bears into instant panicky flight, to get somewhere else than where they happened to be at the moment. Those on the islands generally plunged into the river to get to the shore, and those on shore sometimes plunged into the water to find imaginary safety on the opposite side. Yes, Cap Gullion knew his bears; and, if there was anyone on board who knew how to use a rifle, it was a pretty sure bet there would be fresh bear liver or tenderloin for breakfast. It is reliably reported that as many as twenty-eight bears were seen within three hours from the deck of the *Peace River*— seven at one time—and seventy counted in a single four-day trip up the river.[124]

Shooting bears from the deck of the *Peace River* was about the most convenient form of hunting these animals that it was possible to find. But it was a very different matter for the Indians, half-breeds, and whites who lived in the back-country and had to get their bears in the old-fashioned ways. Still-hunting is fundamentally the same wherever it is practiced—with the feeding or traveling habits of the quarry playing an important part in the art of silent ambush. In the Northwest, however, life of the people of the country took on a somewhat different pattern than was followed in the southern and less rigorous climates. The principal pursuit was trapping fur-bearing animals, which is strictly a winter occupation and took the local inhabitants deep into the hills and mountains when the snow was deep and the weather extremely cold.

Because of the rugged character of the north country the natives have not had the benefit of wide use of the horse, as did the Indians and pioneers in the southern regions. Necessary transportation and search for game had to be done on one's own legs, with only the benefit of snowshoes and the added aid of dogs. Here, certainly, the dog was man's best friend. Sleds or toboggans were used throughout the more open country; but, where travel was too rough, the dogs carried packs on their backs, just as their masters did, and here the dogs have played a very important part in the hunting of bears, even in the sub-zero difficulties of midwinter.

No matter how tough the trip might be the whole family generally went along; and it was common practice to spend night after night in a siwash camp, with little more than a hurriedly improvised lean-to as a shelter, even for a mother's newborn baby.

The Indian dogs of the mountainous regions of the Northwest are for the most part lean and scrawny; but, like their masters, they are as tough as the native copper the Indians once pounded into hunting knives. Most of these canines in the earlier days had a high content of wolf blood in their veins, which was occasionally renewed with a fresh supply by their masters tying the bitches out in the woods at the proper times. Underfed and overworked for many generations, they are in appearance a mongrel lot, without style, habitually fighting savagely with their tails pulled up disgracefully between their bony legs. But they are, even today, extremely good hunters in a crude sort of way, which is the result of many generations of harsh necessity, and they often display a reckless abandon in the face of personal destruction, particularly when grizzly bears are involved. It is a strange paradox that the price of death is always the cheapest, where the difficulties of life are the most severe.

After a long and strenuous day of struggling over deep snow, through timber and thickets, up and down steep, rocky ridges and ravines, the end of the day brings a halt to the Indian or half-breed family. The dogs are relieved of their heavy packs; and, while the mother and kids go to work at setting up a lean-to shelter and bringing in wood for the night, the father will take the dogs to get food. The father may take a son along, if he has one old enough to be of any assistance whatever. They may have only one rifle between them—a rusty old .30–.30, or possibly just a little .22. All the cartridges they possess may be carried in one small pocket. What they find is not nearly so important as getting it, for living off the country day to day is a common practice. A moose or a caribou will be cause for celebration, but the winter den of a bear, whether black or grizzly, will supply the stringent necessities of existence. Nor are the dogs particular. They will take the trail of anything. There may be half a dozen of them in the pack. Some may be young ones who have never even smelled a bear. If they survive, they'll be smarter next time.

Grizzlies prefer to den up for the winter in a high rocky canyon or where they can find a cave that will make a bed-chamber remaining dry until the spring thaws have pretty well cleared the lower country. But, like the black bears, they will sometimes crawl under the upturned roots of a big tree or get under a thick pile of logs or brush where the winter snow will put a good roof over them. Wherever a bear is denned up, no matter how many feet of snow are covering him, his breath and body heat will always make a blowhole to the surface. This may be a few inches or more than a foot in diameter and usually is ringed by a coating of blue ice. The bear is a highly odorous creature, particularly when he has been lying in a winter den for a long time, and a good Indian dog will pick up the scent for a mile or more when the air currents are favorable.

The dogs will spread out and range over a wide area, making half circles a mile or so in radius, swinging back across their master's trail. Sometimes they have the misfortune of meeting up with one or more big timber wolves, which frequently results in a meal for the latter. If they find the den of a bear, the situation is not a simple one, particularly if it happens to be a grizzly.

No bear likes to be rudely routed out of his bed in the middle of a long winter sleep. The barking of the dogs may awaken Old Ephraim and cause him to push his head and shoulders out through the blowhole to find out what the rumpus is all about. His appearance may make the dogs so excited that one or more will rush in close enough to snap a nick or two out of the bear's ears. This generally brings him all the way out. Here's where the inexperienced dogs become wiser ones or dead ones. They may be overly zealous to show their disregard for danger and very suddenly find themselves being torn to pieces.

The bear is not apt to go very far, particularly if the snow is deep; and, when the hunter arrives on his snowshoes, there is a pretty good chance the family will enjoy bear meat for supper. In the case of a grizzly there is also a good chance that the mother left to set up the night's camp may have to lead the kids back to the village without assistance.

If the dogs are smart, they will keep well back from the blowhole, and the bear is apt to keep right on sleeping, probably thinking the noise is just a bad dream. Then it is the hunter's task to slip up close, hope to be able to peek inside and put a bullet into the sleeper's brain, or carefully make the hole large enough to do so. The bear may come rushing out at any juncture of this procedure; or, if the first shot does not kill the animal instantly, the chances of disaster are greater than the prospects of success.

When circumstances permit, heavy logs may be piled over the entrance of the den before the shooting begins. This is not always easy, or possible, when the snow is deep and unless there are two or more husky men in the party, although it has been a common practice among the natives from British Columbia to Alaska. A large grizzly may push his way out through most any barricade of logs that can be heaped over the doorway of his winter den.

In the mountainous regions of the Northwest the use of deadfalls for getting bears by the natives was more commonly practiced than in other regions, and they sometimes used snares of various kinds. But, good hunters that they were, the average Indian hunter generally left the grizzly alone when it was possible to get other game. No matter where he was found, or what size or variety he happened to be, Old Ephraim was a dangerous character and highly deserving of the respect which he was universally accorded.

Chapter XIX

BEARS OF THE SNOWSHOE COUNTRY

THAT bears can stand a lot of extremely cold weather, even in the Far North, was rather forcibly emphasized by an experience I had in Alaska. This occurred on November 19, 1916, practically the middle of winter, on the western end of the Alaska Peninsula. There was about twelve inches of snow on the ground, which is a lot of snow for that region, and the temperature was down toward zero. There was one great bear, however, who had not yet gone into his winter den. The incident has further significance in that this particular grizzly is the only one that ever made an unqualified charge upon me.

During my first two years in Alaska I spent the late fall and winter at the western end of the Alaska Peninsula, devoting my time entirely to hunting, collecting information, and traveling on a little fur-trading boat with Captain Charlie Madsen, the noted Alaskan and Siberian trader. I was only twenty-two years old at the time, living in a little native shack in the village of King Cove—having gotten there by working my way from Seward as a galley slave on the notorious tramp steamer, the *"Dirty" Dora*, under the none-too-pleasant dictates of her Negro cook. This was on my first scientific expedition to Alaska and the Yukon, collecting for a proposed natural-history museum at Ohio State University;

and my none-too-edifying situation was the result of having unwisely spent all my funds trying to climb Mount Logan in the Yukon during the previous summer. I had come to King Cove for the particular purpose of hunting "Kodiak grizzlies" and to spend the winter—with a total capital of fifty dollars. That's the way real adventures are born—but that's another story.

The snows had come and the time to hunt bears had passed. I had previously been fortunate (or lucky) in getting four of these biggest-bears-on-earth, all in one bunch and while hunting alone, and had settled down to collecting a group of caribou and the vast varieties of salt-water ducks and other sea and shore birds, and had become the one-man crew on Captain Madsen's little trading boat, when he made periodic trips out to the Aleutians and up into Bering Sea. There was no pay, but the amiable trader permitted me to hunt wherever he stopped to barter for fur. Between those rough but wonderful trips along the northernmost edge of the Pacific my little shack was a gathering place for many of the natives and the three white men of the village, as a result of which I learned much about such things as the gone-but-not-forgotten sea-otter hunting and the big grizzlies of the country.

One day two half-breed young men came to see me. They lived with their white father and Aleut mother in Thin Point Cove, near the western portal of Cold Bay between King Cove and the end of the peninsula. They had come in a big sea dory to get some supplies and new traps and paid me a visit for the purpose of telling about a monster bear that was interfering with their winter trapping. They had nicknamed him the "Bear Cat," and he was such a monster they were afraid to shoot him. They wanted me to go back with them and shoot the beast. "We show you him, anyday you want."

I talked to Madsen about it. He knew these bears about as well as anyone. Later, for many years until his recent death at the age of seventy-two, he was head of the Kodiak Guides Association and the best-known bear guide in all Alaska. But

Charlie only laughed. "There aren't any bears out this late," he assured me. "Those boys have been drinking too much 'sour-dough.'"

A couple weeks afterward Captain Madsen and I were on our way back from Unimak Island and the Bering Sea coast and got into a stormy blizzard that almost swamped our boat before we could make the nearest shelter. It happened to be Thin Point Cove. Even after we anchored inside it was so rough we had quite a time getting ashore in the rowboat. Thin Point Smith's boys were on the beach to pull us out of the breakers.

That evening as we sat in the warm half-underground bar-rabara, after a big meal of caribou steak and many mugs of strong coffee, one of the boys brought up the "Bear Cat." "Wanta go out in the morning and shoot him?" he asked. Madsen winked at me. But their father insisted we go. "That old bear has been there for years," he vouched. "Every winter . . . sometimes almost till Christmas time . . . and he's the biggest bear I ever saw." Madsen said something about waiting to see how the weather was in the morning, and we went to bed.

When we got up at daybreak the next day the snowing had stopped, but there was still too much of a gale to go to King Cove. So, with nothing else to do, we condescended to go out and shoot the "Bear Cat." It seemed rather silly, but the four of us put on snowshoes and started. In many places the snow in the ravines and drifts was more than five feet deep. We wore fur parkas, *muk-luks*, and heavy mittens, for it was bitterly cold and the wind blasted down from across Bering Sea, continually whipping the snow into our faces like cutting sand.

We headed for Frosty Peak, an extinct volcano that rose in a great white cone six thousand feet into the pale sky about fifteen miles away to the northwest. The boys were very specific as to the place where we would find the "Bear Cat." It was like going to see a prize domestic bull confined in a small fenced pasture. We soon began to see bunches of Grant's caribou, frequently passed flocks of ptarmigan, all white in their winter plumage, strutting about on the snow, and began to see fox tracks, some apparently made since we had eaten breakfast. "Plenty red fox," commented one of the boys, "but too many wolverine. All time steal bait . . . and eat foxes in traps."

As we moved steadily on to where the volcano rose abruptly out of the rolling lowlands, the boys repeatedly pointed out the ridge from which the great grizzly would be seen. They had lost none of their confidence and even began showing some reluctance to participate in the actual shooting.

Finally we climbed the last ridge. It was like sitting in a poker game, with all one's chips on the table, and waiting for the hands to be laid down. Before I was able to see the frozen stream that ran through the center of the wide ravine, I noticed steamlike vapor rising up against the snow on the opposite hillside. Then I saw where it came from. "Hot springs!" exclaimed Captain Madsen.

A thin cloud of vapor rose from a small section of the stream that was entirely free of ice. Quickly our eyes moved from that spot in wide sweeps up and down the ravine, without finding any bear. The boys seemed a little surprised not to see him.

"Are there salmon down there where those hot springs are?" asked Captain Madsen.

One of the boys grunted an affirmative reply. "That why bear go there." Then, as if to apologize for the "Bear Cat" not being where he should be, young Smith added: "Maybe he eat plenty salmon and go for sleep someplace."

We stood there while I used my binoculars to search up and down the ravine, and while I found no bear I quickly picked up what was unmistakably the fresh trail of some large animal along the near side of the stream. The dense alders, bare though they were, made it difficult to see. Madsen took the glasses to look. "Why, sure it's bear!" he exclaimed at the first glance. *"I'll be damned!"*

It wasn't long before we had made our way down through the alders and were beside the open water, where hot springs kept the ice melted for fifty feet or more. Along the bank we found the biggest bear tracks even Captain Madsen had ever seen. He had been there that morning. Freshly broken ice floated on the open water, and the remains of freshly eaten salmon lay bright in the crisp whiteness of the snow. The whole situation was now very clear to us. The warm springs which kept the ice melted attracted what salmon remained in the stream, and these were providing a source of food for this bear. He probably intended to stay out as long as this food supply lasted.

Following the tracks presented no problem, and the big bear had probably gone but a short distance. The trail had been frequently used, although the freshly fallen and wind-driven snow made the most recent tracks stand out boldly. Madsen lost no time in starting out to track down the "Bear Cat," although both of Thin Point Smith's boys seemed to feel they had now completed their part of the deal and announced they would go back up on the ridge and wait for us. Madsen overruled this, however, and they reluctantly brought up the rear as we moved single file along the tracks of what was possibly the largest grizzly on earth.

It was only a short distance to where the base of Frosty Peak rose rather abruptly, and the trail went up into a large area of thick alders, where it was unsafe to follow. We stopped in an open space and again I put my binoculars into use. But the thicket was so dense that I could not even follow the trail up the mountainside.

We had decided that this was to be my bear. I was to do all the shooting. If he got away, that was my bad luck. Of course, if he charged and I was unable to stop him, that was a different matter, which needed no previous understanding. Finally Madsen had one of the boys fire a shot up through the alders; and almost immediately the "Bear Cat" climbed up out of a tiny ravine, where he had been lying down, and stood in plain view. I distinctly remember having the impression that he looked "like a load of hay," silhouetted against the white snow—although he was fully 150 yards away.

"There's your bear. . . ." said Madsen calmly.

I sat down in the snow, to rest my elbows on my knees for a more steady aim of my .30–.40 Winchester, and fired. The first shot hit him, and he started off at an angle, headed for a big ravine to the south. The alders were so thick that I had to wait for another shot. My second one caught him in the rump, for he wheeled around, biting at the place where the bullet struck, and bellowed a loud growling woof. The Smith boys were moving farther away. My third shot hit him full in the chest . . . and with a snarling roar he came for us. I scrambled to my feet before firing again. The next thing I knew my gun was empty—I was fumbling desperately to find more shells and get them into the gun . . . and all the others were firing at the rapidly approaching bear. The speed with which big grizzlies can move through a tangle of alders is phenomenal—particularly when they are coming in your direction.

The most startling part of this situation was that our heavy bombardment did not make the slightest apparent effect upon this giant bear. After he started the charge he did not seem to even flinch at any of the shots. It gave me the very unpleasant feeling that all the shots were missing. But he finally came to an abrupt stop, dropping on his big belly and ramming his snout into the snow. He had evidently been killed instantly by a shot in the brain. He was no more than fifty feet away—which was entirely too close for a charging grizzly of his size and intentions. If it had not been for that one brain shot, which is extremely difficult on a charging bear with such a heavily boned skull, it is reasonable to assume that he would have come the remaining short distance and gotten one or more of us. Captain Madsen always gave me credit for firing the shot that stopped him—with the old reliable .30–.40 lever-action Winchester I was using at the time. Eleven other shots had hit him—all but two in the front part of his body—one squarely in the mouth. As a matter of incidental record, of the twenty-five grizzlies which I have personally killed or aided in shooting only one was killed with a single shot—an extremely fortunate hit in the eye, as the animal faced me at about thirty-feet distance.

We all settled down to have a smoke and wait awhile to make sure he was really dead. Then, with all guns loaded and ready, we went up into the edge of the alders where he lay. After due deliberation Captain Madsen estimated that his weight would go at least 1600 pounds.

The most important part of all this is the fact that this big bear had not gone into his hibernation den, in such cold winter weather, so long after all bears were supposed to have stopped wandering around.

About three months later the hide reached the taxidermist and the measurements were: eleven feet four inches from nose to tail, and ten feet six inches spread from front claw to front claw. He was one of the largest bears on record. I kept that skin for myself; and, after almost forty years, his great open-mouth countenance still looks down from the wall of my library, where these lines are written.

This is by no means the only instance when grizzly bears have been known to be wandering around in midwinter in the Far North. In a good many sections of the broad Northwest there are native and white trappers of long experience who tell of grizzlies wandering around in the sub-zero weather of mid-winter. They frequently refer to this as the "winter walking" of the bears. Vilhjalmur Stefansson refers to such an observation in his book *My Life with the Eskimos:* "While ascending the Horton River [near the mouth of Great Bear Lake] we saw at intervals the nearly fresh tracks of three Barren Ground Bears [a variety of grizzly] on December 29, 1910, and January 1, 1911, going along the river and over the shortest portages, approximately forty miles in approximately a straight line." (P. 521.)

Another well-informed writer, Arthur E. McFarlane, has somewhat more to say about this occasional peculiarity of the grizzly bears of the Northwest, as related in *Outing Magazine* of June 1911: "He [the grizzly] often leaves his den altogether and indulges in what is known locally as 'winter walking'. He may stop at the neighboring streams, break the ice if he can, and attempt to fish, though he rarely has anything to show for it but a coat of frozen snow. Some Peace River hunters will tell you that he goes in the water with the idea of putting on this ice-coat, that it keeps him warm! But sooner or later the walking grizzly is almost certain to direct his march toward the blow-holes of black bear land. And when he has found a blow-hole he goes to work to dig out his swarthy relative. The black bear is slow to grasp the situation at first, but when, getting the sleep out of his eyes, he does grasp it, he at least gives the grizzly a frightful grace before his meal."

On the other hand, in sections of the Southwest where the mild or entirely open winter permits finding food throughout the year, the bears that once inhabited the region did not find it necessary to hibernate. James Ohio Pattie, on his early travels through the Southwest, found grizzlies "in great numbers" in the Rio Grande Valley and other adjacent regions in November and December of 1824 and throughout the following month. One particularly aggressive grizzly is told about, which attacked Pattie's party of free trappers and was killed on the Gila near Cliff on January 31, 1825.[125]

Hibernation is strictly an alternative for living under conditions when food is impossible or difficult to procure.

Chapter XX

THE LONG WINTER SLEEP

THE processes of hibernation have intrigued both laymen and naturalists for centuries. It certainly is one of nature's most amazing phenomena. That the largest and most impressive of the earth's present-day carnivorous creatures should indulge in this strange subterfuge from the struggle to exist gives it considerable added interest. Since man was himself something of a primitive beast, it has given rise to some wild speculations and interesting beliefs. Some of the Indians' legendary associations with the hibernation of bears have already been cited; and such little bits of misbeliefs as the idea that the bears "suck their paws" as a means of subsistence have prevailed through many generations. That the ursines might occasionally have resorted to such idle doodling is entirely possible, although every naturalist now knows that it could have no nutritious purpose in carrying the animals through their long evasion of starvation. Nature, of course, has evolved a much more realistic and practical process.

Many of the earth's creatures, including man, have long practiced the harvesting and storing of surplus food to carry them through more difficult times. Even the most luxuriously kept city dog will bury a bone or extra piece of meat in his mistress's penthouse roof garden, just as he turns round and round on an oriental rug in the motions of padding down the grass to make a place to lie—following the instincts inherited from long ago. The birds and squirrels cache food for a leaner day and establish storehouses of winter supplies. Some of the smaller animals who hibernate in burrows in the ground beneath the snow provide themselves with accessible stores of nonperishable foods. But the bears had to find a different way of supplying the necessary nourishment for their large bodies through the long winter. Just how they learned the method which they have practiced for so many centuries is one of the many mysteries of natural history that man may never understand, although the process itself is, as usual with nature, very simple. They merely subsist on the surplus fat stored up in their own bodies, which is assimilated into their systems to provide the fuel for life, as natural necessity requires it. The deep layers of fat on the outside of their bodies also provide an extra blanket to keep them warm, and they lapse into a lethargic state of quiet half-consciousness, to reduce the fuel requirements. A benevolent nature has further provided a late summer and fall abundance of fat-producing foods, such as berries, nuts, salmon, and the like, and a bear's appetite to get them ready for the long hibernation.

One of the complicating phases of hibernation, and one which gives an even greater emphasis to the wonderful workings of nature, is the birth of young while the mother bear is still imprisoned in the winter den. The little ones arrive as much as two or three months before the mother leaves the winter quarters or is able to provide herself with any sustenance other than the fat stored up in her own body. There may be from one to four baby bears—usually two and rarely four. This is naturally an extra drain upon the mother. But here again is shown the simple and very realistic manner in which nature takes care of such situations. An Alaska brown bear, which may grow to weigh as much as 2000 pounds at maturity, weighs as little as 8 to 12 ounces at birth, is blind, almost hairless, toothless, and quite helpless—about the size of a skinned gopher.

Why are grizzly cubs so tiny when they are born? The answer is simple. The babies are born so very small so they will require but the least possible amount of nourishment from the hibernating mother, until she can get out of the den and find food to replenish her strength. The process of gestation and birth naturally requires an extra amount of that stored-up fat and the energy which it produces; and big, husky babies would require more than it would be practicable to produce under such stringent circumstances.

A number of grizzly cubs have been born in zoological parks, and some actual dates and weights have been recorded. There were two cubs born to a Rocky Mountain grizzly in the Bronx Zoo, New York City, on January 18, 1908. These were weighed by William H. Wright, author of *The Grizzly Bear:* "They were just twelve hours old when I arrived, and the two weighed one pound, that is, eight ounces each. They measured nine inches from nose to tail. The mother weighed about six hundred pounds."[126] Previously, on January 13, 1906, in the same zoo, another grizzly from Colorado gave birth to a cub weighing 18 ounces. Dr. William T. Hornaday, then the director, gives the period of gestation in this instance as "266 days, or from April 22nd to January 13th."[127] It will be noted that this period of gestation is almost identical in time to that of humans.

A further birth record was established as recently as February 7, 1953, when two cubs were born to a Kodiak bear in the Cleveland Zoological Park, Cleveland, Ohio; and Fletcher A. Reynolds, the director, informs me that at birth the male of these weighed 20 ounces and the female 24 ounces. At the end of one month the same baby cubs weighed 37 and 47 ounces respectively; at two months, 52 and 64 ounces; and at three months they weighed 5½ and 6 pounds each. Grizzly cubs, like human youngsters, lose their "baby teeth" quite early and these are replaced by a new set of permanent ones, which are at first as sharp as needles.

It will be noticed there is almost a month's difference in the date of birth of the Rocky Mountain grizzlies and those of the Kodiak, Alaska, mother. This can be taken as a pretty general criterion. The Alaskan cubs are born later, because the spring normally comes later in that northern latitude than it does in Colorado. Therefore the bears mate at a proportionately later date. How closely do the dates for cubs born in a zoo conform to those in a wild state? John Tee-Van, the present director of the New York Zoological Society, has answered this for me, in a letter dated May 28, 1953: "I would say that the birth dates in captivity correspond to what it would normally be in the wild." There is always a consistency to the programs laid down by nature, just as there is always a very realistic reason behind every rule to which wild creatures religiously conform.

Bears do not just suddenly decide to go into hibernation—walk into a den and plop down to suddenly go into a winter-long coma. It is possible they previously eat some special herbs to prepare the organs of their bodies for the long ordeal, and they may eat something in the nature of sleeping potion. Prior to retiring for the winter most bears show a lazy and sleepy disposition. I have noticed this and it is concurred with by other observers. M. P. Skinner emphasizes this in his book *Bears in the Yellowstone*,[128] based on his work as Roosevelt Field Naturalist in the park.

Before going into hibernation they sometimes sleep for a day or so and then come out to wander around a bit. A change to mild weather may bring them out; and it has already been cited that they sometimes come out in midwinter to make trips of considerable length. But usually, when they go into their private sleeping chamber, their drowsy condition increases, and the ultimate lethargy becomes more and more profound. Respiration becomes slower and slower—eventually so slight that it seems almost to stop. We know there is a certain amount of respiration, even in the deepest stages of hibernation, because of the icy rim and slight signs of rising vapor which are to be seen at the blowholes of the winter dens—a sign that water vapor and carbon dioxide at least are being given off—

although this may be due, in part at least, to the animal heat given off by the body. We also know, from examination of smaller animals in a state of hibernation, that the heart beats slower, all the senses become less and less acute, and the unused digestive organs shrink. The strangest part of all is the fact that little or no mental anguish or physical emaciation results from hibernation. In some regions of their northern range the grizzly bears may remain in the winter den, without coming out or tasting any food or liquid whatever, for as long as seven months or even more.

It may be of further interest to here make another comparison with humans. The average person, without any food or water, will starve to death in only seven to ten days; and a person existing on water alone will last about 45 to 50 days. Without water—and bears in hibernation do not taste water— a man's kidneys will shut down and produce quick disaster; and most of his other organs will react in a similar manner, including severe mental repercussions. How do the bears do it for as long as seven months, year after year, as one of life's regular routines? This is just another animal ability which man is not only unable to accomplish but equally unable to understand.

From birth to death the grizzly lives an exceptional life. They have been born to undisputed power in their own natural environment through so many thousands of generations that its dogmatic influence has become an imperishable characteristic. They normally live much longer than most of the land animals with whom they share their environment, for they are a possible exception to the harsh rule of nature which dictates that wild creatures shall not die from the placid consequences of old age. If there is any exception to this omnipotent law of the wilds, it certainly is the grizzly. Not only is he invulnerable to all of life's hazards, except the artificial weapons of man, but he has a cast-iron constitution. As a species, they are just about nature's healthiest children. Susceptible to practically no physical disease or lesser ailments, they have the natural ability of thriving on a remarkably wide variety of diets. Although carnivorous by physical evolution, they are widely omnivorous in adaptability. About the only feeding habit which they do not turn to, upon necessity, is browsing on the leafless frozen twigs of trees and the needles of evergreens. Thus they generally live to a ripe old age.

Most observers agree that the normal life of a grizzly who avoids a disastrous encounter with man is around twenty-five to forty years, possibly longer. They reach maturity around seven or eight years although generally continue to grow larger and heavier, depending on food supply and other advantages of environment.

The records of bears kept in zoological parks give us something of a criterion in this respect. While such an existence provides an animal with ideal circumstances so far as abundance of food and complete protection from enemies, climatic difficulties, and the like, there is nevertheless a serious handicap in being deprived of the benefits a life of freedom, activity, fresh air in the forests and mountains, and so many other things which make existence worth while for a creature so deeply imbued with liberty-loving instincts as the grizzly bear.

On March 22, 1909, a grizzly was chloroformed in New York City's Central Park Zoo that had been obtained from Barnum's Circus in 1884 and had been confined in the menagerie pits through twenty-five years. Just how old this bear was when it left the circus is not known, and it might have survived considerably longer. Two other records are considerably more conclusive. These were Alaska brown bears in the New York Zoological Society's Bronx Zoo. One born in the spring of 1903 died July 8, 1924, at the age of twenty-one and a half years; the other arrived as a first-year cub in 1922 and died September 18, 1946, at about twenty-four and a half years. But in the matter of age we cannot be too hasty in drawing conclusions from any such records as these—for, like humans, some bears just naturally live longer than others, no matter what the circumstances of life may be.

Chapter XXI

A WHOLE SEASON WITH GRIZZLIES

It had long been my desire to spend a whole season right out in a wild country where there were so many big grizzlies that they could be watched and studied every day, under unmolested circumstances—from the time when the first of them came out of the hibernation dens until the snows of another winter came to call them for another long, mysterious sleep. I realized this privilege in 1922.

I left New York City on December 15, 1921, bound for the Bering Sea coast of the Alaska Peninsula, crossed the Alaska Range by log team, arriving on February 18, 1922, at the trading post of Captain John Cunningham on Herendeen Bay, the south arm of Port Moller Bay, on the icebound coast of Bering Sea at about the middle of the peninsula. I took along a gun principally as a precaution for self-defense; and I took along a motion-picture camera to make a record of the story of the biggest of the grizzlies. My going so early was to have plenty of time to search for winter dens before the snow began to melt and to be well organized in the bear country when the first ones came out in the spring.

When I arrived at Herendeen Bay, I hoped that some native or white trapper might be able to direct me to the winter den of one of the giant bears—preferably that of a female with newborn cubs. But I had no such good fortune. Most of the trappers went to their respective territories long after the bears had disappeared; there were no foxes to be caught high up in the rocky altitudes where the dens were located; and none of these men had any particular interest in bears, either in or out of dens.

The bay was frozen solid, which made traveling by dog team very convenient; and I made a number of trips to various places along the coast, searching for bear dens and getting acquainted with the winter habits of fox, caribou, and wolverine.

By May 11 the ice was completely broken up in the bay and the strong spring tides had carried most of it out into Bering Sea. The weather was still pretty "dirty" and there were large fields of slush ice moving in with the tide, although Captain Cunningham had gotten his cabin gas boat into the water and we set out for the head of Port Moller Bay to the east; and it was on May 14 that I finally found the first bear.

It was in a big valley, with high, broken ridges running along both sides and dense alder thickets liberally covering large areas halfway up the mountainsides. A good place for bear, but a tough place to find them.

The day was almost gone and we were well up the valley when a small bunch of caribou inspired us to get some meat. Having come to the conclusion there were no bear in the country, or luck was badly against us, I shot one of the caribou. Running over to catch and bleed the animal—to avoid firing another shot—I was suddenly attracted by a small, bawling sound and stopped to listen.

"*That's a bear cub!*" Captain Cunningham called out to me. As I stood there listening and searching the hillside with my eyes, I saw a big bear racing across an open space about two hundred yards up the mountainside and as far again up the valley. It was a particularly black-colored bear, almost like a dark Montana silvertip, and its luxuriant coat of hair fairly floated with each lopping stride. Too far away for a good chance of bringing down, I nevertheless sent a shot flying in a carefully calculated direction. I fired about three shots before the bear disappeared in the alders.

As Captain Cunningham came up to where I stood, the cub could still be heard, now and then bawling from somewhere up on the mountainside.

"That old bear has *cached* her cub up there and took off for a safer place. . . ." remarked my companion.

Cap stood trying to determine where the cub was, while I hurried over to quickly gut the caribou. Then we climbed up through the alders to find the baby bear which its mother had left behind. The cub was finally found and gave us about the toughest chase of the kind I ever had. He was just a baby, but he could go through the bare alders, and climb up over the rocks, a lot faster than we could. At last, however, we caught him. This cub was about three and a half months old, and I'm sure he did not weigh more than eight or nine pounds.

We waited for the mother to come back, until it was too dark to see sufficiently well to shoot, and during this time we speculated on just why the Old Lady had raced away, leaving her newborn behind. At first I had the feeling that this mother bear had disgracefully abandoned her baby. But now I am even more certain that she had another and much more honorable purpose. The first law of nature is the law of self-preservation, and the preservation of newborn offspring comes pretty much in that same category with most animal mothers. What may sometimes appear to be fearful or undignified behavior is in fact an example of wise judgment. Animals are extreme realists. It is not always wisest or safest procedure to stand and fight. For an animal to hide her baby, or babies, and make a hasty departure is a wise practice among wild creatures. Usually the babies, whether bears or birds, stay silent and motionless, no matter what happens. In this particular instance the cub did not follow the rules. If he had kept silent, we would never have known he was up there on the mountainside, and his mother would have returned to teach him many more wise things about life.

Ten days later I started down the Bering Sea coast in Captain Cunningham's twenty-eight-foot gas boat. The sea was free of ice, but the rough weather of early spring made it a boat trip I was mighty thankful to finish. We had more of a load than the rules of good judgment allow. The captain had a young Nome Eskimo for a helper; and we took along X. B. Jones, my squaw-man dog-team driver, his Eskimo wife, five big Malemute sled dogs, and their summer supplies of grub. To say that the little boat was crowded and overloaded is an understatement. Nor was there a single place to find shelter all the way from Port Moller to Izembeck Bay—about a third of the entire length of the Alaska Peninsula. How we ever made that trip without a catastrophe is an indication of the good luck that has always been mine in all of my adventurous experiences. Making the same trip the next year cost my good friend his life—only parts of the wreckage of the boat being found strewn along the barren beach. Maybe the bears got his body.

Satisfied the bears were still up high, on June 2 I left my heavy movie camera on the boat and we took off from the western end of Izembeck Bay and climbed up into the mountains. On the second day we located four bears, all lying in a bunch on a large snow field that completely covered the head of a wide basin near the highest part of the mountains. It was a big female and her three husky yearlings. Mother bears follow the practice of taking their cubs into the family hibernation den through the next winter after their birth; and they usually travel with her until the approach of the second winter after they come out as newborn youngsters. Mature bears very rarely mate more often than every other year. This particular family was lying near the end of a well-beaten trail, the opposite end of which was at the entrance of the winter den in a cave at the base of a sheer rocky cliff.

Here was another interesting side light on the routine lives of these big grizzlies. That well-beaten trail, which was about thirty or forty yards in length and ran out parallel to the den, was their "limbering-up" place. When they first come out of hibernation they often spend a few days just walking back and forth to get the kinks out of the muscles of their bodies after the long months of lying dormant. They do not seem in any particular hurry to get down in the open country to get food. Back and forth they amble, very leisurely, stretching and yawning, maybe going into the den or sprawling on the snow to rest and snooze. Sometimes they make short trips down to the lower country, to dig a few "medicinal roots," such as the skunk cabbage, which evidently reacts on their innards and prepares the organs of their bodies to return to normal functioning. The most amazing thing about this is the fact that they do not appear skinny and emaciated after living for possibly seven months without a single taste of food or water. Their entire bodies, from the hair on their hides to the bones of their skeletons, have continued to grow in a normal manner—entirely sans food and entirely sans water.

I decided to take this big female for a museum group, and it was decided necessary to make a long, roundabout climb that would bring me directly above where they lay. The shooting which took place is unimportant. What followed, however, is well worth repeating. The big one was hit several times and was finally considered "dead." But the long wall of snow between us and the bear was so steep and so high that we did not dare take the risk of going directly down. Instead we had to make the long trip back the way we had climbed up.

When we eventually reached the place where we had first seen the bears, a big surprise awaited us. All four of the bears had disappeared. The old lady had not only regained consciousness, but she had climbed straight up that high snow wall which we had considered too steep to come down. The first thing we saw was the bold, bloodstained trail leading upward and disappearing over the top, where I had stood to do the shooting. It seemed incredible, but there was the unmistakable evidence.

Hurriedly we retraced our roundabout course once again,

with the hope that we might follow the trail and overtake this amazing bear. That she was badly wounded there was no doubt whatever. I had hit her at least five times—once after we were sure she was dead.

The day was pretty well gone when Jones and I reached the trail on top of the high ridge. Still amazed at what had happened, we took off hurriedly to track her down. We followed the trail until it was too dark to continue and then went back to the boat. We spent all the next day on the trail, but we never saw her again. In spite of the fact that this big bear had just come out of a long winter in hibernation and not tasted food for so many long months, and the added fact that she had been mortally wounded, she had performed a physical feat which, under even normal circumstances, I would have considered impossible.

Chapter XXII

DOWN TO THE SEA FOR SALMON

THE winter-to-winter season that I spent living among the big grizzlies of the Alaska Peninsula provided one of the rarest privileges that could possibly be hoped for by a serious observer. The most of the time I had but one companion, Andy Simons, the famous Alaskan bear guide, who came out from Seward in early June and met me on Unimak Island. We devoted the entire season to watching, studying, and filming the bears. We adapted our daily lives to that of the bears—doing the most of our sleeping in the middle of the days—and most of the time from afternoon to morning we were prowling around the streams where the bears were catching salmon. There were times when we spent as much as a whole week without any tent or blanket, with only our little collapsible canvas canoe to upturn as an improvised shelter from the cold rain; and we had very little to eat. I doubt very much if any individual, in the last hundred years at least, has observed as many grizzly bears, under such ideal circumstances for observation, in a similar period of time. As previously indicated, I saw a total of 197 grizzlies on that trip, 188 of them within forty days, and most of these at unusually close range and, unmolested, going about all their various personal pursuits. I was as close as twelve feet to one and within less than fifty feet of several.

The more journalistic aspects of these and other of my earlier bear-hunting experiences have been recounted in my book *Alaska Bear Trails*,[129] which was published twenty-four years ago. Now, looking back with the benefit of years of further experience and thoughtful retrospect, I am far more interested in the motivations and meanings behind those incidents than the mere excitement which they produced.

One of the early and best lessons I learned from the Cree Indians in British Columbia was that the successful hunter or trapper is the person who finds out where his prospective game is regularly obtaining his groceries. To kill, trap, photograph, or study animals you must be familiar with their daily habits, and the quest for food is fundamental. Bears are no exception. They generally follow definite patterns in their feeding habits. Scientifically classified as carnivorous, they relish widely diversified foods, such as meat of any kind, from tiny mice to whales, and in any state, from freshly killed to ripe carrion, fish, ants, berries, honey, grass, butterflies, roots— in fact, about anything and everything that red man or white man will put in his mouth, and many things that no human would consider eating. This is true of the grizzlies from Mexico to the Arctic, and they adapt their feeding habits to the seasons and to the sources of food available in the districts where they reside. Extremely varied though their menu may be, bears concentrate on any particular course when the supply is sufficient.

The feeding habits of the big bears on the Alaska Peninsula follow a very definite pattern, particularly where they are not disturbed by human enemies. A good many of the grizzlies I observed had never had any previous contact with a human, which gives added interest to some of the things they did when we happened to meet.

There seems to be a difference of opinion as to which of the bears, if any, habitually come out of the hibernation dens first. Some observers insist that the old males are the first to leave the winter sleeping quarters. Mr. M. P. Skinner, the Roosevelt

Field Naturalist in Yellowstone Park, states in his book *Bears in the Yellowstone:* "The pregnant female bear retires earlier, sleeps sounder and is apt to come out later. . . ." (P. 102.) Others agree with this. My own experience, however, has been to the contrary, and natural logic seems to support my observations. The physical processes of gestation and giving birth to offspring certainly require more life-sustaining nourishment for the mother than for a dormant male. It would certainly seem that a female who had brought forth would be far more inclined to get out of the winter quarters and find food to supplement the stored-up fat in her own body at the earliest possible time. My experiences on the Alaska Peninsula, and those with whom I have talked, strongly indicate that females with newborn young are the first to come out and the old males are normally the last ones to leave their hibernation beds. This cannot, however, be taken as an unalterable rule. In fact, there are extremely few if any hard-and-fast rules which do apply to grizzly bears—any more than there are with human behavior.

Within a few days after coming out of the winter den they seek out the hillsides having a southern exposure, where the new spring grass first makes its appearance. When a patch of green grass is found they will graze upon it like a cow in a pasture, and for a time this will constitute about ninety-eight per cent of their diet. The other two per cent will be ground squirrels or whatever carrion may be found left by the melting snow—the carcass of a caribou or of a fox that had been skinned by a trapper during the winter. But grass is the principal diet for one to two months. They have occasionally been called "the great grass-eating bear."

The real feast of these big bears, however, is provided by the salmon that come in from the sea. The Pacific salmon come into the fresh-water streams in the late spring or early summer of each year in successive "runs" or waves, usually beginning the latter part of June and continuing almost until September. These salmon go up to the streams to spawn, sometimes so far up the valleys there is hardly enough water to cover their bodies. They come in by the millions. I have seen many places where they seemed to be like sardines in a can.

The first run of salmon seldom comes at the same time each spring. There may be two or three weeks' difference in the date, sometimes more. But the bears seem to know very accurately when it will be. At the proper time all bear tracks will be leading down to the shore of Bering Sea. At night they may wander along the sandy beach, with the big waves rolling in to burst in white spray and thunder in unending monotony and the chill salty mist wetting their heavy spring coats. They will pick up an occasional dead codfish or crunch the shells of giant spider crabs that the storms sometimes wash ashore by the many thousands. If they find the remains of a seal or sea lion, maybe the victim of a killer whale, they will enjoy a special meal. If a whale should come ashore about this time, it's pretty certain the bears will congregate around it. An Aleut once told me of finding a large whale left high and dry on the beach at low tide, and as he approached three bears came plunging out from the great cavity that once had been the animal's stomach.

Sometimes the salmon seem reluctant to leave the salt water and begin their migration up the streams to spawn and die. A bay may be literally alive with them, although not one has gone into fresh water. The air will be permeated with the pungent smell of the fish, and the bears waiting at the mouths of the streams will become impatient and irritated. I have on several occasions seen them wade out into the bay and try to catch their first fish in deep open water. The first time I saw the "Three Musketeers" these three three-year-olds were romping and chasing each other along the beach near the mouth of a stream at the eastern end of Izembeck Bay. I was watching through my binoculars and could see them occasionally stop at the water's edge to sniff the tantalizing fishy air. Finally all three waded out into the bay until they had to stand on their hind feet, with the water up to their armpits, and they splashed about in a comical display of trying to catch the big salmon that swam about them. At times they were completely submerged. They certainly were too smart to think they would be very successful, but they surely appeared to be having a lot of fun in trying.

After spending a few days on Unimak Island and seeing only a few bears, we had gone on Captain Cunningham's boat through the Isanotski Straits into the North Pacific and up to the head of Cold Bay. We packed my heavy Akeley camera equipment and our meager supplies across the narrow neck of tundra to establish a base camp on one of the streams that runs into the east end of Izembeck Bay. Here Andy Simons and I were to make our headquarters for the rest of the summer and into the fall. Here we had a little silk tent and sleeping bags; but for the long trips beyond, in our collapsible canvas canoe and overland, our only protection from the most miserable of the weather was the clothes on our backs.

It was a wonderful feeling as we drifted down that stream toward the coast. Here was the home of the great Alaska brown bear. The flat tundra stretched for miles in all directions, broken by large areas of wet marshes, and covered with "niggerheads" which made traveling abominable where the ground was solid. Sluggish streams, deep or underlaid with bottomless mires, wound back and forth. To the southwest rose the familiar barren cone of Frosty Peak, where I had gotten my biggest bear five and a half years before. To the east rose the rugged volcanic mountains which form the backbone of the Peninsula—up into the valleys of which we were destined to spend many unpleasant but wonderfully fascinating days. There was not a tree much higher than a man's head for more than six hundred miles—only the gnarled tangles of alders. It is one of the most bleak and foreboding lands on earth. But it teems with life of its own peculiar kind—ducks, geese, swans, snipe, plover, and other water and shore birds in great variety and abundance; ptarmigan, eagles, fox, wolverine,

Barren Ground caribou, and, surmounting all, the great bears which were the purpose of our being there.

Although it was the beginning of July, the first run of salmon had not come in. Along the shore we could see the big tracks of the bear, all leading toward the sea, and we followed them.

The atmosphere was a mixture of the musty aroma of swamps, wet grass, salty sea air with a dash of fish, and the fragrance of flowers. There were acres of ground where the lilies of the valley were so profuse it looked like snow and smelled more like a perfume shop than the bleak tail end of the North American continent. One of the first bears we saw was a big fellow sitting in the middle of one of these magnificent areas of flowers. We put our canoe into the bank and watched him with binoculars as he sat lazily, running his long claws slowly through the stems of the blossoms, as if trying halfheartedly to pick a few. There is no doubt whatever that he could smell and was fully aware of the fragrance, and I am inclined to think he enjoyed it.

It was a little late in the season for mating, although we saw one instance of this. It was also a little early in the afternoon for the bears to be out. But mating is a circumstance which causes bears as well as men to frequently ignore the routine principles of life.

Where the stream swung far to the east it came close to some rolling hills that extended with gradually increasing altitude back to the high mountains, which were still liberally spotted with patches of snow. Drifting quietly along in our small canoe, Andy's keen eyes picked up a big bear lying on the grass at the edge of the alders; and, turning into the bank, we put our glasses into use. There was not just one bear but four, and they were all big ones. As we watched, a husky fellow of unusually dark brown color got up and walked leisurely to a much lighter one that seemed to be lying in the center of the circle. No sooner had the dark one started, however, than two others got up and intercepted him. With our glasses we could see that this was not a friendly encounter. The hair went up on their backs; their mighty heads swung back and forth with snouts twisting forward and lips stuck out in the unmistakable gesture of pugnaciousness. The third one also joined the threatened imbroglio. The fourth member of the gathering continued to lie indifferently.

"That's a female . . . with three males after her," chuckled Andy. And so it was. We lay at the top of the bank and watched them.

These bears are by no means monogamous. It is a common occurrence for a female to have more than one prospective husband at the same time. They apparently like to play hard to get, and when two or more males join in the affair there is apt to be rough competition. An Aleut told me of watching a fight between two big bears who had challenged each other's mating prerogatives. It developed into such a bloody battle that one of the contestants was actually killed and the theoretic winner was so badly ripped and torn that he was unable to enjoy the fruits of his victory. I regret to make the further report that the native shot the survivor—but, finding his hide too badly torn to make a mattress for the bunk in his barrabara, he left the poor Lothario where he fell.

Andy and I made a well-planned stalk on these four grizzlies, carrying my heavy camera in a wide swing up through the thick alders, and cautiously approached the spot where we had hoped to get some pictures. But they had all disappeared when we got there. The wind had been in our favor, and we followed every precaution, but some back draft of an air current had probably carried a warning that sent them all off through the wide expanse of thick alders to some other rendezvous.

Returning to the canoe, we decided to take a position at the bend of the stream and wait for the possible reappearance of these bears. My camera was set up on the bank and camouflaged with the tall dead grass.

The afternoon was settling into dusk when we saw a bear

coming over the bald ridge off to the south. It was quite apparent that this was not one of the original four. He was headed straight toward us, and the prospects of getting some pictures seemed unusually good. After a little while, however, Andy made a disconcerting comment: "That old bear is going to cross our tracks. That may spoil things for us."

It had been at least three hours since we made the stalk on the romantic tête-à-tête of the four bears, and this new bear's course would take him where we crossed an open space which was heavily carpeted with deep moss, in which the tread of our shoepacks had left no more of a track or visible sign than if it had been rubber or solid rock. And the moss was dry. Could he possibly pick up the unexpected scent?

There wasn't the slightest doubt when the bear came to where we had walked. He stopped as suddenly as though he had run into a wire fence. We were watching through binoculars. For a few moments he stood motionless. Then his big brown snout began to shift about as he sniffed the air. It finally was lowered to where he could sniff the moss in front of him, and he gave the telltale scents a very careful inspection. Very methodically he sniffed along in both directions for a short distance. He was determining which way we had gone, and there is no doubt that he correctly determined the answer. Apparently having found out all that he needed to know, he rose up slowly to his full height on hind legs, facing in the direction we had traveled. His nose swayed back and forth in the air for additional clues. Then he dropped down on all fours and, swinging around, started running back in the direction from which he had come. He had not stopped the hasty retreat when he disappeared from our view over the top of the bald ridge.

Chapter XXIII

THE FEAST OF IVAN

W<small>HEN</small> the salmon start coming into the fresh-water streams, they come like tidal waves. Within a few hours every estuary on the bay may be chocked to the surface, as the "silver horde" begins the last short part of its long journey to spawn and die. Not one of the millions that come in will ever return to the salty sea. And here the feast of the bears begins.

After the first run of salmon comes in, the Alaska brown bear eats little else, and a full-grown bear will devour a hundred pounds or more from dusk to dawn, day after day and week after week. As the fish move upstream, the bears move with them, picking out their own favorite fishing spot, to remain close by and come out of the alders regularly every afternoon to renew the abundant repast and eventually move on to a convenient source of supply that is nearest to the winter den.

Once the bears had settled to their fishing, my problem of getting pictures was considerably simplified, and we soon found a successful formula. Before going near a good fishing section of a stream we would carefully observe the daily movements of the bears through our binoculars, from some elevated lookout position as far away as possible. We would watch through the afternoon to find out where each bear came down to the stream and again in the morning to make sure where they went to bed down for the day. We might spend two evenings and two mornings on the lookout. Where the bears had not been disturbed, they would often have their day beds only a couple hundred yards from where they fished; and they would regularly follow the same routine day after day.

When we were certain where the big hairy fishermen were quietly snoozing, and where they would probably amble down the well-trodden trail to the stream, we would slip out during midday to improvise a blind and await their return. It was not just as simple as that, for the direction of the wind and the sunlight and a position of photographic advantage were important factors. There was also a little matter of weather. Time after time all the circumstances seemed to be in our favor, only to have a dense fog and cold rain keep drifting in from Bering Sea. There were occasions when we built a blind in the pleasant warmth of sunshine and the dirty weather closed in just before the bears came out. And, once the bears were made aware of our presence, there was nothing to do but move on to a new location.

We were soon capable of telling a good fishing place as far away as we could see it with binoculars. The bears always picked the "riffles," where the water was shallow and ran over a wide rocky bottom. In these places the water might be only a couple inches deep and the salmon would almost have to crawl upstream through the rocky obstructions. Every minute of the day there would be fish going past these riffles; sometimes they were literally alive with squirming, splashing fish of up to fifteen or more pounds in weight, and it was no problem whatever for a bear to walk out and pick them up, one after another, until his voracious appetite was satisfied. And the bears invariably came down to dinner so regularly each afternoon that we could almost set our watches by their appearance. They kept right on feeding until morning.

It has long been a popular belief that grizzly bears hook the salmon out onto the shore with a swipe of their long-clawed paws. That they are capable of this sort of fishing, and occasionally do so, is beyond doubt; but the more normal method is just to walk out onto a shallow place and pick up the salmon in their teeth. Carrying it out onto the shore, they will strip off the flesh as dexterously as an Eskimo woman using an *oolo* knife. Laying the salmon on its side, the bear will hold it securely with the claws of one paw while he cleverly tears off the whole fillet with his teeth; then, turning it over, he will repeat the procedure—leaving little more than the head, tail, and bony skeleton. Often they will crouch down on their broad brown bellies and take it quite leisurely, nibbling and using the back of a big paw much in the fashion of a plate to catch the crumbs before they fall into the sand.

The feast of the bears was also a feast for the sea gulls. There was generally a flock of the noisy sea birds around the bears' fishing places, awaiting their return. They would hop about from rock to rock, trying to peck out the eyes of the salmon as they swam by. But they were really waiting for the bears. Often these gulls would become impatient and fly, squawking, over the spots where the hairy fishermen were still snoozing in their day beds in the alders, raucously urging them to get started at catching salmon. They would follow a bear down the stream, flying noisily around him and hovering close until the skeleton of a salmon was left on the shore. Then the birds would swoop in and fight over the remains. The gulls were like bird dogs in keeping us informed as to where the bears were and when they were coming down out of the alders.

Andy and I would stay in our blind until it got too late to make pictures. Even in the fog and rain we would wait just to watch the bears, and there was hardly a time we were not rewarded with some new experience of excitement, amusement, or revelation about these fascinating creatures. When we saw one whom we recognized from previous observations, it was like seeing an old friend, and we talked about them in much the same manner. We learned that they were the most cautious when they first came out and their boldness increased as it became darker. Very frequently we had them less than seventy-five feet away, sometimes more than one at a time. There were occasions, however, when we suddenly realized it was almost dark and there were far too many grizzlies prowling around entirely too close, and we made a hasty retreat. Wet, cold, and miserable, we would make our way wearily but happily back to the meager shelter of an over-turned little canvas canoe, with only the wet moss to lie on to get some rest, or maybe just eat a little cold food (we never built a fire when in good country) and eke out the endless night by sitting huddled in the rain and periodically prancing up and down to get warm. It was in the middle of the days that we got our best rest and sleep—just as the bears did.

One evening, as we made our way through the rain to a place of retreat, we ran onto a big bear who gave us a bit of excitement. It was almost dark, due to the heavy, low-hanging clouds, dense fog, and rain. We were traveling along the bank of a stream and saw this old fellow leisurely eating a salmon directly ahead on our course.

"Aw, he'll break and run when we get closer. . . ." assured Andy, as we trudged wearily on our way. We had been travel-ing for a mile or more through marshy country, where there wasn't a place to sit down or rest our heavy packs; and we were in no mood to go six steps out of the way. But this big grizzly showed no signs of budging as we got closer and closer. Finally, at about thirty yards, we stopped and Andy yelled at the old fellow and waved his hat in the air, to try and scare him away. Instead of running the bear got to his feet, and the hair went up on his back as he stared defiantly at us. The wind was blowing at right angles, so he was unable to get our scent. What his weak little eyes told him we were I do not know; but he certainly showed unmistakable signs of aggressive intentions. Andy slipped a cartridge into the cham-ber of his 280 Ross as the bear made a couple of suspicious movements in our direction.

"That bear's apt to charge," warned Andy, although shooting any bear was the last thing we had any desire to do.

We both shouted and waved our hats. But all this didn't seem to mean a thing to Mr. Grizzly. He didn't seem to like our looks or the sounds of our voices and made another couple of menacing steps toward us.

"Maybe if I circle out around him, into the wind until he can get my scent . . . he may stop all this foolishness. . . ." suggested Andy. "Maybe he's never seen a man with a gun before."

The bear stood defiantly watching my companion as he walked slowly out around this arrogant critter to where the wind would carry the human scent to him. His big head occasionally swung back toward me, as he appeared to be trying to figure out just what it was all about. We had already gone so close there was serious doubt that he could be stopped before he got one of us, if he suddenly decided to do so. One of the fundamental rules in dealing with these big grizzlies, among those who know them, is never to let one get closer than you can conveniently and accurately put at least three shots from a high-powered rifle into them where it will do the most good. Andy was so tired, and, with a fifty-pound pack on his back, quick and accurate shooting would be severely handicapped. It was a dangerous situation.

Then, very suddenly, the bear sprang into action, as though a powerful spring had been released. The instant he got the scent he made a wild leap and went splashing across the stream and continued racing away through the tall grass of the marshland, as though a dozen devils were right at his heels. He had not associated what he saw with man, the only thing on earth that is feared by these creatures; but, once he got that human scent, he realized what a cardinal mistake he had made and took off with all the speed of which he was capable.

How different bears are from humans in this respect. They do not depend on their weak little eyes as they do on their much more highly educated noses. It is just the opposite with humans. If we had smelled that bear, for example, we would never have been convinced of his presence until we actually saw the animal; for man depends on his eyesight to the same proportionate degree that bears depend on their sense of smell.

We covered a considerable area of the country, transporting the camera and canvas canoe from one stream to another, carrying everything over the alder-covered ridges, across wide areas of mossy tundra, where walking became an ordeal, or through big marshes, where there was often the hazard of breaking through the floating vegetation into bottomless depths of muddy mire that was as bad as quicksand. Sometimes we just dragged the canoe over the tall, wet grass. We saw bears practically every day, except when we went back to the little base camp to catch up on rest in a sleeping bag and a couple of big meals of hot food for our neglected stomachs. According to entries made in my diary, the numbers of these grizzlies seen on the following consecutive days were: .6—7—9—6—12—none—18 and 10 bears. Our lives became increasingly adapted to the daily routines of the hairy fishermen, with whom we became more and more familiar.

When we were traveling along a stream we never walked on the shore but in the water, where tracks leave no telltale scent. When we carried the canoe and camera ashore, to make a temporary camp or take off overland, we would wash out our tracks from the water's edge to as far back from the shore as we could, using a light tin bucket that was carried as part of the equipment. We also had a special method of camouflaging the overturned canoe if the grass was not tall enough to hide it. I had improvised a net of codfish line, which fitted over the canoe much like a woman's hair net. Into this it was easy to tuck tufts of grass, which gave our shelter the appearance of a hump on the tundra.

One dreary, drizzly early morning we had a visitor, as we lay huddled, shivering, underneath the canoe, half awake and wondering if sunshine would ever come again—and convinced that no human being in his right mind should subject himself to such a personal ordeal, just to watch some grizzly bears all doing what comes naturally to them. Several times during the night we heard bears sloshing along the shore or splashing in the stream, about seventy-five feet away.

As approaching daylight filtered through the fog and drizzle, the great shaggy head of a bear appeared looking down through the grass, not more than ten feet away. Seen through sleepy, half-open eyes, it set off something in the nature of a chain reaction of impulses that was much like a mental explosion. We almost kicked through the canvas bottom of the canoe in a wild scramble to get out. The overly inquisitive bear made an equally sudden and undignified effort to get somewhere else. He almost fell over backward in getting started. By the time we were wide awake enough to know what was actually going on, the big grizzly was trying to cross the seventy-foot stream in a single leap; and he kept right on across the tundra, sending up spray from the wet grass like the wake of a speeding motorboat.

We later found, from his tracks, that this bear had been walking along the bank of the stream and, seeing the unfamiliar hump on the tundra, had ventured over to investigate. About halfway he had stopped and walked back and forth, suspiciously standing on his hind legs to get a better look. Then, curiosity getting the best of his better judgment, the old fellow had ventured to within about ten feet before finding out the mistake he had made. Why this bear had not taken the usual and simple precaution of circling to get the benefit of an explanation via scent on wind I cannot understand. Maybe he was just a dumb bear. He could have smelled us all right, for I hadn't had a bath for three months!

Time after time we watched these creatures in the normal course of their unmolested daily lives. Several times we saw them put their noses to work as they crossed our invisible tracks across the moss-carpeted tundra. They always seemed to show the same attitude toward man. It is doing these creatures an injustice to call this fear, for there was always a haughty aspect to their sudden alarm; and there was invariably an indication of cautious curiosity. One big fellow was more bold, or more inquisitive, than the others. After that first suspicious investigation he slowly followed the trail until it led him to one of the blinds we had improvised with alders stuck into the ground. Every little way he would stand up on his big, flat hind feet and sway his long snout to carefully sniff the air. As he approached the old blind, he became quite excited in his boldness, prancing about nervously as he stood up and stared at the man-made contraption, and a couple of times jumping back, as if fighting a strong impulse to make a wiser retreat. We couldn't help laughing as we watched his antics through our binoculars. Finally, to our surprise, this bear mustered enough brazenness to venture right up to where he could stick his nose inside where we had lain hidden for several hours. The scent must have been strong there. But he did not stay long after this. Apparently satisfying his curiosity and finding out all he wanted to know, he suddenly wheeled about and went racing away.

The most memorable of all these experiences was one evening when Andy and I lay in a drizzling rain on a lookout and watched twelve Alaska brown bears come out of the alders and wander down to fish in a short stretch of the same rather small stream. For about an hour and a half, until it got too dark to see them clearly, they were all in sight at the same time. This was on July 28. They were all big bears, and it was one of the most wonderful experiences I have ever been privileged to witness in all the time I have spent in game country, as well as one of the most informative of my observation of grizzly bears.

I had long realized how definitely and how strongly each grizzly was invested with his own individual character and temperament. We became increasingly aware of this from watching the many bears we saw day after day, and it was this realization that often prompted us to give some of them their nicknames. This particular occasion, however, provided the best evidence we had observed. I do not remember the exact procedure of events, for only remarks of a general nature were ever entered in the notes of my diary; and the recollections which stand out so vividly are important because of their implications rather than the order in which the happenings took place. For instance, one bear would amble leisurely down a trail out of the broad expanse of alders on the low hillside that rose a short distance beyond the stream. Walking out into the shallow water of the long stretch of riffles, he would pick up a salmon in his teeth, like a dog might carry it out onto the bank, would crouch down on his belly and begin methodically stripping off the fillets. As the next one came down the same trail through the grass and approached the first bear already enjoying supper, the second arrival would make a detour out around the first one, avoiding too close a meeting. It was plainly evident that these two were not on friendly terms, and there was no doubt as to which one held the other in unmistakable respect. When the third one arrived, however, the situation was completely reversed, and the first one got up and moved out of the way, standing off to one side while his obvious superior padded along on his way with haughty arrogance. When the next one came along, he might walk directly up to his neighbors; they would touch noses in a most friendly manner and stand eye to eye for a few moments of chummy greetings; then the late arrival would hurry out to get a salmon and rejoin his friend at a table for two. This is not exactly as it happened, but it is a faithful indication of the attitudes of these bears toward one another. Throughout all the time that we watched them, moving back and forth at their fishing along that short stretch of stream and frequently meeting, there was no doubt that each individual and his temperament was a matter of full understanding to each of the others.

Chapter XXIV

A WORLD THEIR OWN

Watching twenty-eight big grizzlies in the course of a single day could hardly be without its interesting moments, particularly when most of these bears were at extremely close range. That is really a lot of grizzly bears—virtually three times the total number of these animals to be found today in the whole state of Colorado. They were practically all big ones, and it was at the same location where Andy and I had watched twelve the previous evening. We named this place "The Bowery," because of the number of rough old characters we saw there.

We were back on the elevated lookout early the next morning to watch where the bears went to day beds in the alders. Several were still fishing, although about half of them had filled their stomachs and retired or wandered off to some new location. It was probably the former, for when not disturbed they seldom moved very far from their groceries. We recognized some of the individuals seen the previous evening, as we lay in the drizzling rain and moved our binoculars from one to another. We also saw a few others ambling among the alders on the moss-covered hills. We had seen ten of the animals by the time the last one disappeared.

As the weather showed signs of clearing we had brought the heavy movie camera along. We had located where several of the bears had bedded down for the day and were confident we knew the trails they would follow in returning to their fishing in the evening. So we curled up in the moss to get a couple hours of sleep before moving down to build a blind beside the stream. The location had been carefully decided on. It would give us a good view of the trails coming down the hillside as well as a considerable section of the stream in both directions. The afternoon light would be at our back, which was good for pictures; the breeze was blowing steadily up the stream; the rain had stopped; and the clouds were lifting and thinning. Everything seemed to be in our favor.

It was about noon when we moved down to build the blind and settled down for another four hours or more of waiting.

The first bear to come waddling leisurely down a trail a couple hundred yards upstream was a medium-sized, straw-colored fellow we had named "Towhead." He was too far away for pictures, even with the longest telephoto lens I had. We watched him closely, for he was not only the first to appear but, being down-wind from us, there was the possibility he might cross the stream and get our scent.

Towhead was hardly at the water's edge when a second bear appeared considerably closer, and after sitting lazily at the edge of the alders for a few minutes, apparently trying to get his eyes open, he too ambled down to supper.

We had about forgotten Towhead when Andy grabbed my arm and directed my attention toward him. The first bear had caught a salmon and was carrying it out on our side. If he had stayed near the bank it would have been better, but he carried the still-flopping fish back in the grass. The worst happened. Suddenly dropping the fish, he reared up on his hind legs and his long snout swayed back and forth in the breeze for a few hasty moments; then, dropping down on all fours, he went splashing away back across the stream and up the trail he had just come down.

"*Oh hell!*" snapped Andy—for this bad turn of luck might spoil the best prospects for pictures we had enjoyed.

The second bear had reached the bank of the stream and was standing lazylike, looking down at the salmon, when Towhead made his dash for the alders. This woke him up rather abruptly. He stiffened in his tracks and watched the hasty retreat. Then his head swung around in our direction. It should be remembered that the one and only thing in all the world for which these big bears have any fear whatever, and which will cause them to take so much as a single step in flight, is their one and only enemy, *man*. The second bear stood staring and sniffing for probably half a minute or less. That the brain which nature had developed in his big skull was functioning in the same manner that mine was is beyond reasonable doubt. He had not gotten the scent himself, although he knew that his neighbor had; and, figuring the situation out for himself, very promptly he too made a hasty retreat to the alders. They both disappeared, leaving us mighty disappointed.

Impatiently we waited, as the northern twilight deepened and the time for making pictures steadily slipped away. Why didn't the other bears come out as they normally did? The wind had been blowing too steadily for any chance of our scent going up into the alders. We could not help but feel that the bears knew we were there. But how?

Finally a third bear appeared a short distance to the north. I swung the camera around and began taking pictures. It was better to get a few distant ones than none at all. But this fellow showed unmistakable signs of suspicion about coming down to the stream. He walked about restlessly, as though he really wanted that first big, fat fish, but better judgment restrained him. And remember, I repeat, that man and man alone could put enough fear in his heart to keep that big grizzly away from his supper.

Then another bear reappeared at the edge of the alders, but he showed the same suspicious attitude about coming down to feed.

It probably should be further explained that our little improvised blind did not present a sufficient alteration of the scenery to alarm the bears. We always took the greatest care in this respect. There was another possibility, however; and that was an audible warning alarm of some kind which we had not been able to hear. Or could it be that animals possess some extra sense, beyond the realm of smell or hearing or sight, which is neither possessed nor understood by man? We frequently refer to it in the vague specific of "mental telepathy." Is it the same sense that tells a dog whether or not a strange man is friendly and lets a horse know what kind of a rider and master a man is, almost before his hand first touches the rein? There is so much about the world in which animals live that we know so very little about, it is dangerous to attempt an explanation.

As Andy and I crouched in our little blind, with binoculars, in hand, and impatiently waited as the clouds closed in and darkness settled, we occasionally caught a glimpse of other bears along the edge of the alders; and farther away on the surrounding hill we saw still more. We counted eighteen of these animals during this one evening; and, with the ten seen in the morning, it made the largest number seen in any one day.

When the time for using the camera passed, I put it in the case, but we waited to see what would happen. We would have to move to a new section of the country anyhow. With the coming of darkness other bears appeared, and then they began coming down to the stream. Their boldness increased with the darkness. First they began catching salmon above and below where we were; and before we left they were actually fishing within fifty feet or less in front of us. As a matter of fact, as it got too dark to see them plainly, we were literally run out of "The Bowery."

All of these bears were full-grown ones and mostly males. We saw no females with young cubs in any of the congregations around the best fishing places. When we did see new families, they were well off by themselves; and they were more apt to be seen traveling in the middle of the day. There was a good reason for this. The big males do not like baby bears, even their own offspring, and will kill them whenever the opportunity is presented. This is one of the few discreditable traits of the grizzly. We did not get acquainted with the families until we went up some of the valleys back in the high mountains and found the safer sanctuaries to which the mothers retreated.

There was one big valley which particularly attracted us, and we paddled our little canvas canoe up the sizable stream which flowed down through its grassy floor. It curved back into a large cluster of rugged barren peaks and offered a pleasant change from the long weeks we had spent in wandering over the flat, swampy tundra and deep moss of the low rolling hills.

It was early on the morning of August 5 that we climbed up to a high bench on the west side of the upper valley. It was mighty good to get our feet on solid ground, and the weather was a pleasant change. For the first time in a good many days we caught an occasional glimpse of blue sky and we could see the rugged brown tops of the mountains. There was a luxuriant warmth to the grass on the solid ground; and as we stretched out and put our binoculars into use we quickly located several bears wandering about farther up the valley. This was virgin country. I doubt very much if there had been a single human being in there at any time when any of the bears were out for a good many years. It was not even trapped in winter, for there was too much better country down below.

Directly across from us was a rather narrow valley that cut back abruptly into the mountains. Out of this ran a small stream that cut down through a rocky canyon. The place attracted us very strongly; and, after deciding that salmon could get up the tumbling creek, we decided to explore the valley.

The weather had become so good that we took the camera along. It was too rough-going to follow the stream, but we swung off to one side and soon came onto the deepest bear trail I had ever seen. It was cut to an average of at least six inches into the solid ground—leading up into the valley. We marveled at how many thousands of footsteps by the padded feet of bears, through the untold expanse of years, it had taken to cut that primeval trail.

What we found was more than we had hoped for. It was the permanent home of two families of bears. One big mother had two cubs, and the other had three. During the ten days that followed we bcame very well acquainted with both of these families. We called the one with two youngsters the "Murphy family" and the other the "O'Flaherty family"—because the mothers were always having a difficult time in keeping their respective offspring far enough apart to avoid free-for-all fights, just like a couple of families of tough little Irish kids might do. And we named this beautiful little valley "The Nursery."

We got better acquainted with the Murphy family than with their neighbors, and we gave each of the Murphy youngsters appropriate names. One we called "Apron Strings," deciding she was the little sister because she was always right at her mother's heels. The other cub we named "Little Roughneck," because he was forever wandering off and going out of his way to get mixed up in trouble of one kind or another. He hobbled about, trying to avoid putting his front left foot on the ground. At first we thought it had been injured, but after watching him through a couple of days we decided that he had made the mistake of getting a bit too intimate with a porcupine and got a paw stuck full of quills. This was quite natural, as these bears, even grown ones, often try to kill these slow-moving little animals, whose only protection is their abundance of easily shed and fast-sticking quills. I once shot a big bear that had evidently tried to crush a porcupine by grasping it in his arms, with the result that the quills had been stuck and badly festered clear across his chest and the inside of both big arms.

The O'Flaherty family had a cave up at the head of a long rockslide that was overgrown with grass. Every afternoon they came down this broad grassy outlet of the high-walled canyon to feed on the salmon in the stream. And the three youngsters always played the same game as they came—much as human children might do. Here and there were large boulders sticking up as much as four or five feet above the surface; and the idea of their game was to see which of the three could be master of the summit and keep the other two from taking his place. They would push and pull and slap and bite, with the one on top always being attacked by the other two. Mrs. O'Flaherty just ambled philosophically down the trail; and, when she got too far ahead, there would be a wild race of the three youngsters to another rock ahead and another wild fight to see who could stay master of the top the longest.

The Murphy family stayed down in the valley, having a special day bed in the alders, which we quickly located. They both had their own special fishing grounds, about half a mile apart.

We were never quite close enough to get good movies of the free-for-all fights between the Murphy and O'Flaherty kids—when their respective mothers had to do some pretty strenuous slapping and biting of baby rear ends to get their families separated and herded on their way again. But we found a terrific interest in watching them through our binoculars. There was another occasion when we saw Little Roughneck get hold of a big king salmon that was almost too much for him to handle. In fact, this fish was so large and strong that the cub was hardly equal to the occasion. But he held on with teeth and claws as though his very life depended on the outcome. They thrashed and splashed about, with the fish occasionally being on top. Even the cub's lame foot was not favored in this battle. But Roughneck stuck at it, and finally the little fellow conquered. Standing up on his hind legs, with the big fish clasped tightly in his arms and its tail dragging between his feet, he walked triumphantly out onto the rocky shore. The salmon was almost as long as he was. When he got it a safe distance from the water's edge, he released it to flop about in the grass; and, without further attention to the prize, he walked tiredly off to one side to lie down for a much-needed rest after his strenuous conquest. Mrs. Murphy left a salmon of her own to walk over to where he sprawled, panting, with his soft pink tongue drooping far out of the corner of his mouth; and she probably made some motherly commendation of pride.

There was one other incident which stands out vividly above all the others. It may be the most significant of all my experiences with bears. Little Roughneck was also the central figure in this instance, and it occurred the very first time that we went into "The Nursery."

As Andy and I came up the deeply cut bear trail that wound among the clumps of alders and led from the big valley up over the rim of the bench, we came abruptly into the open and stopped to survey the beautiful little valley that nestled snugly between the mountains. If there had been no bears at all, the climb would have been worth while. But almost immediately we spotted the mother bear with three cubs coming down the grassy slide about a quarter of a mile away. The youngsters were busily engaged in playing their little game of master-of-the-top-of-the-rock. We quickly ducked back into the alders and got out our binoculars. Soon we had a blind constructed and the movie camera set on its tripod, for we promptly decided to stay where we were, with the hope that the bears would come in our direction after they reached the stream and began fishing.

We were comfortably settled behind our blind and had been watching the family at their fishing for only a few minutes when Andy grabbed hold of my arm. Turning my attention to closer by, my heart gave an extra thump when I saw another big bear walking out of the alders only a couple hundred feet to our right. One cub was already well out in the open, and a second one was tagging along at the mother's heels. This was our first glimpse of the family we came to know so well as the Murphys.

To our joy the sky had cleared and the afternoon sunshine was spreading its wonderful glow through "The Nursery." The bears were apparently pleased at this too, for Mrs. Murphy waddled leisurely out and stood stretching her big neck and swaying her head, as if to say, "Gee, that sunshine feels good!" Then she stretched out on the warm grass, rolling over on her back, with all four legs stuck up in the air in a very unladylike manner.

As the "Old Lady" lay sprawled on the sunny grass, the cub we later called Apron Strings settled down to have afternoon tea. But Little Roughneck had more exciting ideas. He went romping off a hundred feet or more up the valley. Then he suddenly turned around and came galloping back. He walked stiff-legged, limping along, holding the one sore foot up off the ground, sometimes rearing up on his little hind legs. He was so full of energy and devilment that he couldn't stand still.

Finally he started wandering down to our right, which soon gave us serious concern.

"If that cub keeps on going, he'll get our scent," whispered Andy.

There was nothing we could do about this, however, except speculate as to what might happen. We whispered back and forth as we watched the adventurous little cub. There was no doubt in our minds that he had *never before* come in contact with the scent of man. We wondered just what he would do if this happened. Could he possibly recognize the faint scent of the only enemy in all his own little world? This seemed impossible, for he was so young and so inexperienced.

Farther and farther he went, as we watched, whispered, and hoped he would turn back. Then all of a sudden he wheeled around and reared up to stand stiffly erect on his little hind legs, with his nose stuck out and swaying back and forth in our direction. He stood there for only a few brief moments, and, dropping down on all fours, he went racing back to his mother as though the devil was after him. We did not hear him make the slightest sound, although he had hardly gotten started when the "Old Lady" and the other cub scrambled to their feet and both reared up on their hind legs, with noses swaying in our direction; and all three of them went running away as fast as they could.

Andy and I were so amazed that the disappointment of this unfortunate turn of events was almost forgotten. We talked about it for a long time, and we discussed it further on a good many occasions thereafter. The more we thought about this instance, the more significant it became. How could that cub possibly have recognized the first scent of man which had ever come into his baby nostrils? How could he know that the scent represented the one thing in all the world from which he must flee as fast as he could? How had he been able to convey this important information to his unsuspecting mother and to his baby sister? It still puzzles me. I wish I understood. But I like to think, and possibly correctly, that Mrs. Murphy had on more than one occasion sat down with her two children before her and told them about the facts of life which lay ahead and explained about the one enemy which they should learn to fear—in such a manner that, when her Little Roughneck came in contact with the scent for the very first time, he knew what was the wisest thing to do and had the good judgment to run like hell. Wise little fellow that he was, he probably lived to a ripe old age. I hope so.

The extent to which animals are capable of communicating with each other is a field of research which has been but very little explored by naturalists. They certainly have some "language," commonly used between creatures of the same species and to some extent understood by others. My interest in this was aroused many years ago by one of our great authorities on African animal life and lore—Carl Akeley. His understanding of wild creatures was broad and profound. There were many things he told me when I was a young man that made very deep impressions; and among the most memorable was his earnest belief that animals had a language of their own and that different species which lived in the same area were able to understand one another. To illustrate this contention, he related a vivid account of an instance when he was studying elephants in a remote section of Africa. It was back in the days before the motorized safari, and the game knew but very little about the white hunter with a gun. Akeley was making a cautious approach to a large herd that was feeding in dense cover, and the elephants were enjoying their wilderness seclusion and security in unsuspicious and noisy manner. There were also many monkeys, birds, and other animals, all chattering and squawking. Akeley approached with all circumstances of wind and other factors in his favor. The discordant chorus gave the naturalist a pleasant feeling of confidence. But all of a sudden there was complete silence. Every voice stopped with the abruptness of the slash of a knife. As he stood there, listening, some of the birds began flying mutely away, and there was a rustling in the treetops as monkeys scurried off. He later learned that the entire herd of elephants was also moving away, rapidly, but so quietly that he was for a time unaware of their departure. At this juncture of the account Akeley said to me with a religious seriousness: "Some animal, or some bird, that had learned I was there . . . had decided I was dangerous. Its signal of warning had been recognized above all that noisy din; and it was instantly accepted without question or doubt by every other creature in that whole feeding area . . . and they slipped away as silently as ghosts."

It is unfair to make direct comparisons between grizzly bears or other animals and humans. This becomes particularly true when we venture into the vague field of mental intelligence. It is undeniable that bear and man both have a physical brain, nervous system, and all the affiliated sense organs, of almost identical character and purpose, developed through many thousands of generations. But the worlds in which each has lived and struggled to survive have been far apart. What has become important to one is of no consequence to the other. It would be as unreasonable to expect a grizzly to drive an automobile through Manhattan traffic as it would be to ask a policeman to follow a bank robber from the scene of a crime by sniffing the tracks along a city sidewalk, or for a Wall Street broker to hibernate for seven months during a financial depression. It is equally unfair to put too much importance upon single instances or isolated observations. Man and other mammals have each had their own worlds, and each has survived and developed in accordance with his own ability to do so.

The better acquainted I have become with grizzlies, the higher opinion I have had of them; and this applies to their intelligence as well as their dispositions. Practically every guide, hunter, and naturalist whom I know has shared this opinion. It has been strongly expressed by practically every observer whose judgment can be respected.

"I would give the grizzly first place in the animal world for brain-power," wrote Enos A. Mills, from his wide and highly sensitive observations.[130]

"He is superior in mentality to the horse, the dog, and even the gray wolf. Instinct the grizzly has, but he also has the ability to reason," wrote David Star Jordan, the eminent naturalist of Leland Stanford University. "He is the most human of all the beasts."[131]

And there could be no higher tribute than that paid by the primitive Indians, who acknowledged this wild creature as their ancient ancestor.

In hunting as well as observing grizzlies I became continually and increasingly respectful of their dangerous but dignified character. In my younger years the success I enjoyed was more a matter of lacking the good judgment of being afraid, and an unusual amount of good luck, rather than any personal bravery on my part. It is true there was only one unqualified charge in the twenty-five mortal attacks in which I participated; and yet today I would not think of taking many of the aggravated risks that I did as a young man. There is an old saying that familiarity breeds contempt—but this does not apply to grizzly bears.

On dozens of occasions I have been within a hundred feet or so of them, trespassing upon their feeding and other natural pursuits of their private lives, and yet never once has any one of them made an unchallenged or unprovoked fight of our meeting. Furthermore, I do not know of a single instance in which any grizzly has made an absolutely unprovoked attack upon any other person. I have gone to considerable length to get the real facts behind numerous instances in which men have been severely injured or killed by grizzlies, and in each instance there was some good and valid reason of aggravation on the part of the human victim. Many times I have asked the same question to persons whose experience and judgment are worthy of respect: "Do you know of any instance in which a grizzly made an absolutely unprovoked attack?" The answer has invariably been "No." Sometimes this has required an understanding of what Old Ephraim considers an act of provocation—which may be somewhat different than your own opinion—and what may aggravate one will not bother another. But, by and large, they are pretty amiable citizens, so long as they are left entirely to themselves.

Also, to hold to the belief that Old Ephraim is just a "dumb animal," without mental faculties or the endowment of intelligent perception in meeting his own problems of life and existence, is just another fallacy of the great human ego.

Chapter XXV

BORDERLAND OF OBLIVION

THE story of the grizzly bear in the United States is a strange historical paradox. Naturalists and hunters, since the days long before the first white man came to America, have been agreed that this mighty mammal that walks like a man is the greatest living carnivorous creature of this continent, if not the whole world. He has become a present-day symbol of virile strength and bravery in our vocabulary and popular opinion. He stands sublimely among the rough and rugged characters that make up the exciting lore of the Old West, a valiant protagonist of the pioneers who tamed the wilderness. No other wild creature has taken on such a richly legendary stature as Old Ephraim. But, in spite of all these honorable attributes, the grizzly has been subjected to the most disrespectful and intensive attrition ever perpetrated upon any species by man. Since the earliest days of our pioneering and development of the West he has been marked by the cattlemen as an outlaw to be destroyed without valid cause or conviction.

Once abundant throughout practically all of our West beyond the Great Plains, the grizzly is today close to total extermination throughout all of its original range, except for a few struggling survivors in a few scattered areas; and yet he is not now accorded the ordinary game-law protection which we grant to rabbits or skunks. Of the four of our states where the species is still to be found, only one provides the grizzly a partial protection of *"no open season"*; and in one state, where according to the official census only ten individuals are said to exist, they may be legally killed by anyone at any time. Even in Yellowstone Park, which in 1872 was created as a permanent sanctuary for the wild life of the Rocky Mountains, some of the grizzlies have recently been killed on the excuse of being a menace to the welfare of tourists; and hunters make a harvest of those that wander beyond the boundaries of the park.

The extermination of the grizzly in the United States is not an unforewarned eventuality. As long ago as 1906 the eminent zoologist Dr. William F. Hornaday, who was one of the best-informed authorities on big-game conditions in this country, made the following prognostication in his book *Camp-fires in the Canadian Rockies* (p. 172): "In the United States, outside of Yellowstone Park and the Bitter Root Mountains, grizzly bears are now so rare that it is impossible for a sportsman to go out and kill one, no matter where he hunts, and no matter how much money he spends. One of our best known writers on hunting matters, who has hunted in the West at frequent intervals during the past fifteen years, recently announced that he has now given up all hope of killing a grizzly in our country." The situation has steadily worsened, and yet practically nothing has been done to forestall total extermination of the greatest wild creature which has lived in the territory of the United States since the days of the mastodon and the saber-tooth tiger.

To get firsthand the whole story of the present situation with regard to the grizzly bear in the United States, I set out in the early fall of 1953 to do some actual hunting and to make a comprehensive survey of our western states where these animals once were residents. Through more than half a century it had been my strong personal desire to become better acquainted with the grizzly in our own West; and on this recent trip it was my good fortune to be privileged to hunt under extraordinary circumstances, in what was undoubtedly one of the best of the few remaining areas where these bears are still to be found in their wild natural state. The most of my bear hunting had been north of the U.S.-Canadian border.

According to the best of available information assembled by the state fish and game departments and the National Fish and Wildlife Service, there were in 1953 more than five times as many grizzlies in the state of Montana than there were in all the rest of the country combined. The details as to the estimated numbers and other facts bearing on the subject will be gone into later. And of all the specific areas where grizzlies are still to be found, from Mexico to Canada and from the Great Plains to the Pacific coast, there was no place that offered a better opportunity to get one of these animals than the section of the Rocky Mountains known as the Mission Range, which comes within the protective border of the Flathead Indian Reservation in western Montana. Few of our mountainous regions are more rugged and inaccessible than the lofty basins of the high cluster of cathedral peaks around Mount McDonald. White men have not been permitted to hunt there in a good many generations, and the Indians have left the grizzlies pretty much unmolested in this rocky mountain retreat. These circumstances have provided Old Ephraim an isolated sanctuary quite ideal to his natural characteristics and well-being. When the Indian Council of the Reservation met in official session and passed a very special ruling which granted me permission to take one grizzly in this haven of last retreat, I proceeded to Montana with considerable assurance of success.

The autumn air was rich with the pungent smell of spruce and moss in the early-morning sunshine as our nine-horse pack train strung out in single file and started climbing the trail along the mountainside around Lake McDonald. Within half an hour we were on rocky switchbacks, where the horses scrambled and grunted up the steep footholds across the face of cliffs, sending loose rock clattering far below. Within the first three hours we had climbed over the first divide, passing several places where losing a horse, or a man, had been a serious possibility.

The hunt had been arranged by my old friend, George Mushbach, born in Montana seventy-two years before, and whose whole life had been spent in hunting and in the service of the U. S. Biological Survey and the Fish and Wildlife Service, from which he had recently been officially retired. For a good many years he had been in charge of the National Bison Range, which occupies a large area on the Flathead Indian Reservation and is within sight of the Mission Range. Both of our guides had been born on the reservation, and one was a member of the Indian Council.

This was a particularly happy trip for me, for I was accompanied by my son, Harold Conrad McCracken, and I had high hopes of his being able to do the actual shooting of the grizzly which we had a permit to take. This was not his first experience with American big game. He had gotten his first antelope in Wyoming, at the age of fourteen, and on that same trip had been thrice charged by an angry mother grizzly just outside of Yellowstone Park. The incident comes about as close to being an unprovoked attack as any of which I know, and it was little short of a miracle that no one was killed. In company with Ernest Miller, the well-known Montana guide and dude-ranch operator, and the latter's son and a young Indian, they had been making color movies of this she-bear and her two cubs. They had stalked pretty close to this grizzly and her youngsters on three or four occasions, and she had hurried off to find a new retreat. In fact, the movie makers had spent three of four hours "bothering" the bears, when the "Old Lady" suddenly decided she had had enough of this sort of thing and came charging straight for the party, puffing and snorting and slapping right and left with her clawed paws as she went through the group like a plunging fullback. The little group had jumped to one side or the other, and the grizzly went so close she could have been touched with an outstretched hand. Three times she came in the same manner. They had no gun; but on the third charge Ernest Miller struck her in the head with the 16-mm. movie camera on the tripod, with such force that it broke the metal turret to which the lenses were attached, after which the grizzly went back to her cubs—and the movie makers decided it was well past time to go home.

My son had often chided me with the undeniable fact that he had experienced a narrower escape from a grizzly than had come to me in all my years of hunting. Incidentally, Ernest Miller had photographed the grizzly's first charge, and it is one of the best color films of a charging grizzly that was ever made. It has been seen by many hundreds of thousands of sportsmen and other TV viewers in the film *Stalking Big Game in Montana*, which was released by *Field and Stream Magazine*.

I had not been with my son on that occasion; and, though we had hunted together for deer, geese, woodcock, and other upland game birds, this 1953 trip to Montana was our first, and last, bear hunt together.

After the first three hours in the saddle we followed an old Indian trail which hadn't been used for many years and was so overgrown and obstructed with fallen timber that the only advantage in following it was as a guide to the best or only places where it was possible to take horses over the high rocky passes. But we had finally swung around directly in back of Mount McDonald and her cluster of sister peaks, where we made camp, and then climbed up into the lofty rocky basins.

In all my experiences in British Columbia, Alaska, and the Yukon, covering trips of up to two years' duration and in some instances penetrating to where no white man had been before, I had never encountered such rough and difficult hunting country. The heavily timbered heads of the valleys are broken with numerous rocky ridges; and the mountains, being geologically recent, rear their mighty ramparts in high perpendicular hulks of sharp, bare rock. In the cavernous basins lie beautiful little lakes, surrounded by big spruce, pine, and hemlock, with spectacular cliffs rising abruptly into the sky. It is a marvelously beautiful country—damnable for horse and man, but a wonderful haven of last retreat for the last descendants of Old Ephraim.

We frequently saw elk and deer, and nearly every great wall of a mountain had its own group of wild goats. On some of the trips out from the main camp we took along single horses, getting them to places where our Indian guides assured us no horse had ever been before; and we back-packed to more difficult places up amid the little glaciers.

In the evenings, as we sat around the campfire, our guides resurrected from their recollections all the grizzly stories they had heard, particularly those in which men had been badly injured or killed by the mighty bears. The number of these fatal encounters, even in recent years, was a little surprising and gave me a feeling that Old Ephraim realized that his race was facing a last stand, with his back on the brink of annihilation, and was making a final show of desperate defiance. In each case, however, it was quite evident that the man had precipitated the incident. The victim of one of these attacks and a narrow escape was at the time a gasoline-filling-station attendant at the reservation town of St. Ignatius, where I later talked with him and confirmed the circumstances.

We found unmistakable signs of grizzly—where they had been digging, and their distinctive claw marks—on the game trails that led up over the ridges. My son and Benny McDonald, who is a direct descendant from the famous Scotch pioneer for whom the great mountain is named, stayed out all night to watch from a promising lookout. We searched far and wide with our binoculars. But we saw no grizzly.

Finally we decided to back-pack up into the highest basins in the cluster of peaks and were compelled to spend the night on the bare face of Mount McDonald, not many hundred feet from the top. My legs had completely given out under the pack I carried, and traveling was much too dangerous to go any farther without an overnight rest. Although we were high above timber line, the guides managed to get together enough wood to cook a pot of coffee. An even greater problem was to find a place where it was safe to lie in the light eider-down bags we carried. The rocky face of the peak was so precipitous that to roll over just once in one's sleep was almost certain to start a disastrous tumble of more than a thousand feet.

We huddled beside the embers of our tiny fire, waiting for the cold of night; and we talked about grizzly bears and the inaccessible basin we were trying to reach. The only one who had been there before was Benny McDonald. He told us, in his quiet Indian manner, of watching a big grizzly in there on a previous trip, and it is one of the choicest bits of grizzly lore I have ever heard. There had been a recent "hatch" of yellow butterflies, and they were flying together in a swarm, like a swirling little cloud that moved slowly about near the shore of the basin's tiny lake. As Mr. Grizzly ambled along in the afternoon gloaming, turning over an occasional rock or picking an occasional blueberry from the skimpy low bushes, he was attracted by the swirling little swarm of butterflies and hurried over to begin following it about in a curious and rather playful manner. Finally the cloud of yellow wings completely enveloped the great bear; and, standing up on his hind legs, he pranced about, keeping himself in its midst, swiping his powerful paws from side to side, and snapping his jaws, in a rather futile effort to make a bit of supper out of the gossamer bits of life. I had been well aware that Old Ephraim would eat most anything, but this was the first time I had heard of him trying to make a meal on butterflies.

When we all got so cold it became necessary to slip into our eider-down bags—shoes, coats, and all—I tried not to go to sleep and smiled to myself about the big grizzly and the butterflies. I did doze off, however. Starting to shift my position, from discomfort, I woke up with a start. Staring up into the inky sky, it seemed I had never seen so many stars before; and they blinked with unusual brilliance, almost close enough to reach up and touch with my cold fingers. Then I sat up and looked out across the wide Flathead Valley far below, where many other little lights shone more feebly, from windows of farmhouses on the reservation. I noticed the cluster of lights that marked historic St. Ignatius Mission and the other little settlements along the modern highway, where the headlights of an occasional automobile or truck seemed to creep along. We were so close to civilization and yet so far away. I looked up at the stars again. I realized that they had been looking down in the same manner upon this big hulk of mountain for many centuries before even the first Indians came, when the grizzlies ruled alone and supreme throughout all this land. There were probably not half a dozen of all the Indians who had ever been born and grown to maturity throughout that whole valley who had been high up on the mountain where I sat. Certainly none had ever been there in the middle of a starlit night. I also wondered how many of the last-surviving grizzlies had sat up there, as I was, and looked out across the valley and its many little farmhouse lights; and I wondered what thoughts might have passed through Old Ephraim's mind or if he realized how close he sat to the borderland of oblivion.

We spent more than two weeks climbing and searching the high basins. Only three grizzlies were seen by any of the members of our party, and these were observed at such great distances that even their true identity was not entirely certain and it was physically impossible to get close enough for a shot. I did not see a single one. It was an unsuccessful hunting trip—but a revealing commentary on the sad situation to which Old Ephraim has come. It was my son's first grizzly hunt—and the last one for both of us. I went on to make a grizzly survey in the western states. Shortly after this was completed my son was killed in an automobile accident. The last time I ever saw him was when we parted at the end of that hunt together in the Mission Range on the Flathead Indian Reservation.

Chapter XXVI

LAST OF OLD EPHRAIM'S TRIBE

THE great American grizzly is today a creature of the past throughout the United States, except in a few remote and isolated areas scattered over the broad range that these creatures once dominated in plentiful numbers. Where they still exist the numbers are few and the areas into which they have retreated are of such a wild and protective character that it is difficult to determine an accurate census of the species. Each of the states has its own Fish and Game Department, whose duty it is to keep well informed on the year-to-year situation regarding its wildlife population and to recommend such legislation or changes in the laws as may be best suited to the well-being of the different varieties of game. Each state also has the benefit of the U. S. Fish and Wildlife Service and their staffs of professional biologists, most of whom are specialy trained and make lifelong careers of their work. It is only natural that the grizzly bear, because of his glamour as well as his importance as a big-game animal, should receive special interest among these specialists in the field. It was therefore this writer's purpose, during the fall of 1953, to visit the various state and federal offices in the West, to find out as much as possible about the present situation regarding the grizzly where he still exists and, in those states where the species has been exterminated, to get something of the circumstances surrounding the passing of the last member of Old Ephraim's tribe into the limbo of historical recollections.

It should be realized that big-game hunting is big business in a good many parts of our country and the annual toll of animals is high. The inventory compiled by the U. S. Fish and Wildlife Service for the hunting season of 1952 gives a total of 1,246,158 head of big game of all varieties reported as legally taken throughout the United States. This does not include the game killed by Indians, who are not required to report, or the large number which each year are illegally taken or not reported. The actual figure for this one year probably runs close to 2,000,000. That is almost eight times the number of U. S. Army personnel killed in combat during all of World War II. The total big-game population of the United States prior to the 1952 hunting season was estimated at slightly over ten and one half millions.

The state of Montana has a particularly active Fish and Game Department. The state is divided into thirty-seven game-management unit areas, in each of which is carried on a well-organized program of investigations, surveillance, and annual cumulative recording of big-game facts and figures. The 1952–53 state-wide report shows an estimated total big-game population of 336,112—more than all the surviving Indians throughout the United States—and the legally reported kill of big game was 79,313. Special attention was given to the grizzly bears, and they were found to exist in twelve of the management unit areas. The total population of these animals was set at 437, plus 120 in the sanctuary of Glacier National Park. The legally reported kill was 10. The previous year showed a total population of 635 and the kill was 20. This indicates a one-year decrease of 78, or more than 14 per cent. The inventory of the U. S. Fish and Wildlife Service, released in the fall of 1953, shows a more liberal estimate of 758 grizzlies in Montana, although the state census is probably the more accurate.

The one area in the United States where there are today

evidently more grizzlies in their wild natural habitat than any-where else is the Flathead-Sun River district of western Montana. The latest state survey indicates 154 of the animals in this region. The report for 1951 showed 190, and 245 in 1948 —a decrease of almost 60 per cent in four years. The increase in the sanctuary of Glacier Park has only been 20 or about 17 per cent in this same period.

The steadily losing fate of the grizzly, under existing circumstances, is further accentuated by the fact that nowhere else in the United States is there such a large area so well suited to the survival and well-being of these animals as that section of the Rocky Mountains which spreads across the western part of Montana. It has the added advantage of having the great natural sanctuary of Glacier Park on the north and Yellowstone Park on the south; and it offers numerous areas of high and rugged retreats, with thousands of square miles of intervening dense forest, much of which is as wild and difficult to travel as it was a hundred years ago. But there is nowhere the white hunter will not go; and, the grizzly being the exciting trophy that he is, the species is sure to be hunted down and exterminated unless legal protection is promptly given—even in western Montana.

It is only natural to expect that the great state of Wyoming should today provide the haunts for a good many of the descendants of Old Ephraim. Extending down through the central part of the state are the Big Horn Mountains, which not so many years ago were considered one of the finest hunting grounds of all the West. Such notable grizzly hunters of the 1880s and 90s as Teddy Roosevelt, Col. Wm. D. Pickett, J. C. Merrill, and many more chose this area above all others for their exciting exploits. Colonel Pickett, whose experience as a grizzly hunter was probably unexcelled, killed as many as twenty-three of these bears in a single season in the Big Horns. Also occupying a large section of the northwest corner of Wyoming is Yellowstone National Park, embracing well over two million acres of virgin wilderness which in 1872 was set apart as an ideal sanctuary for the preservation of the wild game of the Old West. But the grizzly population of the entire state of Wyoming, outside of Yellowstone Park, according to the 1952 report of the U. S. Fish and Wildlife Service, was only 49. The State Fish and Game Association set the number at 62. In spite of this low figure, the reported kill for the same year was 6, and 14 were taken the previous year—for grizzlies are fair game in Wyoming. It does not take an expert in natural history or game conservation to foresee the extermination of the species, under circumstances which provide no safeguard for their perpetuation.

Even in Yellowstone Park the welfare of the grizzly has become subservient to the whims of the tourists who each summer flock to enjoy the natural beauties of this mountain wonderland. The black bear, unlike his silvertip relative, is of far greater placability of disposition and has been able to adapt himself to the modes of tourists and encroaching civilization. No one can drive through Yellowstone without encountering the black hairy beggars who come out on the highways to stop the automobile travelers and insist on handouts of sandwiches and chocolate bars. On my recent visit I even saw a big male coyote who had adopted the begging tactics of the black bears and brazenly ambled from one to another of the half-dozen autos he had "held up" on one of the main highways through the wilderness. But such prostitution of nature's dignity is below the regal self-respect of Old Ephraim. He has never stooped to be a beggar of man or conciliated his forthright hostility. What he takes he seizes with arrogance; and because of this he has suffered, even in this great sanctuary which was created, just as the Indian reservations were sardonically set aside, for the perpetuation of life and liberty.

Just how many grizzlies remain in Yellowstone Park, surprising though it may seem, is not well established. "We have no figures on the total population of grizzlies in Yellowstone," writes Edmund B. Rogers, superintendent of the park, in a letter dated June 11, 1954. The Fish and Game Commission of the state of Montana, however, set the figure at 180, as a result of their own survey.

To watch the bears come out to feed at the garbage dumps was for many years one of the favorite tourist attractions in Yellowstone. This practice had to be abandoned, however, because the tourists persisted in their desire to get snapshots of Little Susie patting a nice big grizzly bear. On this writer's recent visit not a single members of Old Ephraim's tribe was seen; and he heard the disquieting rumor that these bears "had been killed off, as a menace to the safety of tourists." When queried regarding this, the U. S. Fish and Wildlife Service in Washington, D.C., diplomatically evaded the issue. In the letter above referred to, however, the superintendent of Yellowstone had the following to say: "In April 1954 we killed four adult grizzlies which were especially dangerous in the Old Faithful area. In 1953 one adult grizzly was accidentally killed on a highway by an automobile; one young animal was killed to avoid damage to people and property, and two other young ones were trapped for the same reason and shipped to a zoo. In 1952 only one grizzly, an adult, was killed in the interest of public safety. . . . Only as a last resort do we kill grizzlies. Probably the greatest drain on the Yellowstone population is by hunter harvest along the boundaries in the states of Wyoming and Montana."

The nearest approach to a state-wide protection for the grizzly is in Idaho, where I grew up as a boy and where they once were plentiful. There has been *no open season* on grizzly throughout the state since 1946, although even here they may be killed "if molesting livestock." The official estimated census in the spring of 1954 was set at 67—which hardly presents a serious threat to the livestock industry of Idaho. Most of these are in the extreme northern part of the state.

Idaho is to be congratulated for leading the way in offering game-law protection to Old Ephraim. Sixty-seven individuals of a species is not a great many, but neither does it present an entirely hopeless prospect for the future. The sportsmen by and large will respect the law, although to the farmers, and particularly the many sheep raisers who graze their flocks on the grassy ranges adjacent to grizzly country, the future of Old Ephraim will never be secure, even if he never lays a claw upon any livestock. It is the old theory that the grizzly is Public Enemy Number One to all domestic stock; and this provides an ever-ready subterfuge which can easily nullify the existing law.

The narrow panhandle of northern Idaho is flanked on both sides by states where grizzly are fair game for the hunter. This presents much the same situation as the borders surrounding Yellowstone Park; and it is in the neighborhood of the Idaho boundary, in the northeastern corner of Washington, where most of the grizzlies are taken in the latter state. Unfortunately, however, very little has been done by the Washington Department of Game in the way of conservation or established information on the subject. So far as the inventory of the U. S. Fish and Wildlife Service shows, there are no grizzlies whatever in the state of Washington, although the state's Chief of Game Management Division, in a letter under date of June 3, 1954, supplied the following rather vague information: "There have been several grizzly bears killed in this state during the past three or four seasons . . . I think that one group of hunters from the Spokane area killed two grizzly bears during the past hunting season."

My own native state of Colorado is the fifth in which remnants of Old Ephraim's tribe still survive. In July 1951 "it was established beyond doubt that grizzly bears still exist in Colorado. . . ." according to the Quarterly Progress Report of the state's Department of Fish and Game. More specific information is contained in the Game Commission's official periodical, *Colorado Conservation*, for the same year and month, by one of their wildlife technicians who ironically reported that "the total present grizzly population in the state is estimated at ten or less." Ten grizzlies or less in the whole state of Colorado in 1951! The U. S. Fish and Wildlife Service set the figure for 1952 at 32 grizzlies. When I raised the question of numbers, on my visit to the Game Department's headquarters in Denver in the fall of 1953, however, my informant cited a statement of the commission's manager of their Educational Division, which set the number at 16, although his own opinion was that this was an overly optimistic estimate. Most if not all of these bears were in the San Juan region in the southeastern part of the state. The number of black bears, incidentally, was set at 70,000. And yet Old Ephraim has continued to remain as fair game for hunters in every open season, on the same basis as black bears, and always subject to being killed by more or less apprehensive, or opportunist, livestock men. This combination of circumstances has brought about the virtual extinction of the species throughout the state; and today the only place where one can be sure of finding a Colorado grizzly is in the beautiful Denver Museum of Natural History.

From the foregoing data it would seem there are in the neighborhood of 569 grizzly bears, or less, living in the United States in a wild state, outside of Yellowstone and Glacier National Park. The grand total to be found everywhere in this country, including all parks, is evidently between 850 and 875. Lined up end to end along any highway, that would be quite a tribe of grizzly bears; but, scattered as they are through the wildest sections of the Rocky Mountains, and subject to continual slaughter almost without restraint of protective law, it is a pretty sad state of affairs, by all the standards that nature measures a principal species. To estimate the inevitable trend to the future we have only to look over the vast territory where these mighty creatures are now entirely a historic memory.

In the states of Nebraska, Kansas, and Oklahoma, the Big Plains grizzly that once followed the buffalo herds across the rolling hills and grassy prairies was so long ago that no records are to be found in the game-commission offices and many doubt that Old Ephraim ever was there. There have been no grizzlies even in the Dakotas since the early 1900s; and the last authenticated kill was evidently made near the town of Oakdale, North Dakota, in the fall of 1897, by one Dave Warren.

In the state of Texas, one of the few established records of these big bears being taken was in the Davis Mountains about fifteen miles southeast of Livermore Peak, near the site of McDonald Observatory. This was a large male, estimated to have weighed around 1000 pounds, and was shot November 2, 1890, by C. O. Finley and John Means. The skull was used by Dr. C. Hart Merriam to establish the subspecies known as the Texas Grizzly (*Ursus texensis* Merriam).

Moving westward takes us into a country where the grizzlies were once so numerous that they seriously challenged the right of the primitive Indians to live in the land. It was in those colorful mountains that the remarkable Ben Lilly became famous as a killer of bears and panthers, leaving behind a rich galaxy of exploits that have become legends in the Southwest. This bearded old man of the game trails, in March 1911, followed a lone grizzly from the Animas Mountains of southwestern New Mexico, down into Old Mexico, through the San Luis Mountains of Chihuahua, into Sonora, and back into Chihuahua before finally killing the bear. By the spring of 1917 the official survey set the number of grizzlies still surviving in all of the state of New Mexico at only 48; and by 1927 the species had reached the point of "almost total extermination." Just when and by whom the last one was actually killed is a matter of doubt, although it was evidently twenty or more years ago.

In Arizona the situation is similar. The files of the U. S. Fish and Wildlife Service in Phoenix, which are by far the most complete, indicate that the last grizzly of record to be killed in that state was a two-year-old taken in 1935 in Greenlee County, near the New Mexico boundary, by Richard R. Miller. There was also one killed the previous fall in Stray Horse Canyon. It is doubtful if any grizzly has been taken since, for the publicity alone which would naturally result from such an incident could hardly have escaped the keen attention of the Fish and Wildlife Service naturalists or the State Game Department wardens. There would be no reason for hiding the facts, for if a grizzly should today appear anywhere in Arizona there would be a simple subterfuge to a killing privilege. Section 57-109A of the State Game Law reads: "Any landowner or lessee who is a legitimate livestock operator may authorize the taking of stock killing bear, provided, however, that a witnessed statement, describing in detail the facts of such stock killing, shall be signed by the stockman and filed within thirty (30) days after the bear has been taken, with the Phoenix office of the commission, or local game ranger." Stockmen throughout the West have never required as much as thirty days to find an excuse for killing a grizzly bear—and their excuses, when given, have never been seriously questioned.

In the state of Utah we find the date of August 22, 1923, deeply engraved at the end of the last chapter in the life story of Old Ephraim's tribe. In Cache County, not far from the northern border, there is a large wooden monument and a heap of native rock, put there by local Boy Scouts to mark the passing of the last Utah grizzly, which was shot there by Frank Clark. The epitaph indicates that this creature weighed about 1100 pounds and it stood 9 feet 11 inches in height. The skull is in the Smithsonian Institution, Washington, D.C.

The last of the great bears of record in the state of Oregon faded into the limbo of history on September 14, 1931, when it was shot by Evan Stoneman, on Chesnimnus Creek, in northeast Wallowa County.

There are no established records for the state of Nevada where, according to the Fish and Game Commission, "the grizzly bear has never existed."

Little more than a hundred years ago—and that is a very brief space of time in the history of life on this earth—there were probably more grizzly bears in California than anywhere else in the United States. The big carnivores had been enjoying a prosperous existence in that salubrious land for a million years or more, going back to the days of the saber-tooth tiger and other Pleistocene monsters that roamed the sunny valleys and had fought among themselves for untold centuries. But then came the white man—and within less than seventy-five years every grizzly bear in the state of California had been tracked down and killed.

In 1850, when the gold rush blossomed into full swing and Americans began settling the state's fertile areas, grizzly bears were so plentiful that in many sections they seriously affected the raising of domestic stock and it was considered unsafe for a settler to go along a trail after dark to visit his neighbor. One of the favorite pastimes of the Spanish colonial sportsmen still was the roping of grizzlies to stage bloody fights with domestic bulls. As a present-day evidence of the abundance of these mightiest of bears, some two hundred of the state's topographical features, streams, and towns got their names from the grizzly: Grizzly Peak, in back of Berkeley; Grizzly Mountain, in Trinity County; Grizzly Springs, in Lake County; Grizzly Bluff, in Humboldt County; and no less than twenty-two Grizzly creeks, to mention only a few instances. Even popular Yosemite Park derives its name from a Miwok Indian name for the grizzly bear; and there is no more significant association than the fact the grizzly has been the official symbol of California since 1846, when the American residents revolted against Mexican authority and adopted Old Ephraim as the emblem on their flag. The selfsame figure of this bear still stands boldly on today's official state flag. And what follower of modern athletics is not familiar with the "Golden Bears" of California.

When Americans began settling California in 1850, the records indicate as many as forty grizzly bears were seen in sight at one time.[132] And yet, in Mendocino County, the last grizzly was slain in the fall of 1875, and the last one of record in the Yosemite region was in 1887. In the mountain regions of Southern California the big bears held onto existence somewhat longer. There are accounts of them being lassoed in Los Angeles County in 1857, for the popular bear-and-bull fights at the mission; and as late as the winter of 1879–80 a 500-pound grizzy was killed in the vicinity of Pasadena. There were still a few in the San Gabriel Mountains in the early 1890s. The last grizzly of record to be killed in Southern California, according to the authorities Grinnell, Dixon, Linsdale, was on October 28, 1916, in Tujunga Canyon, about two miles northeast of Sunland, in Los Angeles County. This bear had been enjoying a few grapes in the vineyard of Cornelius B. Johnson, who caught it in a steel trap and finished its career with a rifle.

The last of all the grizzlies in the state of California, according to the best information, was shot in August 1922 at Horse Corral Meadows, Tulare County, by Jesse B. Agnew, a cattle rancher. Thus came to an end the million-year-long history of the beast that walked like man and was the rightful native son of the state of California.

Where the members of Old Ephraim's tribe still survive in the United States, the ragged margin which separates them from total extinction has been steadily narrowing. The day when the last of the species will go down into that black abyss comes closer and closer into the foreseeable future, as surely as the sun goes down in the west. He survived through the centuries and ages of time—through geographic holocausts that radically changed the shape and climate of the whole continent on which he lived. He endured and perpetuated where hundreds of other mighty species failed. Nothing endangered his robust defiance to all enemies, both natural and unnatural, until the white man invaded his native land. This nemesis struck swiftly and destructively.

We have excused ourselves for subjugating the Indian and destroying his culture, and for sweeping the herds of buffalo of the plains, to make a place for our farms and our towns. The best we can claim on behalf of the grizzly is that he pro-

vided a questionable menace to the welfare of domestic livestock. To be sure, he has taken a toll of stock, as well as men,
although the extensive investigations of experts have proven
that this claim is as poorly founded as the excuse for our attitude toward the Indian. The grizzly has never been considered
worth the powder as a source of food or for the value of
his hide, as the buffalo and other game animals have. Certainly we have not required the sort of land where he likes
best to live. Everyone, from the naturalists to the sportsmen
and even the cattlemen, have acknowledged him the greatest
wild creature that has lived on this continent within the history
of man. Silent and sagacious, he has asked very little for himself—only to be left alone in the wildest and most worthless
parts of the remaining wilderness. And yet, from the earliest
times, we have marked him for extermination. From cubhood
to patriarchal old age he has been subjected to an intensive
Armageddon by every means of destruction which the white
man has been able to devise. In spite of all this, Old Ephraim
has marched proudly down the trail of inevitable expropria-
tion, haughty and steadfast in his harsh ideology. Never has
he lost his bold arrogance or his savage dignity, nor has he
ever bowed to the subjugation of what the white man chooses
to call his own civilization—choosing instead, it seems, to pay
the price of annihilation, to the last member of his race.

APPENDIX

Appendix

FOOTNOTES

CHAPTER II

1. *Note on a Gigantic Bear from the Pleistocene of Rancho La Brea,* by John C. Merriam. University of California Publications. Bulletin of the Department of Geology, No. 6, April 18, 1911, pp. 163–66. (This paper describes remains found in 1906.)
2. "Two Fossil Grizzly Bears from the Pleistocene," by J. Willis Stovall and C. Stuart Johnson. In *The Journal of Geology.* Chicago, February–March 1935.
3. *The Pleistocene Mammals of Iowa,* by O. P. Hay. Iowa Geological Survey, Vol. XXIII, 1912.
4. *Preliminary Report on a Recently Discovered Pleistocene Cave Deposit, Near Cumberland, Maryland.* Proceedings, U. S. National Museum. Vol. XLVI, 1914.

CHAPTER III

5. *When Buffalo Ran,* by George Bird Grinnell. New Haven, 1920, p. 38.
6. Ibid., p. 27.
7. *Old Indian Trails,* by Walter McClintock. Boston, 1923, p. 16. (This book is a particularly rich source of Indian culture.)
8. Several lexicographers as well as anthropologists have endeavored to establish the word "Amerind" (composed from the first syllables of "American Indian") as a substitute for this inappropriate term. Introduction of the term "Amerind" was apparently first suggested by an American lexicographer in 1899 (*Handbook of American Indians.* Bureau of American Ethnology, 1912, p. 49). A plea by Dr. W. J. McGee for its general adoption appeared in 1900 in the *Journal* of the Anthropological Institute of Great Britain. Use of the word was

also suggested at the International Congress of Americanists, in New York, in 1902, bringing forth a discussion in which it was supported by some and attacked by others. (See: *Science*, n.s., XVI, 892, 1902.) The name has since found its way into some scientific literature, although it has never found popular acceptance.

9. *Bear Ceremonialism in the Northern Hemisphere* (a thesis), by A. Irving Hollowell. Philadelphia, 1926.

10. Ibid., pp. 43 *et seq.*

11. *An Introductory Discourse, delivered before the Literary and Philosophical Society of New York*, on May 4, 1814, by Dewitt Clinton, Ll.D., New York, 1815, p. 27.

12. Ibid., p. 75.

13. "Zoology of North America," by George Ord. In *Gutherie's Geography*, second American edition, Vol. II. Philadelphia, 1815.

14. DeWitt Clinton, op. cit., p. 27.

CHAPTER IV

15. See "The Great Grizzly Bear." *True Bear Stories*, by Joaquin Miller. Chicago, 1900, pp. 96–105.

16. *Digging for History at Drake's Bay*, by Lawrence A. Williams. In *Pacific History*, published by the California Academy of Science. Vol. VI, No. 4, July–August 1953, p. 12.

17. *Handbook of American Indians*, Bureau of Ethnology, Vol. II, 1912, p. 528.

18. "The Ute Bear Dance," by Verner Z. Reed. *The American Anthropologist*, Vol. IX, July 1896, pp. 237–44.

19. Ibid., p. 237.

20. Ibid., p. 239.

21. Ibid., p. 242.

CHAPTER V

22. *Journal d'un Voyage Fait par ordre du Roi dans l'Amérique Septentrionale; Adresse à Madame la Duchesse Delesdignieres. Par le P. De Compagnie de Jesus*. Paris, 1744, Vol. 5, pp. 169–75.

23. Walter McClintock, op. cit., pp. 290–95.

24. See "Bear Mother," by Dr. Marius Barbeau. *Journal of American Folklore*, Vol. 59, No. 231, January–March, 1946.

25. *The Thompson Indians of British Columbia*, by James Teit. *Memoirs* of The American Museum of Natural History. Vol. II, No. IV; New York, April 1900.

26. *A Journey from Prince of Wales's Fort, in Hudson's Bay, to the Northern Ocean . . . in the years 1769 to 1772.* Dublin, 1796. Footnote on p. 372.

27. *The Story of the Indian,* by George Bird Grinnell. New York, 1896, pp. 206 *et seq.*

28. *Blackfoot Lodge Tales,* by George Bird Grinnell. New York, 1892, pp. 65–69.

29. Walter McClintock, op. cit., pp. 174–78.

30. "The Grizzly Bear's Medicine," by George Bird Grinnell. In *The Punishment of the Stingy.* New York, 1901, pp. 87–113.

CHAPTER VI

31. *Early Narratives of the Northwest, 1634–1699.* Edited by Louise Phelps Kellog, Ph.D. New York, 1917, pp. 133–34.

32. "The Career of Henry Kelsey," by James F. Kenny, Ph.D. In *Transactions of the Royal Society of Canada,* Section II, May 1929, pp. 37–71.

33. "The Journal of Henry Kelsey," by Charles Napier Bell, President—The Historical Society of Manitoba. *Transactions:* No. 4 (New Series). Winnipeg, May 24, 1928, p. 33.

34. *The Kelsey Papers,* with an Introduction by Arthur G. Doughty and Chester Martin. Published by the Public Archives of Canada and the Public Record Office of Northern Ireland. Ottawa, Canada, 1929. In 1926 certain documents were presented to the Public Record Office of Northern Ireland by Major A. F. Dobbs, of Castle Dobbs, Carrickfergus. These interesting papers had presumably remained buried in the major's family possession since they were collected by his illustrious ancestor, Arthur Dobbs, who from 1754 to his death in 1765 was governor of North Carolina, British colony in America. In this collection of documents was found the 128-page handwritten journal of Henry Kelsey, together with letters and other related memorandums. The journal was dated in the year 1693, at which time, according to the records of the Hudson's Bay Company, Kelsey was on a visit to his home in England. The documents were subjected to a careful examination and substantiation by checking against the excellent records that were kept by the Hudson's Bay Company and various other related facts.

35. James F. Kenny, op. cit., pp. 37–71.

36. *New Voyages to North America.* Edited by Reuben Gold Thwaites. Chicago, 1905, Vol. V, p. 169. Original 1703 Edition, p. 346.

37. *Journal d'un Voyage Fait Par Ordre du Roi dans L'Amerique Septentrionale . . .* Paris, 1744.

38. *Journal . . . of . . . Charlevoix.* Edited by Dr. Louise Phelps Kellog. Chicago, 1923, 2 vols.

39. *Pennant's Arctic Zoology.* London, 1784, Vol. I, pp. 62–64. (Charlevoix, Nouv. Fr., Paris, 1744, pp. 169–74.)

40. *Journal of a Voyage to America . . . of Pierre Xavier de Charlevoix . . .* Edited by Louise Phelps Kellog. Chicago, 1923, Vol. I, p. 173.

41. *A Journey from Prince of Wales's Fort, in Hudson's Bay, to the Northern Ocean . . . In the years 1769–1772,* by Samuel Hearne. Dublin, 1796, p. 372.

42. *The Present State of Hudson's Bay,* by Edward Umfreville. London, MDCCXC.

Chapter VII

43. *History of the Expedition under the command of Lewis and Clark. To the Sources of the Missouri River, thence across the Rocky Mountains and down the Columbia River to the Pacific Ocean, performed during the years 1804-5-6, by Order of the Government of the United States. A New Edition Faithfully Reprinted from the only Authorized Edition of 1814, with Copious Critical Commentary, Prepared Upon Examination of Unpublished Official Archives and Many Other Sources of Information, Including a Dilligent Study of the Original Manuscript Journals and Field Notebooks of the Explorers,* etc., by Elliott Coues, etc. In four volumes. New York, 1893. (Limited to one thousand copies.) The original edition used by Coues was titled: *History of the Expedition under the command of Captains Lewis and Clark to the sources of the Missouri, thence across the Rocky Mountains and down the River Columbia to the Pacific Ocean. Performed during the years 1804-5-6. By order of the Government of the United States.* Prepared for the press by Paul Allan, Esquire. In two volumes. Vol. 1 (II). Philadelphia, Bradford and Inskeep; and Abm. H. Inskeep, New York. J. Maxwell, Printer. 1814. (8 vo. Vol. I., pp. i–xxviii, 1–420, with one large folding and 2 small maps. Vol. II, pp. 1–ix, 1–522, and 3 small maps, also 5 copper plates. This being the original and only authoritative history of the expedition. Elliott Coues.) (The absolute date of publication of this work was February 20, 1814—McCracken.)

The 1814 edition was by no means the earliest account of the Lewis and Clark Expedition that was published and brought the work of these explorers to the attention of the American public and the world. The eminent Dr. Coues has the following to say regarding this, in his Bibliographical Introduction, which further explains the present author's choice of quotes and footnotes which have been used:

"Publication of the results of this memorable undertaking was attended by the untoward circumstances that neither Lewis nor Clark became the ostensible author, and that, pending the preparation of their MSS. for the press at other hands, two separate sources of incomplete information respecting their Expedition became available. These were eagerly seized by certain dishonest publishers, who appreciated the lively and general interest which the intrepid explorers had awakened. The result was the appearance of several spurious books which purported to be, in one way or another, the 'Narrative', 'Travels', or 'Journey', of 'Lewis and Clark' . . . and quotation of 'Lewis and Clark' has too often been made with reference to the bogus books."

First was the *Jefferson Prodrome and the Apocrypha*, a message of the President dated of February 19, 1806, when the expedition was still in Oregon, and subsequent *State Documents* in the same year. These formed the basis for several publications which shortly followed. Dr. Coues refers to these in such terms as "motley volume," "wretched meretricious compilation," and characterizes the author of another as "a bold man . . . Whereas the compiler, editor, thief, or whatever he may have been . . . retired behind an anonym." There was, however, the "perfectly authentic" *Journal* by Patrick Gass, which was published in 1807. Gass accompanied the expedition and was "an intelligent and observant person of very limited education, who kept a diary of his own." The first authentic history of the expedition which has come down to us, however, was not published until 1814.

44. Coues, footnote 6, p. 90.

45. Ibid., p. 91; original Lewis and Clark, p. 60.

46. Ibid., p. 200; L. & C., p. 288.

47. Ibid., p. 187.

48. Ibid., p. 200; L. & C., p. 288.

49. Ibid., pp. 297–98; L. & C., pp. 207–8.

50. Ibid., pp. 306–7; L. & C., pp. 214–15.

51. Ibid., footnote 21, p. 307.

52. Ibid., pp. 309–10; L. & C., pp. 216–17.

53. Ibid., pp. 370–71; L. & C., pp. 264–65.

54. Ibid., p. 381; L. & C., p. 274.

55. Ibid., p. 393; L. & C., p. 283.

56. Ibid., Chapter XXV, "Botany and Zoology." Vol. II, pp. 841–42; L. & C., pp. 165–66.

57. Ibid., Vol. III, footnote 39, pp. 841–42.

58. Ibid., pp. 1029–30; L. & C., Vol II, pp. 303–4. It is quite obvious that this is a distinction between the grizzly, which was referred to by these Indians as *hohhost*, and the brown color phase of the black bear, which they recognized as *yackah* and an entirely different animal.

CHAPTER VIII

59. *Frank Forester's Field Sports,* by Henry William Herbert. (New edition.) New York, 1848, Vol. II, p. 188.

60. See Appendix, *"Principle Scientific Descriptions."*

61. *Geographical, Historical and Commercial Grammar; and Present State of the Several Kingdoms of the World,* by William Gutherie, Esq. In 2 vols. Philadelphia, 1815. Volume II contains Ord's "Zoology."

62. The history of existing known copies of the original "Ord's Zoology" is briefly summarized in the following statement taken from a letter under date of July 2, 1953, to this writer, by (Mrs.) Venia T. Phillips, Librarian, the Academy of Natural Sciences of Philadelphia, which is quoted in part: "We have the original article by Ord, that is, pages 291–360, as a separate. The Union Catalog of Philadelphia reports a copy of the entire Volume II of the *Geography* at the Historical Society of Pennsylvania here in Philadelphia. I hoped this might be the copy that had come from Dr. Cohen's library, but the Historical Society's librarian states that the one they have was donated by Mrs. C. B. Bartlett in the early 1900's, and it has no annotations whatever. Our bibliographic data indicates that the Cohen copy was George Ord's and annotated by him with notes in pencil. This one at the Historical Society cannot, therefore, be Dr. Cohen's copy. The Library of Congress has an imperfect copy of Volume II of the Geography, one in which the title page and table of contents are badly mutilated or missing.

"At the suggestion of the librarian of the Historical Society here, I called a bibliographer in this city who knows the son of J. Soles Cohen, and he believes it will be next to impossible to trace the (original) copy."

63. The complete title page reads: *A Reprint of the North American Zoology by George Ord. Being an exact reproduction of the part originally compiled by Mr. Ord for Johnson and Warren, and first published by them in their Second American Edition of Gutherie's Geography, in 1815, Taken From Mr. Ord's Private, Annotated Copy. To which is added an appendix on the more important Scientific and Historical Questions Involved. By Samuel N. Rhoads. Published by the Editor. Haddonfield, New Jersey, 1894.*

CHAPTER IX

64. *The Cheyenne Indians,* by George Bird Grinnell. New Haven, 1923, 2 vols., Vol. I, p. 291.

65. *Report of Explorations and Surveys . . .* [of a] *Route for a Rail-*

road from the Mississippi River to the Pacific Ocean, by C. B. R. Kennerly. Washington, 1856. Vol. IV, pt. 6, pp. 1–17.

66. *Mammals of New Mexico,* by Vernon Bailey. North American Fauna, No. 53. Bureau of Biological Survey, Washington, D.C., December 1931, p. 365.

67. *Sporting Adventures in the Far West,* by John M. Murphy. London, 1879, pp. 30–31. (There is also an American edition of 1880.)

68. *The Kentucky Rifle,* by Townsend Whelen. New York, 1918.

69. See: "The Percussion Plains Rifle," by T. B. Tryon. In *The American Rifleman,* November 1936.

CHAPTER X

70. *Hunting the Grisly and Other Sketches,* by Theodore Roosevelt. In *The Works of Theodore Roosevelt,* Executive Edition, New York, n. d., pp. 56–57.

71. Ibid., p. 67.

72. *Thirty Years of Army Life on the Border,* by Bvt. Brig. Gen. R. B. Marcy. New York, 1874, p. 353.

73. Vernon Bailey, op. cit., p. 6.

74. Ibid., pp. 357–58.

75. *Voyages and Travels in Various Parts of the World—During the Years 1803 to 1807.* London, 1814 (Russell Reprint, 1927), pp. 82–83.

76. "Grizzly Bear Lore," by Henry G. Tinsley. *Outing Magazine,* November 1902.

77. The writer of this present book, during a research survey in the fall of 1953, visited the California Department of Fish and Game, at Sacramento; and, among other inquiries, an effort was made to substantiate this statement or add to the facts. While no records directly bearing upon it were available, it is presumed that the capable editors of *Outing Magazine* had sufficient justification for printing the statement; and, based on this writer's personal knowledge of the numbers of Alaska brown bears killed by commercial hunters on the Alaska Peninsula, there seems no reason why this early California figure should not be accepted.

78. Marcy, op. cit., pp. 284–85.

79. *Mountain Men,* by Stanley Vestal. Boston, 1937, pp. 160–61.

CHAPTER XI

80. *The Song of Hugh Glass,* by John G. Neihardt. (Date unknown.)

81. *James Bridger,* by J. Cecil Alter. With which is incorporated a

verbatim copy, annotated, by James Bridger . . . by Maj. Gen. Grenville M. Dodge. Salt Lake City, Utah, 1925.

82. *James Clyman—American Frontiersman* (*1791–1881*). Edited by Charles L. Camp. California Historical Society, Special Publications No. 3, Cleveland, 1928, p. 25.

83. J. Cecil Alter, op. cit., p. 26.

84. Stanley Vestal, op. cit., p. 62.

85. See: *The Travels of Jedediah Smith*, by Maurice S. Sullivan. Santa Ana, California, 1934. Also: *The Way to the West*, by Emerson Hough. Indianapolis, 1903. Also: *Jedediah Smith and the Opening of the West*, by Dale Morgan. Indianapolis, 1953.

86. Charles L. Camp, op. cit., pp. 25–26.

87. *The Fur Trade and Early Western Exploration*, by Clarence A. Vandiveer. Cleveland, 1929, p. 258.

88. *The Wilderness Hunter*, by Theodore Roosevelt. New York, 1893, p. 9.

89. *Life of Kit Carson*, by Charles Bardett. Philadelphia, 1869, p. 143.

90. Ibid., p. 229.

91. Emerson Hough, op. cit., p. 223.

92. *The Life and Adventures of Kit Carson*, by DeWitt Clinton Peters. New York, 1853.

CHAPTER XII

93. *The Wilderness Hunter*, Roosevelt, op. cit., pp. 258–59.

94. Marcy, op. cit., pp. 404–9.

95. *Hunting the Grisly*, Roosevelt, op. cit., p. 122.

96. "Ba'tiste the Bear Hunter," in *Outing Magazine*, February 1903. Also see: "Some Bears," by Arthur E. McFarlane, *Outing Magazine*, May 19.

97. *Hunting the Grisly*, Roosevelt, op. cit., pp. 143–44.

98. *Reminiscences of a Ranger . . . in Southern California*, by Maj. Horace Bell. Los Angeles, 1881.

99. Ibid., p. 359.

100. Ibid., pp. 359–60.

101. *Hunting Grounds of the Great West*, by Col. Richard I. Dodge. London, 1877, pp. 214–15.

CHAPTER XIII

102. *Fur Bearing Mammals of California*, by J. Grinnell, J. S. Dixon, and J. M. Linsdale. Berkeley, California, 1937, 2 vols., Vol. 2, p. 77.

103. Maj. Horace Bell, op. cit., p. 254.

104. Marcy, op. cit., pp. 331–33.

105. *Three Years in California*, by J. D. Borthwick. London, 1857.

106. *Helena Weekly Herald*, Helena, Montana. October 8, 1868, Vol. 2, No. 45, p. 8.

Chapter XIV

107. There is a Boston reprint of the same year; also a briefer account, *Life of J. C. Adams,* presumably an autobiography, printed in New York late in 1860. The original edition was reprinted in 1911.

108. See: "The California Grizzly—Emblem of the Golden Gate State," by Macy I. Stover and Lloyd P. Tevis, Jr., *Pacific Discovery.* California, July–August 1953, pp. 22–27.

Chapter XV

109. Vernon Bailey, op. cit., p. 360.

Chapter XVI

110. *The Grizzly—Our Greatest Wild Animal,* by Enos A. Mills. Boston, 1919, pp. 275 *et seq.*

111. Ibid., p. 13.

112. Joaquin Miller, op. cit., pp. 114–15.

113. Vernon Bailey, op. cit., p. 360.

114. Ibid., p. 365.

115. *Hunting the Grisly,* Roosevelt, op. cit., pp. 61 *et seq.*

116. Ibid., pp. 62–63.

117. *Hunting Trips of a Ranchman,* by Theodore Roosevelt. New York, 1897 edition, pp. 326–27.

118. Enos A. Mills, op. cit., pp. 155–56.

119. Ibid., pp. 155–58.

Chapter XVII

120. See the following books by Theodore Roosevelt: *Hunting Trips of a Ranchman* (1885); *Ranch Life and the Hunting Trail* (1888); *The Wilderness Hunter* (1893); *Hunting the Grisly and Other Sketches* (1893); *Big Game Hunting* (1898); *Good Hunting* (1907).

121. *Hunting Trips of a Ranchman*, Roosevelt, op. cit., p. 328.

122. "Trail and Camp Fire." *Book of the Boone and Crockett Club*, Editors George Bird Grinnell and Theodore Roosevelt. New York, 1897, pp. 230 *et seq.*

123. *The Grizzly Bear*, by William H. Wright. New York, 1909.

Chapter XVIII

124. *Outing Magazine*, May 1911, p. 171.

Chapter XIX

125. *The Personal Narrative of James O. Pattie, of Kentucky, during an Expedition from St. Louis through the Vast Regions between That Place and the Pacific Ocean* (a reprint of the original edition of 1831) in *Early Western Travels, 1748–1846*. Vol. 18, Cleveland, 1905.

Chapter XX

126. William H. Wright, op. cit., p. 200. (There is also a photograph of one of the newborn cubs on the opposite page.)

127. *Camp Fires in the Canadian Rockies*, by William T. Hornaday. New York, 1906, p. 173.

128. *Bears in the Yellowstone*, by M. P. Skinner. Chicago, 1925, Chap. VI.

Chapter XXII

129. *Alaska Bear Trails*, by Harold McCracken. New York, 1931.

Chapter XXIV

130. Emos A. Mills, op. cit., p. 5.

131. "Introductory Notes" in *True Bear Stories*, Joaquin Miller, op. cit., p. 7.

Chapter XXVI

132. *Fur Bearing Mammals of California*, by J. Grinnell, J. S. Dixon, and J. M. Linsdale. Berkeley, California, 1937. 2 vols. Vol. 2, pp. 69–70.

DESCRIPTION AND CLASSIFICATION
OF THE GRIZZLY BEAR

by DeWitt Clinton

In his *Introductory Discourse*, presented before the Literary and Philosophical Society of New York on May 4, 1814, and printed the following year, DeWitt Clinton recorded the following relative to the grizzly bear:

"The white-brown or grizzly bear; the ferocious tyrant of the American woods . . . a distinct animal from the *ursus arctos*, or polar bear, with which it is confused. (The Linnæan name for the polar bear is given as *ursus maritimus;* the common bear of Europe is *ursus arctos;* and the common black bear of America, *ursus americanus.*) The grizzly bear has no scientific name."

In his Note 14 (pp. 74–75) of the published work, DeWitt Clinton gives the following more complete estimation: "The white-brown, or grizzly bear, is of all colors; from a brown to almost a perfect white. It is much taller and longer than the common (black) bear; the belly is more lank. It runs much faster, and its claws, tusks, and head, are much larger and longer, and it has a large tuft on the back of its neck.

"One was shot on Lewis and Clark's expedition, which weighed between five and six hundred pounds at least; and measured eight feet seven inches and a half from the nose to the extremity of the hind feet; five feet ten inches around the breast; three feet eleven inches around the neck; one foot eleven inches around the middle of the fore leg; and his talons, five on each foot, were four inches and three-eighths. Its talons are much longer and more blunt than those of the common (black) bear; its tail shorter; its hair longer, finer, and more abundant; its liver, lungs, and heart much larger, even in proportion to its size; the heart particularly, being equal to that of a large ox; its maw ten times larger; its testicles pendant from the belly, and in separate pouches, from two to four inches asunder; whereas those of the black bear are situated back, between the thighs, like a dog; its track in the mud and sand has been sometimes eleven inches long, and seven and a quarter wide, exclusive of the talons.

"It is principally carnivorous, and will generally attack a man whenever it sees him. These animals are numerous, and their tenacity of life is wonderful. No wound except through the head, is mortal; and they have escaped after being shot in several places through the body.

"The Indians never attack him but in parties of six or eight persons, and even then are often defeated with the loss of one or more of the party; and when they go in quest of him, paint themselves, and perform all the superstitious rites customary when they make war on a neighboring nation. The Indians say these bears have killed numbers of their bravest men . . .

"It has long been supposed that this animal was the *ursus arctos* of Linnæus, and his is so characterized in the 6th volume of the Philosophical Transactions . . . I am sorry to say, that such is the low state of natural knowledge among us, that Dr. Belknap the inestimable historian of New Hampshire, has even represented our common bear as the *ursus arctos*."

DESCRIPTION AND CLASSIFICATION
OF THE GRIZZLY BEAR

by George Ord

Complete title of original work:

Geographical, Historical and Commercial Grammar; and present state of the Several Kingdoms of the World, by William Guthrie, Esq. In two volumes. Philadelphia, Johnson and Warren, 1815.
(This is the *Second Edition* of the publication, being the first to be printed in the United States; and George Ord's "Zoology" appears for the first and only time in this American Edition.)

Complete title of the Samuel H. Rhoads's reprint, from which the following quotes are taken:

A Reprint of the North American Zoology by George Ord. Being an exact reproduction of the part originally compiled by Mr. Ord for Johnson and Warren, and first published by them in their Second American Edition of Gutherie's Geography in 1815. Taken from Mr. Ord's Private, Annotated Copy. To which is added an appendix on the more important Scientific and Historical Questions Involved, by Samuel N. Rhoads. Published by the Editor. Haddonfield, New Jersey, 1894.

ZOOLOGY OF NORTH AMERICA
CLASS Mammalia; GENUS Ursus

Grizzly Bear . . . *Ursus horribilis*

"*Grizzly Bear:* 'This animal,' says Mr. Brackenridge,[1] 'is the monarch of the country which he inhabits. The African Lion, or the Tiger of Bengal, are not more terrible or fierce. He is the enemy of man, and literally thirsts for human blood. So far from shunning, he seldom fails to attack; and even to hunt him. The Indians make war upon these ferocious monsters, with the same ceremonies as they do upon a tribe of their own species; and in the recital of their victories, the death of one of them gives the warrior greater renown than the scalp of a human enemy.

" 'He possesses an amazing strength, and attacks without hesitation, and tears to pieces, the largest Buffalo. The colour is usually such as the name indicates, though there are varieties, from black to silvery whiteness. The skins are highly valued for muffs and tippets; and will bring from twenty to fifty dollars each.

" 'This Bear is not usually seen lower than the Mandan villages. In the vicinity of the Roche Jaune, and of the Little Missouri, they are said to be most numerous. They do not wander much in the prairies, but are usually found in points of wood, in the neighborhood of large streams.

" 'In shape, he differs from the common Bear in being proportionally more long and lank. He does not climb trees, a circumstance which has enabled hunters, when attacked, to make their escape.' "[2]

[1] *Views of Louisiana; together with a Journal of a Voyage up the Missouri River, in 1811.* By H. M. Brackenridge, Esq. Pittsburgh, 1814.

[2] "*Zoology of North America*," by George Ord, p. 299; Brackenridge, p. 55.

The original Ord introductory account continues: "In the history of the expedition under the command of Lewis and Clark, we have much interesting information relating to this dreadfully ferocious animal. These enterprising travellers made many narrow escapes from the attacks of this monster, who in some instances was not brought to the ground until he had received seven or eight balls through his body. As a wonderful proof of the tenacity of life of this animal, one that was killed on the nineteenth of May, 1805, ran at his usual pace nearly a quarter of a mile, after having been *shot through the heart*.

"The Grizzly Bear has been long known to naturalists; but the above travellers were the first to give us a particular account of this monarch of the American forests. One killed by them near the Porcupine river measured as follows:

	Feet	Inches
"Length from nose to the extremity of the hind foot	8	7½
Circumference near the fore legs	5	10½
" of the neck	3	11
" of the middle of the fore leg	1	11
Length of the talons		4⅜

"His weight, on conjecture, was between five and six hundred pounds. But this was not the largest Bear that was killed by the party. They give an account of one which measured *nine* feet from the nose to the extremity of the tail; and the talons of another were six and a quarter inches in length. It is said that this animal when full grown and fat will exceed a thousand pounds."[3]

In Ord's classification of the mammalia of North America (p. 291) he establishes three varieties of bears, under *Genus Ursus:* the Polar Bear (*Ursus maritimus*); the American (Black) Bear (*Ursus americanus*); and the Grizzly Bear (*Ursus horribilis*). The accepted classification in present-day nomenclature for the first two of these has been changed. The popular name of "grizzly" which George Ord gave to this animal has become universally accepted. The Latin name of *Ursus horribilis*, which he gave, has been accepted as a basis of the more recent and elaborate classifications of this genus and related forms, species, and subspecies, although Ord's name has been appended only to the one

[3]Ord, pp. 299-300.

particular variety which he described—known as the Big Plains Grizzly, *Ursus horribilis horribilis* Ord. Thus it came to be, however, that George Ord established the common name of this animal and all his closely related kin as "grizzly bear," in recognition of its color characteristics; and he gave the Latin name of *horribilis* as a recognition of its pugnacious and aggressive nature.

There are certain addenda by Samuel N. Rhoads to his reprint of George Ord's "Zoology," which are included in the Appendix added to the original work and which have a direct bearing on Ord's naming of the GRIZZLY BEAR—*URSUS HORRIBILIS.* These carry the authority of the Philadelphia Academy of Natural Sciences, which Mr. Rhoads represented; and this is probably the best place to include them: "This of Ord's is the first tenable name for the West American form, which many eminent naturalists consider too intimately related to *Ursus (sic) arctos* to form a distinct species."[4]

This indication of scientific confusion, it should be remembered, as indicated by one who spoke with authority, was written seventy-nine years after Ord's "Zoology" was published and eighty years after the Lewis and Clark journal was published.

Rhoads goes on to state: "Because of the endless controversy among zoologists respecting the status of black, brown and grizzly bears of America and their affinities with *Ursus arctos*, this original description and naming of *Ursus horribilis* has done more than anything else to keep the name of Ord prominently in scientific notice. This interest has been increased by the absolute lack of other references to Ord's description than the synonymatic ones made to it by Say, Goodman and Baird.

"Owing to the disappearance of the only known copy of Gutherie from which Baird took his references, it has been impossible to improve upon them until now. It may be disappointing to many, who now for the first time scan the description, to find that Ord in this, as in similar cases, makes no personal deductions or diagnosis of the case, as presented by Brackenridge, which might absolutely fix the type and type locality of this form as contrasted with others in the United States nearly related to it. Ord's quotations being wholly taken from Brackenridge's account (in which are included the Lewis and Clark quotations

4Reprint of Ord's "Zoology," Appendix, p. 13.

made by Ord, their sequence only being changed), we may justly define the typical habitat of *horribilis* to the western North Dakota, eastern Montana and north-eastern Wyoming. Brackenridge's description, apart from its Lewis and Clark quotations, is unquestionably taken from hearsay rather than personal experience and we must therefore base conclusions mainly on Lewis and Clark's narrative of the Bears in this region. [It is for these reasons that the Brackenridge material has not been specifically included as a separate part of this book—McCracken.] The type specimen of horribilis is the 'brown bear' (Coues' 1893 ed.; L. & C., pp. 297, 298) whose measurements Brackenridge and Ord copied from Lewis and Clark. This specimen is described as the largest they had seen up to that time; it was killed May 5, 1805, near old Fort Charles at the mouth of Little Dry or Lackwater Creek, flowing into the Missouri, in Dawson County, northeastern Montana.

"In a recent paper *'On the Character and Relationships of* URSUS CINNAMOMEUS Aud. & Bach.'[5] Mr. Arthur Erwin Brown gives a résumé of the relationships of the North American Bears to each other and to those of Europe, deciding finally that *Ursus arctos* should stand as the type, *isabellinus, syriacus, horribilis, cinnamomeus* and *americanus* being only subspecifically distinct therefrom. A strong consensus of opinion today is largely in agreement with this view. Nevertheless it is a patent fact that a trustworthy, representative series of kins, with accompanying skulls and full data, of these bears does not exist in all the museums of the world, nor is it likely that they will be secured for many years to come. Until such a collection shall have been made, the verdict cannot be final, though it is likely that it will closely approximate the conclusions of Mr. Brown. . . .

"It should be stated that the type specimen and given habitat of the *cinnamomum* of Audubon and Bachman indicate, with considerable certainty, that it is identical with Ord's *horribilis* as now defined, and that Mr. Brown's brown and yellow Bears are nothing more or less than the 'brown' and 'white'[6] Bears which con-

[5]*Proceedings of the Academy of Natural Sciences,* Philadelphia, 1894, p. 119.

[6]This is a reference to the "brown-gray" bear in *Journal of the Voyage and Travels of a Corps of Discovery,* by Patrick Gass. Philadelphia, 1811.

tinually harassed the westward march of Lewis and Clark from the Mandan villages to the eastern slopes of the Rocky Mountains. This is corroborated by the description of a skull of a 'brown bear' killed on the Missouri (sup. cit., p. 307) which mentions the 'sharp projection of the center of the frontal bone' and the great thickness of the skull, as defined by Mr. Brown for his *cinnamomeus*. The evidence, so far as I can sum it, makes cinnamomum a pure synonym of *horribilis*. [This deduction was later borne out —McCracken.]

"The California Grizzly is thought by some to represent a type subspecifically distinct from that of the Missouri Valley. [A true deduction—McCracken.] Should this be agreed to, the only applicable *existing* name is *horroeus*, applied by Baird[7] to a small Sonoran form which he thought differed from the Grizzly of Northern California. If possible, this name should be retained in preference to giving a new one."[8]

This pretty well covers the grizzly bear's advent into the dignified society of classification in scientific nomenclature. We must, however, wait through a period of 103 years after the publication of Ord's "Zoology" for the definitive classification of these bears by Dr. C. Hart Merriam.

[7]"Mammals of the Boundary," by S. F. Baird (founder of the National Museum). In *Mexican Boundary Survey*, under Lt. Col. W. H. Emory. Washington, 1859. Vol. II, pt. II, p. 24.
[8]Reprint of Ord's "Zoology," Appendix, pp. 28-29.

A CHECK LIST
OF
THE GRIZZLIES AND BIG BROWN BEARS
OF NORTH AMERICA

The accompanying check list is based on the scientific classification covering all the varieties of grizzlies and big brown bears of North America, established by Dr. C. Hart Merriam, of the U. S. Biological Survey and Smithsonian Institution. It includes all of the 86 varieties described in his *Review of the Grizzly and Big Brown Bears of North America,* North American Fauna No. 41, Washington, February 8, 1918.

It should be pointed out that Dr. Merriam's classifications were made very largely on a study of the extensive collection of skulls in the National Museum. In a number of instances there is no general description, for a single skull may have been the only available basis of information. The eminent biologist admitted that the number of varieties which he described "will appear to many as preposterous." This view is shared by most naturalists. However, Dr. Merriam goes on to state that "it is not the business of the naturalist to either create or suppress species, but to endeavor to ascertain how many Nature has established." Critical though they may be, it is not the prerogative of the layman to disclaim the findings of a qualified scientist; and the list is here given in full. Whether it may be incomplete or preposterously exaggerated, there is little that can be done to make a definitive reclassification because of the total extinction of these animals throughout the great majority of the territory where they once were found.

The various species and subspecies in the following list have been rearranged as nearly as possible to their geographic distribution, rather than the scientific grouping followed by Dr. Merriam. Few liberties have been taken with the established type localitites or range of habitat; and only the most fundamental descriptions have been included here, with some additional notes from various sources. For a more detailed scientific description the reader is referred to the original work and to the other sources cited.

Order *CARNIVORA* . . . Family *URISIDÆ* . . . Genus *URSUS*

Common names: Grizzly, grizly, white bear, gray bear, silvertip, roach-back, range bear, bald-face, big brown bear, Old Ephraim, Moccasin Joe, and other local names, as well as the various type names established in the following classification. The name grizzly is now universally recognized as the common name for all varieties except the big brown bears of Alaska and Arctic Canada.

General characteristics: This genus embraces the largest in size of all present-day carnivorous mammals on earth. They are characterized by a massive, muscular body, covered with moderately long, coarse hair, basically brown in color and grizzled or washed to a varying degree with lighter shades. The general color varies widely from a light straw color to almost black. They have high shoulders, of varying degrees; large, flat feet, heavily padded with moderately flexible soles, and are *plantigrade,* or walk with the whole foot upon the ground, like man, and not on their toes as the dog, cat, and deer families. The most common characteristics are their large, moderately curved claws of the front feet, small eyes and ears, and almost rudimentary tail. Although classified as carnivorous, they are omnivorous in their feeding habits (will eat almost anything); are solitary in their routine living habits; promiscuous in mating; hibernate in winter, except under abnormally warm climatic conditions; and are normally aggressive and dangerous in character, when provoked.

Principal Scientific Descriptions:

1784—*Grizzly Bear* (a variety of Brown Bear). Thomas Pennant's *Arctic Zoology,* Vol. I, p. 62–64.

1790—*Grizzle Bear.* Edward Umfreville, *Hudson Bay*, p. 168.

1801—*Grisly Bear.* Alexander Mackenzie, *Voyages*, p. 160.

1808—*White, or Brown-Gray Bear.* Gass' *Journal of Lewis & Clark's Expedition*, pp. 45, 116, 346.

1814—*Grisly, Brown, White & Variegated Bear (Ursus ferox).* Lewis & Clark's Voyages . . . Vol. I, pp. 243, 284, 343, 375; Vol. II, pp. 25, 268, etc.

1814–15—*Grissly Bear.* DeWitt Clinton, *Discourse* . . . Read May 4, 1814; published 1815, p. 27, 74, etc.

1815—*Ursus horribilis* (Grizzly Bear). George Ord, in *Gutherie's Geography*, 2nd (American) Edition, pp. 291, 299, 300.

1820—*Ursus cinereus.* Demarest's *Mammals*, No. 253.

1822—*Ursus horribilis.* Day, Long's *Expedition*, Vol. II, p. 244, note 34.

1826—*Ursus canadensis.* Hamilton Smith, in *Griffith's Animal Kingdom*, Vol. II, p. 229; Vol. V, p. 320.

1839—*Ursus ferox.* Richardon's *Fauna Boreali-Americana*, No. 10, pp. 24–29.

1918—*Ursus horribilis.* Dr. C. Hart Merriam, *Review of the Grizzly & Big Brown Bears of North America.* The first complete classifications of all species and subspecies.

Species and Subspecies of Genus Ursus

1. BIG PLAINS GRIZZLY—*Ursus horribilis horribilis* Ord. The first of the grizzlies to be formally described, named, and entered in accepted scientific nomenclature; by George Ord, in *Gutherie's Geography*, 2nd (American) edition, pp. 291, 299–300, in the year 1815. Based on the "white bear" of the Lewis and Clark Expedition, particularly the specimen taken on May 5, 1805, in what is now northeastern Montana, on the Missouri River, near mouth of Poplar River (called the Porcupine River in their *Journal*).

According to Dr. Merriam, the type characteristics are: size huge; skull long and massive; claws long, moderately or slightly curved, and usually streaked lengthwise with whitish or yellowish. Color variable, usually light. Sometimes referred to as "the huge buffalo-killing grizzly of the Great Plains."

2. BLACK HILLS GRIZZLY—*Ursus rogersi bisonophagus* nobis. Sundance National Forest, Black Hills, in northeast corner of Wyoming (collected in February 1887), and ranging through Black Hills of South Dakota. Characteristics: size large; skull long, slender and rather low. . . . Muzzle pale brown; head and face blackish, becoming slightly grizzled posteriorly . . . entire body, legs, and feet very dark brown overlaid on back by wash of light tips.

3. ABSAROKA GRIZZLY—*Ursus absarokus* Merriam. Head of Little Bighorn River, Bighorn Mountains, Montana (May 1893); ranging Laramie and Bighorn mountains, eastern Wyoming, Black Hills region, South Dakota, and northward along Little Missouri to Missouri and Yellowstone rivers.

4. ROGERS GRIZZLY—*Ursus rogersi rogersi* nobis. Graybull River, Absaroka Mountains, northwestern Wyoming (collected in fall of 1890 by Archibald Rogers). Skull very large and long.

5. WASHAKIE GRIZZLY—*Ursus washake* Merriam. Absaroka Mountains, western Wyoming (between Bighorn Basin and Yellowstone National Park). Skull rather short and high, moderately arched and broad, as distinguished from previous varieties; and apparently not so large in body.

6. YELLOWSTONE PARK BIG GRIZZLY—*Ursus imperator* Merriam. Yellowstone National Park. Size large; skull massive . . . closely similar to *horribilis.*

7. YELLOWSTONE PARK GRIZZLY—*Ursus mirus* nobis. Yellowstone National Park. Size medium; skull long, rather narrow and low arched.

8. IDAHO GRIZZLY—*Ursus idahoensis* nobis. North Fork Teton River, eastern Idaho. (Killed by "Beaver Dick" Richard Leigh, September 23, 1874.) Much smaller than horribilis, and shorter than *rogersi.*

9. FLAT-HEADED GRIZZLY—*Ursus planiceps* nobis. Colorado; probably in the foothills or along the western edge of the plains. Skull rather large, low, and flat. (Collected by Dr. F. V. Hayden, c. 1869.)

10. TWIN LAKES GRIZZLY—*Ursus macrodon* nobis. Twin

Lakes, Colorado. Size large; humps (at shoulders) evident. Resembling some of the Alaska brown bears; general body color rich brown, darker on humps and lightly washed with pale-tipped hairs on upper part of back. Skull rather large and flat. (Collected July 28, 1876.)

11. BAIRD GRIZZLY—*Ursus bairdi* Merriam. From San Juan Mountains, southwestern Colorado, through Wyoming and Montana, perhaps to southeastern British Columbia. Probably a mountain animal. Size large; skull long, with narrow elevated frontenasal region.

12. SHOSHONE GRIZZLY—*Ursus shoshone* Merriam. Mountains of Colorado and Wyoming. Size much smaller than *horribilis* and *bairdi*. Skull rather long and high, with flattish, short-pointed, long-sloping frontal shield.

13. UTAH GRIZZLY—*Ursus utahensis* Merriam. Southern Wasatch and Pine Valley mountains. Skull long, narrow, and high, but not arched.

14. TEXAS GRIZZLY—*Ursus horriæus texensis* Merriam. Davis Mountains, Texas, and mountains of southern Colorado. Size small; evidently a light colored or yellowish bear. Skull small; frontal shield low, narrow, flat.

15. MOUNT TAYLOR GRIZZLY—*Ursus perturbans* Merriam. Northern New Mexico. Size very large; general ground color dusky or dark brown; face and head dark brown; body dusky, back grizzled with dark golden tips; legs and feet black. Skull very long and narrow, with high crest. This may have been the grizzly that Coronado mentions when he first visited the Zuni Indians in 1540 (Bailey).

16. NEW MEXICO GRIZZLY—*Ursus horriæus* Baird. Southern New Mexico, south to Casa Grandes, Chihuahua, Mexico, and probably into eastern Arizona. Skull long, low, narrow, and flat. This is the *Coppermine Grizzly* of Vernon Bailey (1931), who describes the same skull as "short, wide and massive," and states "there is no known specimen . . . except the type skull."

17. ARIZONA GRIZZLY—*Ursus arizonæ* Merriam. Escudilla Mountains, Apache County, Arizona. Size of skull rather large, long and narrow, with broad rostrum; size of body rather large, color dull brown with yellow tips to the long hairs.

18. APACHE GRIZZLY—*Ursus apache* Merriam. White Mountains, eastern Arizona. Skull short, broad, low, rather massive, with broad frontal shield and exceedingly broad outstanding postorbitals. Bailey gives the body size as "medium; color dark brown or blackish, muzzle grizzled with yellow-tipped hairs on back and sides."

19. NAVAHO GRIZZLY—*Ursus navaho* Merriam. Navajo country near Fort Defiance, Arizona (Mollhausen); type probably killed in 1856 in Chusaka Mountains, on boundary between northeastern Arizona and northwestern New Mexico. Size small; skull short, broad, and slightly disked.

20. NELSON GRIZZLY—*Ursus nelsoni* Merriam. Sierra Madre of Mexico from northwestern Chihuahua and northeastern Sonora south to southern Durango. Smallest of all the grizzly bears. General color pale buffy yellowish, varying to grayish white, grizzled from darker color of underfur. Muzzle pale brown, much darker around eyes. Skull small and wolfish.

21. SONORA GRIZZLY—*Ursus kennerlyi* Merriam. Mountains of northeastern Sonora, Mexico. (Collected in June 1855.) Size rather small; pale brownish yellow with amber tinge. The tips only are of this color, the basal and larger portion being of a dark chestnut brown, passing into blackish; legs blackish brown (Baird). Skull long, narrow, and high.

22. SOUTHERN CALIFORNIA GRIZZLY—*Ursus magister* Merriam, Santa Ana or Trabuco Mountains, Cuyamaca and Santa Rosa Mountains, and probably San Jacinto Mountains. (Killed in August 1900 or 1901.) Size of male huge (estimated weight over 1400 pounds), largest of known true grizzlies, considerably larger than *horribilis*, the great buffalo-killing grizzly of the Plains. General color dusky or sooty all over except head and grizzling of back. Muzzle gray or mouse brown, palest above; top of head and neck very dark brown, sparsely grizzled with pale-tipped hairs; back dusky grizzled with grayish; legs and underparts wholly blackish. Skull exceedingly large, long.

23. HENSHAW GRIZZLY—*Ursus henshawi* Merriam. Southern Sierra Nevada Mountains, Kern County, California. By far the smallest of the California grizzlies. Skull long, narrow, and rather low.

24. CALIFORNIA COAST GRIZZLY—*Ursus californicus* Merriam. Humid coast region of California from San Francisco Bay south about to San Luis Obispo. Size large; claws long and smooth; pelage variable. Skull long and narrow.

25. TEJON GRIZZLY—*Ursus californicus tularensis* Merriam. Dry chaparral hills of interior coast ranges between the San Joaquin Valley and Los Angeles plain, and probably San Bernardino Mountains, and ranging northward, doubtless covering San Rafael and Gabilan Ranges. Size large, but smaller than *californicus*. General color very dark brown, almost dusky; grizzled on upperparts by admixture of pale-tipped hairs; muzzle reddish brown. Skull large, rather broad and flat frontal.

26. MENDOCINO GRIZZLY—*Ursus mendocinensis* Merriam. Mendocino County, California. Size rather large. Skull short, broad, highly arched.

27. SACRAMENTO VALLEY GRIZZLY—*Ursus colusus* Merriam. Sacramento River Valley, California, and perhaps also San Joaquin and adjacent foothills; westerly in the hot interior coast mountains to Dobbins Creek canyon on the boundary between southeastern Humboldt and southwestern Trinity counties. Size large . . . skull large and long.

28. KLAMATH GRIZZLY—*Ursus klamathensis* Merriam. Siskiyou Mountains of northern California and southern Oregon, to Fort Klamath region and Rogue River Valley, to lower Willamette Valley (presumably same species); south in Sierra Nevada. Size of male large; skull large and high.

29. CHELAN GRIZZLY—*Ursus chelan* Merriam. Cascade and Cassiar mountains from northern Washington to upper Stikine River and Dease Lake, British Columbia. Skull of medium or rather large size.

30. BROAD-FRONTED GRIZZLY—*Ursus phæonyx latifrons* Merriam. Rocky Mountains of western Alberta and eastern British Columbia from Jasper House northwesterly to region between headwaters of Parsnip and Great Bend of Frazer River and thence to headwaters of Stikine River. Size medium or rather large.

31. FOREST GRIZZLY—*Ursus selkirki* Merriam (*Ursus hylodromus* Elliot—described from skull, in 1913, as a black bear!) Rocky Mountains region of western Alberta and eastern British

Columbia, including Selkirk Range. Size of male large, female small; skull medium size, long, low arched, and of medium breadth.

32. RINDSFOOS GRIZZLY—*Ursus dusorgus* nobis. Jack Pine River, Alberta. Skull large, broad, and massive.

33. HIGH-BROW GRIZZLY—*Ursus ophrus* Merriam. Eastern British Columbia. Skull short, strongly disked, remarkably high.

34. CANADA GRIZZLY—*Ursus shoshone canadensis* Merriam. Eastern British Columbia. Size medium; color brown, grizzled with buff; claws short for a grizzly; muzzle very pale drab brown, changing to darker brown on head, face, and chin, darkest around ears, head, back, and thighs washed with buffy whitish; foreleg and lower part of hind leg, feet, and underparts dark brown. Skull of medium size, rather long, low, and narrow, flat in frontal region.

35. KLUANE GRIZZLY—*Ursus kluane* Merriam. Southwest corner Yukon Territory and northwest British Columbia to Mount McKinley region in Alaska, and McConnell River, Yukon. Skull medium, rather long, narrow.

36. INDUSTRIOUS GRIZZLY—*Ursus kluane impiger* nobis. Columbia Valley, British Columbia. Similar to *kluane*, but shield of skull narrower.

37. LILLOOET GRIZZLY—*Ursus pervagor* Merriam. Interior of southwestern British Columbia. Size rather large; skull long, rather narrow and high.

38. KOOTENAY GRIZZLY—*Ursus pulchellus ereunetes* nobis. Kootenay District, British Columbia. Size rather small.

39. KWAKIUTL GRIZZLY—*Ursus kwakiutl* Merriam. Coast region of British Columbia from southwestern corner to Bella Colla. Size large; color dark; ears densely furred; head and face from front of eyes very dark brown, slightly grizzled on occiput by golden-tipped hairs; skull long but little arched.

40. JERVIS INLET GRIZZLY—*Ursus chelidonias* nobis. Jervis Inlet, British Columbia. Size very large; skull very large, massive, flat on top.

41. ATNARKO GRIZZLY—*Ursus atnarko* nobis. Atnarko

River, upper fork of Bella Koola, British Columbia. Size large; skull long and narrow.

42. WARBURTON PIKE GRIZZLY—*Ursus kwakiutl warburtoni* Merriam. Atnarko River, British Columbia, Stikine River, to southeastern Alaska coastal mountains. Skull large and masssive, rather long and flattish on top.

43. STIKINE GRIZZLY—*Ursus stikeenensis* Merriam. Region about head of Finlay River and Dease Lake, northern British Columbia, into Yukon. Size medium; skull short, broad, and highly arched, with pugged face; general ground color dark brown, grizzled with pale-tipped hairs; top of head in front of ears washed with yellowish brown; legs and feet blackish.

44. BIG-TOOTH GRIZZLY—*Ursus crassodon* nobis. Third South Fork, Stikine River, British Columbia. Frontal shield broad. Molars enormous for size of skull.

45. TAHLTAN GRIZZLY—*Ursus tahltanicus* Merriam. Middle and upper Stikine-Skeena region, British Columbia. Size medium; entire body and legs almost coal-black, lightly grizzled on shoulders and anterior back by tips of golden brownish.

46. RUNGIUS GRIZZLY—*Ursus rungiusi rungiusi* nobis. Headwaters of Athabaska River, Alberta. Size small; skull low and flat. Collected September, 1910, by Carl Rungius.

47. STIKINE BROWN BEAR—*Ursus hoots* Merriam. North branch of Stikine River. Size medium or large; skull massive, slightly disked, and rather short, flattish on top.

48. TOWNDSEND BEAR—*Ursus towndsendi* Merriam. Mainland of southeastern Alaska. Skull large, long, massive, rather low, and flat-topped, with extremely small teeth.

49. GLACIER BAY GRIZZLY—*Ursus orgilos* Merriam. Glacier Bay, southeastern Alaska. Size medium; skull long, rather narrow, flat on top.

50. LYNN CANAL GRIZZLY—*Ursus caurinus* Merriam. Coast of mainland of southeastern Alaska from Chilkat River Valley and Lynn Canal south an unknown distance. Size rather large; skull long and rather narrow; color of upperparts yellowish buff; face and most of head pale brown or drab; ears, hump, and underparts darker; legs and feet dark brown or brownish black.

51. SITKA GRIZZLY—*Ursus eltonclarki* Merriam. The Sitka Islands, Baranof and Chichagof, southeastern Alaska. Medium or rather small in size; color very dark brown and rich; occiput and neck grizzled golden brown; back pale, overlaid by buffy tips; legs and feet blackish brown; skull small, long, narrow, and rather low.

52. SITKA BROWN BEAR—*Ursus sitkensis* Merriam. Sitka Islands, Baranof and Chichagof, southeastern Alaska. Size large; coloration very dark brown, washed on back of head, neck, and shoulders with yellowish or golden; skull large and massive.

53. ADMIRALTY ISLAND GRIZZLY—*Ursus kwakiutl neglectus* Merriam. Admiralty Island, southeastern Alaska. Skull rather large and massive, flat-topped and with rather broad outstanding postorbitals.

54. STRANGE GRIZZLY—*Ursus mirabilis* Merriam. Admiralty Island, southeastern Alaska. Size medium; a true grizzly; skull of medium size, short, rather broad, and highly arched.

55. ISLAND GRIZZLY—*Ursus insularis* Merriam. Admiralty Island, southeastern Alaska. Size medium; frontal shield of skull broad and flattish.

56. ADMIRALTY ISLAND CRESTED BEAR—*Ursus eulophus* Merriam. Admiralty Island, southeastern Alaska. Size large; color rich dark brown; muzzle paler; legs, feet, and belly dusky; neck and shoulders sometimes grizzled with yellowish-tipped hairs; claws blue-black, of moderate length; skull large, long, high, and rather narrow.

57. SHIRAS BROWN BEAR—*Ursus shirasi* Merriam. Admiralty Island, southeastern Alaska. A huge brown bear; head highly arched; color black, except muzzle, which is dull brown; a brownish wash along middle of back; skull large, broad, massive, strongly disked, and highly arched.

58. ALSEK GRIZZLY—*Ursus orgiloides* nobis. Coast regions southeast of Yakutat, Alaska. Skull of medium size, long, low, and smoothly rounded and rather narrow.

59. YAKUTAT GRIZZLY—*Ursus nortoni* Merriam. Limited apparently to coastal plain on southeastern side of Yakutat Bay, Alaska. A true grizzly of large size; head grizzled yellowish or

golden brown; muzzle pale brown; neck and shoulders to middle of back pale buffy; hinder back and rump dark, well washed with pale brown tips; lower part of legs and feet dark brown; skull large, massive, and very broad.

60. DALL BROWN BEAR—*Ursus dalli* Merriam. Malaspina Glacier and region northwest of Yakutat, Alaska. Size very large; general body color dark brown, grizzled with pale-tipped hairs; skull large, fairly high but not arched.

61. CHITINA BEAR—*Ursus cressonus* Merriam. Chitina River Valley and adjacent Skolai and Wrangell mountains, westerly doubtless through Chugach Mountains to west side of Cook Inlet, Alaska. Skull large, narrow, high, and strongly disked.

62. MONTAGUE ISLAND BEAR—*Ursus sheldoni* Merriam. Montague Island, Prince William Sound, Alaska. Size large, color variable, from light to dark brown, sometimes yellowish tipped, color darkest on belly, legs, and feet; skull broad and massive.

63. NUCHEK BROWN BEAR—*Ursus nuchek* Merriam. Hinchenbrook Island, Prince William Sound, Alaska. Size large; skull long, narrow, and moderately high.

64. ALEXANDER GRIZZLY—*Ursus alexandræ* Merriam. Kenai Peninsula, Alaska. Size very large; general color grayish brown, legs and feet slightly darker, entire body remarkably unicolor; skull large, long, rather narrow, and high sagittal crest.

65. KENAI GIANT BEAR—*Ursus kenaiensis* Merriam. Kenai Peninsula, Alaska. Size large; appearance that of big grizzly; rather dark brown; top of head, neck, and back washed on tips with buffy; legs and feet much darker; skull large, broad, and massive.

66. TANANA GRIZZLY—*Ursus phæonyx* Merriam. Tanana Mountains between Tanana (Alaska) and Yukon rivers. Size of male large; female small; color of upperparts buff to dark grizzly color; underparts and muzzle pale brown; legs very dark brown; skull medium to rather large, broad, and short.

67. TOKLAT GRIZZLY—*Ursus toklat* Merriam. Alaska Range, vicinity of Mount McKinley. Size medium; color variable, upperparts ordinary grizzly-bear color to creamy white; claws usually dark; skull medium size, rostrum high, rather long.

68. CRESTED GRIZZLY—*Ursus rungiusi sagittalis* nobis. Southwestern Yukon. Size small; skull low and narrow; sagittal crest very high.

69. PALLAS GRIZZLY—*Ursus pallasi* Merriam. Southwest corner of Yukon and eastern border of Alaska; easterly to Mc-Connell River and Teslin Lake, and south into northern British Columbia. One of the smallest of grizzlies, skull moderately elevated, flattish on top.

70. LIARD RIVER GRIZZLY—*Ursus oribasus* nobis. Upper Liard River, Yukon. Size large; hump absent or inconspicuous; general ground color dark brown to dusky; muzzle golden brown; dark ring around eyes; top of head, nape, and shoulders strongly washed with yellowish buff; rump dark brownish. Legs and feet dusky blackish; skull rather large.

71. UPPER YUKON GRIZZLY—*Ursus pulchellus pulchellus* nobis. Ross River, Yukon. Size small; frontal shield and rostrum narrow; vault of cranium well arched.

72. PELLY GRIZZLY—*Ursus pellyensis* nobis. Pelly Mountains, Yukon. Skull of medium size, rather long and narrow.

73. THICKSET GRIZZLY—*Ursus crassus* nobis. Upper Macmillan River, Yukon. Size large; moderate hump; general color dark; top of head and neck strongly washed with golden buffy; shoulders and back lightly tipped with same; legs and feet dusky; skull rather large, short, broad, rather high, and unusually massive.

74. ANDERSON BEAR—*Ursus andersoni* nobis. Great Bear Lake, Mackenzie. Size medium or rather large.

75. MAC FARLANE BEAR—*Ursus macfarlani* nobis. Anderson River, Mackenzie. Skull medium size, massive, broad, flat.

76. MACKENZIE DELTA GRIZZLY—*Ursus russelli* Merriam. Lower Mackenzie River region. Size rather small; color a curious pale drab brown, somewhat darker on legs and feet; ears conspicuously hairy; skull of medium size, rather short and broad.

77. PATRIARCHAL BEAR—*Vetularctos inopinatus* nobis. Rendezvous Lake, northeast of Fort Anderson, Mackenzie. General color varying from whitish buff to pale yellowish buff, darkening to dull reddish brown on ankles, feet, and median line of belly; fur everywhere full, soft and woolly; skull small, mod-

erately arched above. (Strictly not a grizzly or brown bear, although included here.)

78. BARREN GROUND BEAR—*Ursus richardsoni* Swainson. Original description based on old male collected on Bathurst Inlet, shore of Arctic Ocean, by Richardson, August 1, 1821, although species previously reported by Hearne in 1795. According to Preble (North American Fauna, No. 27, 1908), "this famous bear occurs in various parts of the Barren Grounds"; and Dr. Anderson (*My Life with the Eskimos*, Stefansson, 1913) "found the center of greatest abundance of the Barren Ground Bears in the country around Langton Bay and on Horton River." From all reports (and the present writer's observation of skins) these bears are closer allied to the Alaska Brown Bears than to the true grizzlies. Anderson indicates two varieties: "long-snouted and short-snouted . . . reddish brown and dark dusky brown, with tips of hairs on dorsal surface light grayish brown or fulvous."

79. ALASKA BOUNDARY GRIZZLY—*Ursus internationalis* Merriam. Alaska-Yukon Boundary and adjacent mountains, from Arctic coast to the Yukon-Porcupine. Size medium or rather large; color pale yellowish brown; skull massive and strongly arched; and has other characteristics of big-brown-bear type.

80. INNUIT BEAR—*Ursus innuitus* Merriam. Seward Peninsula, Alaska, from coastal region of Norton Sound northward. Size large. Merriam gives no color characteristics; but skins I have examined indicate a close affinity to the big brown bears.

81. ALASKA GRIZZLY—*Ursus horribilis alascensis* Merriam. Norton Sound region, Alaska, southerly over the Nushagak and Kuskokwim rivers to Cook Inlet. Small skull, broad, flattish, very short-pointed posteriorly.

82. TUNDRA BEAR—*Ursus kidderi tundrensis* Merriam. Tundra region of northwestern Alaska from Norton Sound southerly across lower Yukon, Kuskokwim, and Nushagak rivers to Bristol Bay and north side of base of Alaska Peninsula. Size medium; skull long and heavy, frontals broad and flat, and rather high. Known to the natives as "Red Bear."

83. KNIK BEAR—*Ursus eximius* Merriam. Head of Knik Arm, Cook Inlet, Alaska. Size rather large; color uniform rich dark brown; muzzle paler than rest of head; back of head and neck

lightly sprinkled with pale-tipped hairs. Skull long and narrow, with narrow, highly arched frontals.

84. KODIAK BEAR—*Ursus middendorffi* Merriam. Kodiak and adjacent islands. Size huge; skull of male exceedingly broad, high, and relatively short, frontal shield domed. (Merriam does not give a color description.) This is the true "Kodiak Grizzly."

85. KIDDER BEAR—*Ursus kidderi kidderi* Merriam. Alaska Peninsula for its entire length and adjacent Unimak Island. Size large; female nearly as large as male; general color yellowish brown, darkest on belly and legs; skull long, rather low, narrow, and massive.

86. PENINSULA GIANT BEAR—*Ursus gyas* Merriam. Entire length of Alaska Peninsula and adjacent Unimak Island. Size huge, heavily humped at shoulders; the *largest living bear* or second only to the great Kodiak Bear (*middendorffi*). Color variable, from light brown to dark brown and washed on back with buff; skull massive, long, but not highly arched.

INDEX

Abnaki Indian, 38; cited, 35
Absaroka Grizzly, 294
Academy of Natural Sciences (Philadelphia), 90, 278
Adams, James Capen, 146–59
Adaptability, of grizzlies, 191
Admiralty Island Crested Bear, 300
Admiralty Island Grizzly, 300
Adventures of James Capen Adams, Mountaineer and Bear Hunter, The, cited, 147
Adventurers, in Old West, 106, 107, 109
Afterlife, 54
Afterlife, of Indians, 54
Africa, 186
    language among animals in, 248
Aggressiveness, of grizzly, 115–17. *See also* Grizzly bear
Agnew, Jesse B., 269
A Journey from Prince of Wales's Fort, in Hudson's Bay to the Northern Ocean ... in the years 1769 to 1772, cited, 275, 276
Akeley, Carl, 247–48
Alamo, 123
Alaska, 21, 191, 200, 201, 202, 255
    grizzlies in, 201, 205, 206, 207
    hunting in, 22
    Indians in, 100

Alaska Bear Trails, cited, 222, 282
Alaska Boundary Grizzly, 303
Alaska Brown Bear, 21, 31, 32, 210, 214, 225, 229, 236, 279
Alaska Grizzly, 303
Alaska Peninsula, 18, 192, 201, 215, 218, 221, 222, 279
Alaska Range, 215
Alberta (province), 69
Aleutian Islands, 202
Alexander Grizzly, 301
Alexis, Grand Duke of Russia, 183
Allan, Paul, 276
Allouez, Claude Jean, 66
Alsek Grizzly, 300
Alter, J. Cecil, 112, 114–15, 279, 280
American Anthropologist, The, cited, 274
American Fur Company, 129
American Museum of Natural History, *Memoirs,* 274
American Rifleman, The, cited, 279
Ancestral association, of Indians and bears, 35, 40
Ancestral worship, 99
Anderson Bear, 302
Anderson, Dr., 303
Animal ancestry, 47–48
Animal worship, 51, 63. *See also* Indians